HUMAN RESOURCE MANAGEMENT: A NORDIC PERSPECTIVE

T0372563

Sweden has one of the lowest national debts in Europe, a well-educated work-force, and the country consistently ranks in top positions of the best places to live and work in the world. *Human Resource Management: A Nordic Perspective* offers a unique and valuable insight into the working practices of HRM in Sweden, which has been explicated for an international audience. The book offers readers outside of the country alternative methods for improving efficiency and well-being in their own workplace.

A team of experienced contributors based in Sweden discuss and analyse the Nordic tradition of inclusive and participative management and present different perspectives on creating a work-life suitable for every person involved. The first part of the book includes chapters on general issues in HR work such as development and learning, selection, teamwork, career paths, and cooperation within organisations. The second part addresses diversity, inclusion, and how discriminatory practices can be avoided.

This book will be a valuable resource for students of HRM, business, management, education, psychology, sociology, as well as human resource management professionals who are seeking new ways to balance economic and human values.

Helene Ahl is a professor of business economics and management at the School of Education and Communication at Jönköping University, Sweden.

Ingela Bergmo-Prvulovic, Ph.D., is a senior lecturer in education at Jönköping University, Sweden.

Karin Kilhammar, Ph.D., is a senior lecturer in education at Linnaeus University, Sweden and a former HR manager.

'This volume is a very timely addition to the HRM literature, providing insights on topics from careers to creativity, and from "co-workership" to ethics. The strong focus on multiple dimensions of diversity highlights the added value of the Nordic perspective.'

Elaine Farndale, Associate Professor, The Pennsylvania State University, USA and Tilburg University, the Netherlands

'Building on a tradition of democracy and co-workership, inclusion and trust, Nordic countries have demonstrated remarkable results in terms of economic performance as well as quality of life. It is evident that Nordic HRM does something right. This book opens new perspectives and gives invaluable insight into how this works in practice.'

Juergen Deters, Professor of Human Resource Management and Leadership, Leuphana University, Germany

HUMAN RESOURCE MANAGEMENT: A NORDIC PERSPECTIVE

Edited by Helene Ahl, Ingela Bergmo-Prvulovic, and Karin Kilhammar

LONDON AND NEW YORK

First published 2019
by Routledge
2 Park Square, Milton Park, Abingdon, Oxon OX14 4RN

and by Routledge
711 Third Avenue, New York, NY 10017

Routledge is an imprint of the Taylor & Francis Group, an informa business

British Library Cataloguing-in-Publication Data
A catalogue record for this book is available from the British Library

Library of Congress Cataloging-in-Publication Data
Names: Ahl, Helene, editor. | Bergmo-Prvulovic, Ingela, editor. |
Kilhammar, Karin, editor.
Title: Human resource management: a Nordic perspective /
edited by Helene Ahl, Ingela Bergmo-Prvulovic, and Karin Kilhammar.
Description: Abingdon, Oxon; New York, NY: Routledge, 2019.
Identifiers: LCCN 2018026263 | ISBN 9781138592834 (hbk) |
ISBN 9781138592858 (pbk)
Subjects: LCSH: Personnel management—Scandinavia.
Classification: LCC HF5549.2.S34 H86 2019 | DDC 658.3—dc23
LC record available at https://lccn.loc.gov/2018026263

ISBN: 978-1-138-59283-4 (hbk)
ISBN: 978 1 138 59285 8 (pbk)
ISBN: 978-0-429-48976-1 (ebk)

Typeset in Bembo
by codeMantra

CONTENTS

FIGURES

TABLES

CONTRIBUTORS

Helene Ahl is a professor of business economics and management with a special interest in gender and learning. She has many years' experience of gender research within companies and organisations, at various social levels, and even at the policy level. She teaches about gender and organisations at the undergraduate and postgraduate levels. Her work is cited in many international publications on the areas of gender, entrepreneurship, motivation, and adult learning. Her current research projects include how women combine business ownership with maternity, and an investigation into the role of women in rural development.

Vezir Aktas holds a doctor's degree in social psychology from Turkey. He has researched topics such as aggression and prosocial behaviour. His other research interests include social representations, attribution, stereotypes, group dynamics, and conflict. Current projects include a study of the impact on academic scholars as a result of changing conditions for academic work in contemporary Turkey.

Ingela Bergmo-Prvulovic holds a doctor's degree in education and works at Jönköping University. In her research, she has studied what the concept of 'career' entails for different people, and what the consequences are when different parties hold different understandings of this concept. She has researched the influence that changes in the work-life have on careers and the effect such changes have on people and their daily work, and the effect this has for professions that deal with career questions. She lectures on career development and guidance, work-life pedagogics, lifelong learning, communication, leadership, professional communication, and conflict resolution. Ingela has a great deal of experience of working with adults in career-related processes of change.

Cecilia Bjursell is an associate professor of business administration and is the director of Encell, the National centre for lifelong learning. Her current projects include learning and the elderly, intergenerational learning, university–industry collaboration, education management, and learning in organisations.

Ann-Kristin Boström holds a doctor's degree in international education. Her research area includes international and comparative education with a focus on lifelong learning, learning across generations, and social capital. She has many years of experience as an educational advisor and as a specialist. Ann-Kristin has worked on an OECD report on migration and has been a Special Advisor for the Swedish Government regarding international education.

Annika Engström is an assistant professor in work organisation and her research focuses on the role of interaction for task management and on learning in work teams and organisations. Her interests lie with management and organisation of human communication and the meetings that are used to complete and develop work-related tasks. She is currently researching how management curates the force behind innovation – human resources – in the day-to-day management of a 'lean-inspired' industrial company. Annika has a great deal of experience as a consultant in operations management, as well as in group- and organisational development.

Claudia Gillberg holds a doctor's degree in education, specialising in organisational development and learning organisations. She has taught work-life education and professional development at the university level. She has been involved in the further development of the HR programme at three universities and she has considerable experience of cooperative projects with several county councils in Sweden. As of late, she has published work on different methodological and theoretical standpoints concerning participation, democratic sustainability, and learning within the workplace and outside the workplace, with focus on questions about social justice in the labour market.

Joel Hedegaard holds a doctor's degree in education. He graduated in 2014 with a dissertation on how the organisational ideals which are propounded by New Public Management influence the conditions for communication about the delivery of equitable healthcare. Joel has also studied the conditions in various regions of Sweden where work is done (i) to reduce the feeling of isolation that some people experience and (ii) to increase the rate of employment for the youth, people with an immigrant background, and for people with disabilities. Another of his research areas includes work on how high-functioning autistic young adults can be integrated into the employment market.

Martin Hugo holds a doctor's degree in education and has conducted extensive research on how one can change from a state of exclusion to a state on inclusion. His dissertation presented an investigation into the conditions of several high school students who had been let down by the school system. This initial investigation was followed up on with a 4-year-long research project on the school system that is provided to adolescents who have been forcefully removed from home and who live in special youth facilities in Sweden. His latest study deals with inclusion at the workplace via an apprenticeship system for high-functioning autistic young adults (in collaboration with Joel Hedegaard).

Karin Kilhammar holds a doctor's degree in education. Her research area includes co-workership and how it can be developed within organisations. She teaches courses on work-life learning and Human Resource Development, including teamwork, leadership, learning and change, and courses on practical aspects of HR work. Her first degree was in Human Resources Development and Labour Relations. She has many years of experience of working with HR questions within organisations.

Ylva Lindberg is an associate professor of comparative literature. Her research covers a range of literary topics: gender and *fin-de-siècle* literature in Scandinavia, literature and virtual worlds, comic art, modern poetry, Sub-Saharan Francophone Literature, as well as literature in global cultural transactions. She manages and teaches a creative writing course, which was recognised as the most popular course for 2017 at Jönköping University, Sweden. Her book *De la Belle époque à Second Life* (2013) explores the concept of 'creativity' in a technology-dense society where learning has become teacherless.

Frida Ohlsson Sandahl has a bachelor's degree in sociology, with focus on gender, diversity, and work sciences. She works as an organisational consultant and teaches queer theory, feminism, and intersectionality at university and at many other organisations. She is the author of the book *Inkludera: Jämställdhet och hbtq i organisationen* (Inclusion: Equality and lgbtq in Organisations) as well as *Diskrimineringslagen – handbook för chefer* (The Discrimination Act – A Handbook for Managers).

Roland S. Persson is a professor of educational psychology. His research areas include high-performing people (talented people), gifted people, and the macrosocial dynamics that are related to these. Earlier projects that he has worked on have included investigations into musical communication and learning, giftedness at different levels of the education system, and the knowledge climate that prevails in different European countries. His latest projects now include more general research into the individual, society, and social evolution.

Dag Raudberget holds a doctor's degree in mechanical engineering from the Chalmers Institute of Technology and conducts research in the area of modularisation and set-based concurrent engineering. These methods are aimed at making product development more effective and have been tested in a number of industrial development projects with good results. Dag has also been responsible for the Product Development and Design undergraduate programme at the School of Engineering at Jönköping University.

ACKNOWLEDGEMENT

We gratefully acknowledge the work of Dr Robert Ryan (www.textworkshop.org) who translated this book from Swedish.

PREFACE

Today's workplace is informed, to a high degree, by a strict economic perspective where *cost efficiency* and *growth* are key catchwords. Even HR departments tend to subscribe to this perspective and work in this direction. In this book, however, we wish to highlight the role that HR departments have in taking care of the human resources within organisations, by creating a balance between human values and economic values. We claim that achieving this balance brings about advantages for both the individuals and the organisations concerned, and is crucial to establishing and maintaining a long-term, sustainable work-life. By drawing on the Nordic experience, this book presents a collective understanding of HR's strategic role in elevating people as a resource in organisations, especially in the context of today's changeable work environment.

The content of this book is arranged thematically into two parts. The first part presents *general issues in HR work* and provides a view of the entrance and exit of human resources within organisations, and their development and learning. Some of the areas that are dealt with include the supply of competence, teamwork, career paths, and cooperation within organisations. These are areas which, in many regards, characterise the day-to-day work done by HR departments, but these areas also constantly need to be examined in the light of current trends and prevailing challenges.

The second part of this book addresses questions related to *maintaining diversity within organisations, the importance of inclusionary policies*, and *how discriminatory practices can be avoided*. These are questions which have become more and more relevant in conjunction with certain demographic changes in society, and with the emergent mobile, and changeable work-life that many people are faced with. We examine the effects that change brings about for different groups of people and their importance for the work that HR departments perform.

In the introductory chapter, Helene Ahl discusses the Nordic approach to Human Resource management and provides the reader with a detailed presentation of each of the chapters of this book. In the final chapter, Ingela Bergmo-Prvulovic and Karin Kilhammar focus on the central issues raised in this book and they present a number of challenges that HR departments face. They also discuss the competencies which a HR department needs to possess so as to deal with these challenges successfully in its daily work. We hope that the various chapters of this book will stimulate the reader to reflect over some of the issues raised here and that they will provide basis for discussion and practical tips for HR practitioners, future and present, managers, and work teams who are interested in the topic areas and issues that are treated in this book.

The book has come about thanks to the conversations and continual exchange of ideas which the authors have enjoyed during the years that they have researched organisations and work-life. They have all taught HR-related courses at the university level, including courses on leadership, organisations, communication, and changes in the workplace. This book has brought together researchers who have different research areas and points of departure, but all of these researchers are interested in the development and caring for of human resources in organisations and at the workplace.

Helene Ahl
Ingela Bergmo-Prvulovic
Karin Kilhammar

INTRODUCTION

Nordic perspectives on human resource management

Helene Ahl

The literature on international, or comparative, human resource management, cross-cultural management, or human resource management in a multinational context typically compares HR practices that have been developed in Western (predominantly Anglo-Saxon countries) to those HR practices present in Asia and the global south (Dowling, Festing, & Engle, 2017; Syed & Kramar, 2017). But one does not need to leave the West to find HR practices that differ from mainstream practices – the Nordic countries are a case in point. Whilst the five Nordic countries do differ from each other in many respects, they share enough features to allow us to speak of a unique Nordic way of approaching the organisation of social life. Since HR practices are always embedded in their economic, cultural, and institutional context, Nordic HR practices will also display a number of unique features.

Nordic organizations have a very long tradition of workplace democracy, flat organizations, low power distance, open and informal communication, co-determination, and close co-operation between management and labour unions (Lindeberg, Månson, & Larsen, 2013). This is anchored in, and a reflection of, the Scandinavian welfare state that developed as a result of the political ideology of social democratic governments that came into power after WWI (Esping-Andersen, 1990, 2009), but also the result of a historical and cultural tradition that differs from the Anglo-Saxon tradition, as well as from continental Europe in some important respects (Berggren & Trägårdh, 2015). According to the World Values Survey (www.worldvaluessurvey.org), people in the Nordic countries treasure individualism and personal autonomy, and embrace secular-rational values to a higher extent than anywhere else. Sweden is actually counted as the most extreme place in the world in terms of individualism, yet it is not a place with cut-throat competition and large income disparities; quite the contrary – egalitarianism is deeply anchored in the culture. The seeming paradox between individualism and egalitarianism is solved by a safety net that is provided by the State. Berggren and Trägårdh (2010) speak of "statist individualism", which is an informal contract between the individual and the state. Put bluntly, Swedes do not like to depend on others on a person-to-person basis, but recognise that, in order to have a decent and equal society, those in need must have their needs met; so they outsource this responsibility to the State and gladly pay for it with their taxes. The Nordic countries have had an overarching ambition "not to socialise the economy, but to liberate the individual citizen from all forms of subordination and dependency within the family and in civil society" (Eklund, Berggren & Trägårdh, 2011: 14). These countries have large public sectors that provide extensive welfare services, such as healthcare, education, childcare, care for the elderly, and social insurance. The system is made possible by low levels of corruption, transparent institutions, and extensive social trust – in other people, in the market, and in the State. The Nordic countries score very high on all three of these dimensions (Eklund et al., 2011).

Government policies include a generous family policy which makes a dual breadwinner system possible. The family policy includes paid parental leave (18 months in Sweden), public subsidised and universal day-care, child allowances, free education, student loans for everyone, and individual taxation of spouses. The results of these initiatives are high levels of labour market participation for both women and men and a fertility rate which is higher than in many other countries where women must choose between work or family. Other results of this policy are a highly educated workforce and a dominance of knowledge-intensive industry and services which employ 75% of the labour force, and where well over half of operating costs are labour costs (Lindeberg et al., 2013). The often-repeated phrase that "people are an organisation's most valuable resource" is not an empty one in the Nordic countries.

The combination of generous sick leave and the availability of unemployment insurance and liberal labour laws results in a flexible labour market. In Denmark, a system called "flexicurity" has received much international interest (Madsen, 2014). Trade union density is high, ranging from 52% in Norway in 2015, to 92% in Iceland. The corresponding figure for Sweden, Denmark, and Finland was around 67%, according to ILO statistics.[1] Salary levels and many other workplace regulations are determined by collective bargaining between strong unions and equally strong employer federations. Legislation about union representation on company boards and about employee codetermination exists and is closely adhered to. Comparatively peaceful labour market relations prevail, in which unions have looked beyond their immediate, short-term interests and have assumed a macroeconomic responsibility (Eklund et al., 2011). Since the HR manager deals with the strategically important cooperation with the unions, HR managers are also members of the top executive teams in most companies (Lindeberg et al., 2013). Another defining feature of Nordic HRM is the decentralization of HR responsibilities to line managers. Line managers are often responsible for recruitment and employee selection, particularly in knowledge-intensive operations (Lindeberg et al., 2013). There is thus no clear-cut dividing line between HRM and general management issues.

The Nordic model has been proven successful. The Nordic countries consistently score very high on indices of desirable places to live, not least with respect to equality between men and women. In the World Economic Forum's 2011 competitiveness index, which measured twelve different dimensions such as infrastructure, education, innovation and market efficiency, the Nordic countries outclassed the European Union on every single dimension, and beat the United States on nine out of twelve of the dimensions (Eklund et al., 2011). Whilst the Nordic countries are in no way immune to economic and financial crises, they have shown a remarkable ability to deal with them resolutely and rebound quickly. After the downturn in 2008, the Nordic countries recovered much faster than other European countries. Andersen and Hällsten (2016) speak of a 'Nordic resilience tradition' and attribute it precisely to the factors discussed above: an institutional context characterised by trust, transparency, and cooperation, which is reinforced by HR practices that are focussed on individual development.

However, globalization and contemporary, neoliberal management trends do present a number of challenges to the Nordic model. Different methods for managing employees, or perhaps more accurately put, to get the employees *to manage themselves* in alignment with the organisation's goals, have been launched across the world. These methods include *Total Quality Management* (TQM), *self-managing groups, empowerment, lean* processes in industry (Rigby & Bilodeau, 2015), and *New Public Management* (NPM) in the public sector (Czarniawska & Solli, 2014). With the introduction of these new methods and models, we observe an increase in monitoring and measuring performance, and reporting on the employees' efforts and the business' results. Activities of all types are quantified and reduced to numbers, in as much as this is possible.

The public sector was also influenced by this trend, as a result of the spread of NPM and buy-and-sell systems. Critics spoke of 'new Taylorisms' – claiming that these models were just old systems in new clothes. They argued that they were just new (admittedly sophisticated) ways by which the employer could exercise discipline over the workforce, so that the employees could become self-regulating, interchangeable cogs in the wheels of a well-oiled machine (Boje & Winsor, 1993; Brandon, 2001). These developments, whilst enthusiastically adopted by businesses and organizations, present a serious challenge to the ideal of mutual trust on which the Nordic model rests.

However, in parallel to these changes described above, opposite trends were in operation. These were, in part, a result of demographic changes and a result of customers demanding ethical and environmentally sustainable production methods, and sustainable goods and services. The change in Western Europe's age demographics has resulted in a situation where more and more elderly people need to be cared for by fewer and fewer young people. Moreover, there is a mismatch problem on the labour market, leading to a skill shortage; namely, a shortage of well-educated workers in many job sectors (Rauhut & Kahila, 2008;

Saco, 2015). People will become *less* interchangeable. This problem is exacerbated by rapid technical advances, which results in the employee's knowledge becoming quickly outdated. Many organisations try to solve this problem by recruiting newly educated personnel, but this is not a sustainable solution. People who have completed their education and who can be productive workers from day one are not to be found standing in a line, looking for a job. These trends speak for a renewed emphasis on the focus on individual development in the Nordic model, and indicate that it also may have something to offer to other contexts. Certain HR questions become particularly relevant: including questions about how one is to retain and develop one's existing workforce; which career opportunities one can offer; how teamwork, knowledge transfer, and knowledge management takes place within the organisation; how one is to stimulate one's colleagues' creativity; and questions about whether one has a realistic vision of the recruitment process.

In addition to the above, these circumstances raise relevant questions about one's view of other human beings. In a situation where competent personnel is a scarce resource and where organisations are expected to take on social responsibility via programmes such as CSR – *corporate social responsibility* – it is of strategic importance for the organisation to include all types of people and to treat them equally. To ensure the long-term, strategic survival of the business, the HR specialist thus needs to possess knowledge of how to help business managers adopt a realistic view of their employees; a view that is inclusive and allows the business to benefit from the contributions that all different types of people can make to the business. It is precisely this area of knowledge that this book aims to explore and present to the reader. The first part of the book addresses general, strategic issues for human resource management, whilst the second part of the book focuses on diversity and inclusion. The chapters report on in-depth, empirical research and/or draw together recent literature on different topics. In so doing, the book aims at unpacking the "black box" of HRM practices, thus answering Alvesson's (2009) call for not just a discussion of correlations between HRM practices and performance, but for a demonstration of what actually goes on. In other words, we discuss not just those areas where Nordic HRM appears to be successful, but we also describe and discuss *actual* practices, including how contemporary challenges have been, or ought to be, met.

★★★

In Chapter 1, **Karin Kilhammar** explores the concept of 'co-workership' which perhaps could be said to be the essence of the Nordic model. The concept of 'co-workership' has become widespread in Nordic organizations since the end of the 1990s. Various development projects have been instantiated in the name of co-workership programmes or 'co-worker ideas', and a number of consultants sell services in this area. Co-workership is usually associated with taking responsibility, higher degrees of employee engagement, participation, and influence. 'Co-workership' emphasises the importance of the employees for the organisation and its operations. The concept is unique to the Nordic countries and can be considered to be a continuation of the tradition of co-determination and democracy at the workplace. However, it is a concept that allows for a variety of interpretations, depending on the party who is making the interpretation. Consequently, a number of internal conflicts may emerge with this concept. Kilhammar has investigated the implementation of co-workership programmes at two different organisations. These organisations used two different strategies in this regard; the one being more *bottom-up* than the other. The two cases of implementation thus produced different results. Using the results of her research in this area, Kilhammar identifies the various content that is associated with the concept of 'co-workership' and the conflicts that can arise as a result of different interpretations of this concept. In addition, she reports on the different factors which promote or hinder the development of co-workership within an organisation.

It is also noted, however, that co-workership is just one side of the coin. The other is *leadership*. Notwithstanding the fact that leadership creates the conditions for the development of co-workership, leadership itself is influenced by the practice of co-workership. In the final part of the chapter, the author interrogates the interplay between co-workership and leadership, and identifies that which is of importance in leadership with respect to the development of properly functioning co-workership.

Kilhammar stresses the importance of good communication between the different levels and parts of an organisation, as being foundational to a common platform on which co-workership can be developed. In Chapter 2, **Annika Engström** continues on this theme and presents a discussion of how one may create effective cooperation and 'organisational learning' within an organisation. This turns out to be a bit of a 'black art'. For her research, Engström attended a number of different types of teamwork meetings in a manufacturing company. The meetings that were called to attend to short-term assignments or were focussed on finding a solution to a particular technical problem with existing products were meetings that went smoothly and produced the desired results. However, if a meeting was called to discuss issues that addressed fundamental organisational or strategic developmental questions, then the meeting often came to nothing – simply put, there was no proper forum for such discussions. Furthermore, she noted that there was a lack of communication between the different work teams. Arguments and conflicts of interest of various sorts tended to be swept under the carpet, something which, according to Engström, was completely wrong, since it is tension, interruptions, and obstacles that provide opportunities for learning and development. To achieve this, there needs to exist a goal-directed meeting structure. Furthermore, proper leadership and knowledge of how to deal with and lead the communication and information that is shared during such meetings is also needed. Engström concludes her chapter with practical advice for HR specialists and others who find themselves responsible for creating a goal-directed infrastructure for meetings and teamwork.

To a large extent, the communication that takes place during meetings is concerned with the transmission of knowledge and information. In Chapter 3, **Cecilia Bjursell and Dag Raudberget** examine *knowledge transfer*. Organisations deal with knowledge, which is possessed, when all is said and done, by individual employees. However, this knowledge has to be shared, otherwise the organisation is at risk of inventing the wheel over and over again, incurring unnecessary costs. The relevant question in this context is: *How is knowledge best preserved, shared, and developed within an organisation?* Bjursell and Raudberget studied how a large industrial company solves these problems and have come to the conclusion that in every such knowledge management system there exist a number of dimensions and internal tensions. They advise that people who are responsible for designing and constructing a knowledge management system should deal with these tensions by taking into account the conditions that exist within a specific business or organisation. Questions such as *How should one find a balance between a focus on development* versus *a focus on project management?* and *How do we resolve the tension between product research and product standardisation?* are raised. The first issue may be of importance to the long-term survival of the company, whilst the second may ensure profitability from a short-term perspective. Another contrasting pair of issues is *technical knowledge* v. *administrative knowledge*. Forging a career path in a manufacturing business often entails abandoning the practical technical work for the benefit of completing administrative or management work. Is this the best path for the individual and for the business as a whole? Is it possible to create career pathways that solely focus on technical work? Bjursell and Raudberget conclude their chapter with some thoughts on how HR departments might create such scenarios.

The theme of 'careers' (and 'career pathways') is also addressed by **Ingela Bergmo-Prvulovic** in Chapter 4. She discusses a number of different understandings of the concept 'career', and what these different understandings entail with respect to how a particular organisation might map out, or construct, a career pathway within the said organisation. The traditional take on 'a career' is that it is like climbing a ladder – a climb upwards in terms of position and in terms of increased compensation. However, this interpretation is a consequence of thinking that increased effort should be rewarded with promotion and/or a pay increase. Such traditional career pathways, however, are rapidly disappearing. The latest trends in organisations such as delegation, 'flat' organisations, and goal management place emphasis on questions of competence. Consequently, focus is placed on the supply of competence, validation, competence development, workplace learning, and learning organisations, so as to facilitate the organisation's and the individual's ability to quickly reset themselves and face new challenges. Attempts have been made to redefine the concept of a 'career' in terms of personal development instead of a 'climb to the top', but this has not been adopted by most employees.

When hierarchical organisation structures, stable working conditions, contracts of employment, and predictable, transparent career pathways become more and more unclear and unpredictable, this results in insecurity and the impression that the application of increased effort will not result in what one might expect (in terms of promotion and/or a pay increase). This, in turn, creates dissatisfaction and frustration. To re-establish the balance between effort and reward, organisations need to revise the career pathways that they offer their employees, and the HR department needs to clearly define what is meant by the term *career* and investigate how this definition coincides (or fails to coincide) with the employee's interpretation of what a career is, according to Bergmo-Prvulovic.

In Chapter 5, **Ylva Lindberg** investigates how a creative work climate can be stimulated or brought about within an organisation. This is, in fact, a contradiction: an organisation, by definition, necessarily entails certain degree of management and control over the activities that occur within the organisation, so as to achieve common goals. All of these factors can act as disincentives for creativity. However, creativity is currently in great demand, along with independent thinkers and people who can create new things. Most businesses are dependent on new ideas and rejuvenation, so that they do not get left behind by their competitors. It is possible to reconcile this seeming contradiction, however. Lindberg takes up the challenge of examining the delicate balancing act which needs to be mastered so as to solve this problem. The solution is to find the balancing points between freedom and control, between playfulness and seriousness, and between the community and the individual. Lindberg also discusses the importance of a diverse workforce, and what a manager who wants to stimulate creativity should be equipped with.

In Chapter 6, **Roland S. Persson** investigates a commonly ignored, but quite relevant, problem, namely the frequent use of 'personality tests' during the recruitment process. Every organisation needs to recruit people who are suited for, and interested in, just that particular organisation's operations. However, claims Persson, there is an exaggerated sense of belief that a candidate's suitability for a job lies in the candidate's personality, and that people who possess the 'right' personality can be identified by conducting psychological tests. By performing a thorough examination of the literature on this topic, Persson shows that a common conception, that a person's personality is a stable entity, is actually a misconception. One's personality is just as much the result of cultural and environmental factors as it is the result of one's genetic inheritance. This forces us to conclude that 'personality' can change according to circumstance, and that such tests, which are formulated in a particular cultural context, are not at all suitable for other contexts. Second, Persson argues that the assumption that there exists a correlation between 'personality variables' and work performance is also incorrect; no such correlation exits. The only factors that show a certain degree of correlation with work performance is (i) a person's general intellectual ability and (ii) evidence of *previous* successful work performances. The only function of these personality tests, according to Persson, is to provide work for well-heeled consultants and to relieve managers of part of the burden of making decisions about recruitment (the test makes the decision for the manager, in some respect).

This chapter concludes with advice which may assist HR specialists and employers being more 'grounded', when it comes to choosing more realistic and properly thought-out processes for the recruitment of new employees.

Whilst the first part of this book explores some more general aspects of the work done by HR departments, in the second half of the book, we examine, in particular, topics that deal with the notion of 'inclusion' and how HR departments can, and should, work so as to take advantage of *all* of the resources that are available on the employment market. In Chapter 7, **Helene Ahl** discusses the topic of 'gender equality'. Gender inequality continues to exist in many organisations, which leads to negative consequences for both individuals and for the organisation. A particular responsibility with regard to improving gender equality at the workplace lies with the judiciary and the laws which govern employers, and, by virtue of their legal status within organisations, managers, and HR specialists. Often, this involves dutifully writing up a gender equality policy, which is then merely archived. This is a strategic error, claims Ahl, because it may result in the creation of dysfunctional workplaces and an underexploitation of existing competence. In this chapter, the most common failures in enforcing gender equality are presented. Ahl explains terms such as *glass ceiling* and *vertical, horizontal,* and *internal gender segregation*, and she provides an overview of what laws against discrimination demands of employers so that they can work against discrimination. This is a research area which has prompted the sharing of many different opinions and views. Ahl assists HR specialists in their work by closely examining and explaining the most common arguments that are present in the debate on gender equality. She deconstructs several arguments – even in cases where they are made in support of increased equality – which sometimes compete against each other. Ahl ends this chapter with an argument for justice, but provides a new twist to this argument by aligning her own argument for justice with the proper use of resources. Ahl notes that people who feel that they have been treated unjustly also take up an adversarial stance towards the organisation, irrespective of their gender. Organisations which systematically disfavour women (even if this occurs unintentionally) are not using their human resources to their full benefit. Equality between men and women is thus a necessary condition for the good health of an organisation, and allows all available competencies within the organisation to come to the fore.

Continuing the topic of inclusion, in Chapter 8, **Frida Ohlsson Sandahl** discusses how invisible norms about heterosexuality permeate society and the workplace, and what consequences people face who challenge or do not comply with these norms. Ohlsson Sandahl explains how one can evaluate, challenge, and change norms at the workplace in an effort to *include* others, and not to exclude them. Terms such as *LGBTQ, queer, trans,* and *cis* are examined and defined so that they can be properly used to challenge hetero-norms.

In many workplaces, age discrimination is also prevalent. In Chapter 9, **Ann-Kristin Boström** presents a discussion of the somewhat odd fixation on age and the segregation of different generations that occurs ('age segregation'), which often leads to the underutilisation of competence within organisations. It is noted that young managers prefer not to employ older workers. They fail to understand that older people actually have competence, and thus they do not know what competence these people have and what the organisation fails to take benefit of. Older managers who have many younger employees working for them, however, do not always understand the younger employees' way of working; for example, they might think that a virtual, online meeting is just as socially satisfying as a physical, face-to-face meeting. Positive relationships between people are important for successful cooperation, and these relationships are also pre-conditional to the trust that is needed when problems are to be discussed and where employees are expected to be innovative. Crucial to this is a fundamental understanding of the differences across different generations and the different circumstances in which people have grown up. Knowledge of technology and IT plays a role, but differences in historical and cultural experiences also influence relationships at the workplace and thus influence the general work environment. Boström reviews international research on this area which may help HR specialists to understand the importance of the dimension of age and may provide these specialists the necessary tools to overcome any obstacles or problems which may arise in connection with age differences. Again, this is done so that *every* person's competence, irrespective of their age, can be used within the organisation.

Cecilia Bjursell continues to examine the theme of 'age' in Chapter 10, where she discusses competence development for older employees. Her point of departure is the same as in Chapter 9: given certain demographic changes and given that we need to work for longer into our 'old age', we have to ask ourselves how we can most effectively deploy (take advantage of) and develop the competence that older employees possess. Research has shown that older employees are reliable, service and customer orientated, and that they possess institutional knowledge, demonstrate good work ethics and life experience, and are productive. The ability to learn exists in older employees. Employers thus show wisdom and foresight when they provide competence development programmes for their older employees. Another relevant dimension to this situation is the need for the transfer of knowledge from older employees to younger employees within the organisation. At some stage, employees will go on pension, and it is thus important that the organisation does not lose important knowledge and skills. In this chapter, Bjursell presents a model for learning at the workplace which is based on the system of 'study circles', which, to some degree, is a system that is used under different names, including 'research circles', 'quality circles', or 'communities of practice'. What these arrangements all have in common is that the participants search for, and develop knowledge themselves, and they subsequently share this knowledge between themselves.

Immigrants are another category of people whose competence is not fully made use of. In Chapter 11, **Roland S. Persson and Vezir Aktas** discuss the issue of human migration, particularly from the perspectives of skilled labour.

Why is it that when most employers around the world are in dire need of highly qualified individuals with experience, they nevertheless tend to reject job applicants if they have a different cultural background. Instead, employers show preference for lesser qualified individuals from their own country. The number of individuals with both university degrees and considerable experience is increasing. In a time of 'Talent Wars', they represent an often untapped resource for organisations and businesses who are short of skilled staff. Understanding the ordeals that immigrants often have to suffer before they finally get a job (a job which is not likely to match their qualifications or level of experience), the authors suggest several HR practices which would both facilitate their employment as well as allowing the skilled foreign labour to be effectively integrated into the organisation. The most important point made in this chapter is the fact that the reluctance behind employing immigrant experts is rarely made manifest intentionally or on ideological grounds. Rejection of immigrant job applicants is, instead, the result of an unhappy, and largely inevitable, consequence of lacking experience of cultures other than one's own. With such experience and relevant knowledge of other cultures in place, discriminatory behaviour towards foreign skilled labour is likely to lessen considerably. The chapter is concluded with a number of suitable HR practices that facilitate this development and with a number of suggested readings.

Another group whose competence is not properly exploited, because of discrimination and preconceived opinions and attitudes, is people who have different disabilities. This is another situation where employers must consider how the workplace and work assignments can be adapted to accommodate people with disabilities, so that they can be included as members of the labour force. There exists many different types of disability – physical as well as mental disabilities – and each one demands different types of change in the workplace. Once such changes are made, however, most people who have disabilities can actually work. In Chapter 12, **Joel Hedegaard and Martin Hugo** report on a study of a project which aimed to provide people who have high-functioning autism (who were previously diagnosed with 'Asperger's Syndrome') with an education in IT. This education programme was aimed at preparing them to enter the labour market. People with high-functioning autism are often very intelligent, have an eye for detail, and have the ability to concentrate on a task for a considerable amount of time. There are examples of IT companies which *only* employ such people, and view their employees' abilities as providing the company with a competitive advantage. However, not every company thinks this way because high-functioning autistic people have difficulty in interpreting social codes and may have difficulty in taking the initiative. Based on the results of their study, Hedegaard and Hugo provide potential employers with a number of recommendations. These include changes to the work environment: high-functioning autistic employees should have their own, undisturbed, room to work in, and not be asked to sit in an open landscape office with multiple employees. Another recommendation that they make is that work assignments that are given to high-functioning autistic people should have very clear instructions and be properly structured. It is best that only one task at a time be tackled by such workers. Finally, work managers are needed who (i) can understand the situation and conditions that high-functioning autistic people work under and (ii) can create good personal relationships with such workers.

In Chapter 13, **Claudia Gillberg** continues on the theme of 'inclusion' and presents a discussion on how one can respond to, and properly exploit, the competencies of employees who are off sick from work (for extended periods of time) or who have a diminished ability to work (caused by a health-related condition). At the workplace, one is often either 'on' or you are 'off'. One is either considered to be fit and healthy and ready for work, or one is sick and completely unable to work. This often causes additional suffering for the individual in the form of isolation from the workplace. In addition, the business loses out on the competence and skills which actually continue to exist within the employee. Based on peoples' experiences of being off from work because of chronic illnesses, Gillberg discusses the actions that can be taken that can be of benefit for both the employee and the employer. We again are provided with specific recommendations on how work can be changed, not the physical workplace, but rather, how one views (i) what work is and (ii) what constitutes the workplace. In knowledge-intensive organisations especially, claims Gillberg, it is unnecessarily limiting to define the workplace as a physical building and a typical 'eight to five' work shift. A great deal of knowledge-intensive work can be done from a distance by using IT, at times and amounts of work that suit the employee who is ill. It is also limiting to think that one must physically meet one's manager or customer; today, there are many excellent video telecommunication systems that are available for such purposes. This is positive for both the sick employee and for the organisation: the organisation can utilise the intellectual capital that is possessed by the worker, and the worker has the continued opportunity to contribute to the organisation, be gainfully employed, and feel like a person who is 'needed' by the organisation. Gillberg ends her chapter with a number of practical recommendations for managers and HR specialists.

In Chapter 14, **Roland S. Persson and Vezir Aktas** address the question of how an organisation can best engage with employees who possess special gifts and talents, and what challenges and benefits that such people entail for the organisation's business. *Talent Management*, which is the art of recruiting and retaining the very best, talented people, has developed in response to globalisation and the development of the 'knowledge society', where an individual's knowledge and talents are seen as the company's primary competitive factor. Persson and Aktas argue, however, that just because one is highly talented or very creative does not entail that one is an ideal employee. Very intelligent people (with an IQ of 130 or more) can be very individualistic and may find it difficult to work in a group. Their co-workers may view them as antisocial, difficult to work with, or as troublemakers; all the while the highly gifted employee might be experiencing frustration at work or may be terribly bored. According to Persson and Aktas, the solution is to provide such talented employees room in which to manoeuvre and a large degree of freedom and self-determination at work. This advice runs contrary to another trend in the knowledge society, which is the increase in control and management of work details by the use of sophisticated performance measurement tools and reporting systems. Persson and Aktas' advice is that the employer who wishes to recruit and retain talented employees should adapt the work tasks according to the employee, and not *vice versa*. Furthermore, employers should put trust in such workers, give them freedom and suitably challenging work tasks, and avoid confronting such workers with bureaucracies and formalities.

In the final chapter of this book, the Conclusion, **Ingela Bergmo-Prvulovic** and **Karin Kilhammar** state that there are three important strategic challenges that face future HR work. Bergmo-Prvulovic and Kilhammar's formulation of how these challenges can be met is informed by the content of the preceding chapters and the observations made by each of the authors of these chapters: (i) HR departments should deploy a properly informed and critical attitude towards current trends and conditions, (ii) HR departments should deploy a relational and holistic perspective with respect to the work that they perform, and (iii) HR departments should deploy a positive view of other human beings and an ethical stance towards the work that they perform. The final chapter ends with a discussion of the particular competencies that HR specialists need to develop so as to successfully meet the challenges described above.

Note

1 www.ilo.org/ilostat/.

References

Alvesson, M. (2009). Critical perspectives on strategic HRM. In J. Storey, P. M. Wright, & D. Ulrich (Eds.), *The Routledge Companion to Strategic Human Resource Management* (pp. 52–67). London, UK: Taylor & Francis.

Andersen, T., & Hällsten, F. (2016). Nordic HRM: Distinctiveness and resilience. In M. Dickmann, C. Brewster, & P. Sparrow (Eds.), *International Human Resource Management: Contemporary HR Issues in Europe* (pp. 100–114). London, UK: Routledge.

Berggren, H., & Trägårdh, L. (2010). Pippi Longstocking: The autonomus child and the moral logic of the Swedish welfare state. In H. Mattsson & S.-O. Wallenstein (Eds.), *Swedish Modernism: Architecture, Consumption and the Welfare State* (pp. 10–23). London, UK: Black Dog Publishing.

Berggren, H., & Trägårdh, L. (2015). *Är svensken människa?: Gemenskap och oberoende i det moderna Sverige.* [Are Swedes Human? Fellowship and Independance in Modern Sweden] Stockholm: Norstedts.

Boje, D. M., & Winsor, R. D. (1993). The resurrection of Taylorism: Total quality management's hidden agenda. *Journal of Organizational Change Management, 6*(4), pp. 57–70.

Brandon, J. A. (2001). The new Taylorism. *International Journal of Human Resources Development and Management, 1*(2–4), pp. 162–170.

Czarniawska, B., & Solli, R. (2014). Hur går det för New Public Management i svenska kommuner? [New Public Management in the Swedish county authorities] *Organisation och samhälle, 1*(2), pp. 26–30.

Dowling, P., Festing, M., & Engle, A. (2017). *International Human Resource Management* (7 ed.). Andover, UK: Cengage.

Eklund, K., Berggren, H., & Trägårdh, L. (2011). The Nordic Way. *Report presented at World Economic Forum, Davos.*

Esping-Andersen, G. (1990). *The Three Worlds of Welfare Capitalism.* Cambridge, UK: Polity Press.

Esping-Andersen, G. (2009). *The Incomplete Revolution: Adapting to Women's New Roles.* Cambridge, UK: Polity Press.

Lindeberg, T., Månson, B., & Larsen, H. H. (2013). HRM in Scandinavia—Embedded in the Scandinavian model? In E. Parry, E. Stavrou, & M. Lazarova (Eds.), *Global Trends in Human Resource Management* (pp. 147–162): London, UK: Palgrave Macmillan.

Madsen, P. K. (2014). The Danish road to 'Flexicurity': Where are we compared to others? And how did we get there? In R. J. A. Muffels (Ed.), *Flexibility and Employment Security in Europe: Labour Markets in Transition* (pp. 341–362). Cheltenham: Edward Elgar.

Rauhut, D., & Kahila, P. (2008). *The Regional Welfare Burden in the Nordic Countries.* Nordregio working papers 2008: 6.

Rigby, D., & Bilodeau, B. (2015). *Management Tools & Trends 2015.* London, UK: Bain & Company.

Saco. (2015). *Framtidsutsikter: Arbetsmarknaden för akademiker år 2020.* [Future Prospects: The Labour Market for Academics, 2020] Retrieved from www.saco.se.

Syed, J., & Kramar, R. (2017). Introduction: Theory and practice of HRM in the choppy waters of a complex global context. In J. Syed & R. Kramar (Eds.), *Human Resource Management: A Global and Critical Perspective* (pp. xxvi–xli). London, UK: Palgrave.

PART I
General features of HR work

1

DEVELOPING CO-WORKERSHIP IN ORGANISATIONS

Karin Kilhammar

'Co-workership' is a concept which has become more and more widespread in the Swedish workplace. This can be confirmed by the products sold by consultants who offer solutions for 'co-workership development' and other internal organisational arrangements in an effort to develop co-workership amongst employees. In many HR policy documents, co-workership receives a natural, and often prominent, treatment. Sometimes, such documents are titled as 'co-workership policy' or 'co-workership ideas'.

The concept of 'co-workership' and its use provide us with clues about the importance of the employees for an organisation and its operations. When we consider the HR department's role in showing how important the employees are for the organisation and their support of the development of human resources, it is quite clear that the development of co-workership is an obvious area for HR specialists to work in. However, despite the fact that 'co-workership' is a well-established concept in Sweden and neighbouring countries, it can be interpreted by some as somewhat vague. 'Co-workership' is both a multifaceted and a flexible concept, which results in a variety of interpretations and different forms of implementation in different organisations. In this chapter, we examine what is usually assigned as the content of this concept and the various conflicting interpretations that it can give rise to. When co-workership is developed in cooperation with the organisation's management team, then issues of leadership that are relevant to the development of a properly functioning co-workership are affected. Furthermore, this chapter examines the factors which promote or hinder the development of co-workership, and the important issues that should be considered when co-workership development is to be implemented in an organisation.

'Co-workership' – a multifaceted and flexible concept

When I lecture on 'co-workership', I usually ask the audience what they think the concept is about. Often, the answers are tentative and diffuse, but on the whole, certain aspects repeatedly come to the fore. The content assigned to the concept during these discussions is congruent with the common features apparent in the interpretation of the concept which I have identified in my research in this area.[1]

Fundamental to co-workership is that focus is placed on the employees and that it is concerned with how employees deal with their role within the organisation. By using the concept, the employees' importance for the organisation is revealed. It places demands on the employees as well as provides opportunities for their development. The most central aspect of co-workership is *taking on responsibility*. The discourse[2] on co-workership emphasises individual responsibility, meaning that the employee is active and takes the initiative, even though group responsibility is also included as a dimension to this. Furthermore, *participation* and *influence* are also considered to be fundamental to co-workership, which can be seen as a precondition to *taking on responsibility*. To be able to take on responsibility and to contribute to the organisation's development, the employees need to be familiar with the organisation and have a complete, holistic overview of the organisation (Kilhammar, 2011).

One way to describe co-workership is to claim that it deals with the employees' *relationships* at work. This includes relationships with other people who employees interact with at work, for example, managers, clients, and colleagues, but also the employee's relationship with work itself, with the employer and organisation, and last but not least, the employee's relationship with himself/herself and his/her own private life (Hällstén & Tengblad, 2006).

Despite the fact that there exist common features which most people agree with in the various interpretations of the concept of 'co-workership', there are differences in how these features are ranked. These differences in ranking, or emphasis, tend to be related to the perspective that is taken on co-workership; there is a clear difference between the employer's perspective and the employee's perspective in this regard. The results of previous research (Kilhammar, 2011) show that those who represented the employer emphasised *taking on responsibility* as part of the concept of 'co-workership' more so than the employees, and they also associated *participation* and *influence* with *taking on responsibility* more clearly than the employees. The employees took the position that *participation* and *influence* were of value in themselves to a higher extent. There were also differences in the relationships that were emphasised. From an employer's perspective, the employee's relationship to managers, the employer, and the work itself were considered to be central, whilst the employees primarily associated co-workership with their relationships to their colleagues.[3]

Three areas of tension can be used to further clarify the differences in interpretation of the concept, in cases where the interpretation and the realisation of co-workership differ (see Figure 1.1). These areas of tension form a continuum

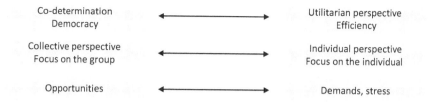

Co-determination
Democracy

←——————————→

Utilitarian perspective
Efficiency

Collective perspective
Focus on the group

←——————————→

Individual perspective
Focus on the individual

Opportunities

←——————————→

Demands, stress

FIGURE 1.1 The areas of tension found in the various interpretations of co-workership (Kilhammar, 2011: 222).

between two poles. While both poles are present in interpretations about co-workership, one pole may be more dominant than the other.

The first area of tension represents the orientation of 'co-workership' and how the concept is used. Is the primary goal of co-workership one of participation, where democratic values are guiding lights, or is the aim of co-workership to achieve the organisation's goals and advance efficiency? In the second area of tension, a collective perspective is contrasted with an individual perspective. The individual perspective emphasises each individual's taking on responsibility and the individual's actions, whilst the collective perspective focuses on the group and how the group functions together. The third area of tension represents how the notion of 'co-workership' is conceived as impacting on the individual: whether 'co-workership' is considered as providing opportunities for development and is something that makes the employee stronger or whether it is considered as a source of increased demands, leading to stress and, in the long run, a cause of illness for the employee (Kilhammar, 2011).

As demonstrated above, 'co-workership' is a multifaceted concept. A superficial consideration of the concept may lead one to think in one particular direction, but a deeper analysis shows that things are more complicated. Opinions about what co-workership represents can differ between different actors within the one and the same organisation. Before large-scale efforts to develop co-workership within an organisation are made, it is thus important to initially make the concept clear to everyone involved and to come to an agreement about its content and the type of co-workership which one wants to feature within the organisation.

'Co-workership' is also a flexible concept. Within the framework of 'neo-institutional theory', we are confronted with the metaphor of popular ideas journeying into, and between, organisations (Czarniawska & Joerges, 1996). Organisations adopt fashionable ideas and translate these ideas so that they suit their own needs. Doing so creates legitimacy and demonstrates that the organisation is 'keeping up with the times', whilst it can also generate ideas that might solve certain problems that the organisation faces.

The growth and use of 'co-workership' over time

The concepts 'co-worker' and 'co-workership' have changed over time, according to different purposes, and have thus been endowed with different meanings.

During the 1950s and 1960s, these concepts were used from a labour union perspective, with the aim of opening up workplace democracy in additional areas where the employer and employee could develop common interests (Stråth, 2000). Accordingly, we note that co-determination and other democratic values were central features at that time.

During the 1970s, employers appropriated the concept of 'co-workershp' and used it from their perspective. This entailed binding employees closer to the company so that their work became part of their identity. A further aim with this was to weaken the employees' strong labour union membership by creating individualised employees (Mahon, 1994; Stråth, 2000, 2002).

It was only during the 1990s that 'co-workership' first began to be used more widely in Sweden. The trend at the time included 'flat' organisational structures with a limited number of managers, which demanded that the employees took on a greater amount of responsibility and participated at the workplace in a way that was different, compared with earlier decades. One result of this change was that the employees, to some degree, took on some of the work assignments which had previously been performed by managers (Hällstén & Tengblad, 2006). Co-workership was sometimes used at the time as a means to change employees' attitudes so that they would adapt to the new working conditions which were being introduced (Jonsson, 2003).

Whilst co-workership during the 1990s primarily resulted in employees taking responsibility for tasks which traditionally had been part of the management's responsibility caused by the very flat leadership structures prevalent at the time, in the 2000s, we note an increased emphasis on *reciprocity* between co-workership and leadership, and the interaction between these two groups (Tengblad, 2011). How co-workership is ultimately realised is dependent on how the management is structured, and *vice versa*. Management structures are needed, but management leaders need to take on different roles, than previously.

The leadership that is needed to develop co-workership

How do we describe the leader's new role as we examine 'co-workership'? What is demanded of management if the goal is to achieve properly functioning co-workership within an organisation? A fundamental condition for this is that management must adapt its leadership role so that it is in total agreement with the form of co-workership that the organisation wishes to achieve. In other words, it is necessary that management be compatible with co-workership. Managers also need to possess the ability to drive the development of co-workership forward within their domain of responsibility and create the necessary conditions for learning (Kilhammar & Ellström, 2015).

The actual manner in which the management structure needs to be arranged so as to achieve total agreement with co-workership is, of course, dependent on the form of co-workership which is desired. Notwithstanding this, there are several fundamental features of management that are necessary to achieve a developed form of co-workership.

First, the management needs to practice a leadership that is generous and delegatory. If employees are to take on increased levels of responsibility and begin to influence the organisation, then managers need to allow for this and delegate certain assignments to the employees and create conditions where taking on responsibility is possible for the employees. This will not happen if the manager is too authoritarian and controlling. Instead, the manager should provide space for the employees' participation, their exercise of influence within the organisation, and even their independence.

Second, a supportive, coaching leadership style by the management is crucial. Employees may also need active support in their roles and in the development of co-workership. It is thus of importance that managers are percipient, support the professional development of the employees, and provide them with constructive criticism.

Finally, management leadership must act as a guide and set standards. Even though the development of co-workership encourages taking on responsibility and independence, leaders are needed who possess a complete overview of the issues at hand, delimit the scope of the work to be done, and provide the work with a clear direction. From the employee's perspective, this may entail that the manager possesses the ability to lead the whole group of employees, in the same direction (Kilhammar, 2011).

Strategies for developing co-workership – two examples

It is not uncommon that centrally coordinated, large-scale efforts are made within organisations, where more or less structured programmes for employee development and the development of co-workership are implemented. How these programmes are implemented and for what purpose can vary, however. This is illustrated by Kilhammar's (2011) study of two initiatives for the development of co-workership in two different organisations and how these initiatives played out.

These organisations had a common, basic motive for the implementation of co-workership, namely to promote the employees' contribution to the effectiveness and quality of the operation of the organisations. However, certain differences were identified; in part, with respect to which concrete problems needed to be solved in each organisation, and, in part, with respect to perceptions of how the goal of co-workership would be achieved. These differences demonstrate the flexibility found in the concept of 'co-workership', where its content and implementation are adapted to an organisation's specific needs (Czarniawska & Joerges, 1996).

In one of the organisations, a county council healthcare provider, the point of departure for the implementation of co-workership was the perceived need for development and participation that was assumed to be included in what "the modern worker" represented. This move was in concert with the council's wish to provide an attractive workplace for its employees so as to ensure the long-term provision of competent employees. At the time, the council had experienced problems with many employees who were on long-term sick leave. The belief was that the development of co-workership would improve the workplace environment. This, in turn, established the conditions for the employees to deliver good quality work, which was also expected to result in the creation of increased quality and efficiency within the organisation, and thus the provision of better healthcare for the patients. The purpose of the development programme was to provide the employees the *conditions* within which they could assume responsibility and perform the work well.

The other organisation, a state-owned service company, had undergone a large-scale restructuring as two separate companies were merged together. In conjunction with this restructuring, a new way of working, *shared service*, was introduced, which placed new demands on the workforce. Co-workership development was then seen as a means by which the workers could satisfy these new work demands. The primary goal was to change the organisational culture and to encourage the workers to become more proactive. The goal of the co-workership development was thus to achieve a direct change in behaviour and attitude, thereby requiring the workers to 'step up' and take on greater responsibility.

What strategies were used to achieve these different goals in these organisations with respect to the development of co-workership? Similarities and differences were identified in the organisations' implementation of their respective co-workership development programmes. The content and structure of the supporting materials were generally the same; these materials dealt with themes touching on everything from 'taking on individual responsibility' and 'cooperating in groups', to 'organisational overviews' and 'customer relations'. The supporting materials were based on short sections on theory, workshop exercises, and discussion questions. The major difference between the two organisations' approaches to the co-workership development was found in the general strategies that were employed by the organisations. The state-owned company used a *top-down strategy* (cf. Sabatier, 1986), whilst the county council employed a strategy which was based on a *learning and development perspective* (cf. McLaughlin, 1976).[4]

In the state-owned company, co-workership development was, to a large degree, directed by the company's management since they had decided on (i) the nature of the work that was to be done in implementing co-workership and (ii) the content of co-workership that was to be treated. The co-workership programme was presented as an educational programme, designed as a series of seminars based on different themes which everyone should attend. The seminars took place either at the local place of work or included staff members from different units who were led by a unit manager and/or a specially trained co-workership coach. Owing to the fact that the structure and content of the programme was so centrally determined by the organisation's management, the workers themselves enjoyed but a very limited amount of influence over what was to be treated during the seminars and how it was to be treated.

A different approach was used by the county council. Despite the common ground which was established for everyone, there was a great amount of freedom provided in how the co-workership development was to take place, according to local needs. The intention was that co-workership development be adapted to the local conditions and that the work to be done in this area be performed with a large degree of participation by the workers themselves. Local plans were formulated in conjunction with managers and workers, as they used the supporting materials that had been prepared according to their choices and their needs. Accordingly, the co-workership development could be more clearly integrated, more so than in the state-owned company above, into the daily work and more readily respond to local needs and solve problems which were directly related to the work situation.

The study focussed on particular units within each organisation: an intensive care unit at the county council and two work groups at an IT unit at the state-owned service company. The results of the study were that, at the unit level, a more comprehensive development of co-workership took place at the intensive care unit than at the IT unit. The unit manager and employees reported that increased levels of participation and a better working environment resulted from the co-workership programme and that they enjoyed a better understanding of each other. They reported that these changes were directly related to the particular areas within co-workership which they actively worked on in developing. At the IT unit, the employees saw no change at the group level as a result of the content of the programme. Notwithstanding this, some employees reported that that cooperation between the two IT groups who had undergone the co-workership programme together had improved as a result of their meetings and the opportunity to learn about each other. At the level of the individual worker, what the co-workership programme had provided was the same for both the intensive care employees and the IT unit employees. In summary, they associated co-workership development more closely with personal development than to the work done at their respective workplaces. Their sense of personal development included 'better self-awareness', 'increased inner strength', and 'increased understanding of others' (Kilhammar, 2011).

What can be learnt from these two examples?

If we examine the differences in the implementation strategies that were used for co-workership development in the two examples discussed in the previous section, three factors can be identified which may have influenced how co-workership development resulted in more widespread and deeper effects at the intensive care unit when compared with the IT unit.

The first factor can be characterised as *the degree of local adaptation*. Implementation research has shown that if a particular idea is to be accepted at the local level, then a mutual process of adaptation needs to take place where the idea is related to, and adapted to, the local context and local needs (Majone & Wildavsky,

1979/1984; McLaughlin, 1976). In the examples above, it is apparent that this was the strategy that was employed by the county council's programme and was implemented at the local level at the unit that was studied. In the state-owned company, the programme was more directed and controlled with respect to the co-workership themes, which were to be treated at the local level, and the degree of adaptation to the local context was minimal (Kilhammar & Ellström, 2015).

The second factor is concerned with *the degree to which co-workership development is integrated into the daily work*. A necessary condition for this integration is that the employees understand the connection between (i) the material and concepts that are dealt within the co-workership development programme and (ii) the work that is done at the unit. However, whilst this understanding is necessary, it is not sufficient; understanding must be translated into practice. In this context, the line managers play a crucial role in creating the space and structures for learning and development at work (Ellinger & Bostrom, 1999; Ellström 2012). At the intensive care unit, the integration of co-workership development and the employees' daily work was strong and the development of co-workership and the unit's ongoing operations went hand in hand. The IT groups engaged in co-workership development separately from their daily work, and the level of co-workership at this organisation was hardly affected outside the seminar sessions in the programme. Note that previous research has shown that it is difficult to transfer that which has been learnt in formal contexts over to work situations (Ellström, 1996; Goldstein & Ford, 2002), thereby providing an explanation as to why the development of co-workership, at the unit level, did not take place for the IT groups.

The third factor identified is *the degree of participation* in the development work. Participation is a necessary condition for the adaptation of the co-workership development to local needs because it is the employees and unit managers who know the local conditions and needs best (Kilhammar & Ellström, 2015; McLaughlin, 1987). The employees' increased participation may be assumed to positively influence levels of motivation and engagement in the development work (Eklund, 2003; Ellström, 2006a). Research exists which shows that participation at the local level in implementation processes is necessary for sustainable change to occur (McLaughlin, 1976, 1987). At the county council, and more specifically at the intensive care unit that was studied, the level of participation by the employees was high during the whole process. Employees were highly involved in taking stock of their needs and in the choices of what they were to work on. They were also engaged in the development work that took place on a broad plane. At the state-owned company and in the IT groups that were studied, the level of participation was limited, including the choice of co-workership areas that were to be dealt with within the groups.

At the level of the individual employee, the similarities in the results of the co-workership development can be explained by the fact that the employees in both organisations were provided with opportunity to reflect over their role as an employee and over the actions that they take in this role. Reflection is important for deep learning, not least reflection that takes place within a dialogue (Boud,

2006; Ellström, 2006b; Mezirow, 1991). However, it may be sometimes difficult to translate what one has learnt from such reflective practices into one's daily life, if there is a lack of support for this to happen (cf. Ellström & Ellström, 2014) and if no practical work is done with the development of co-workership which is related to the actual tasks performed at the unit.

Challenges that HR face in co-workership development

In the introduction of this chapter, it was stated that co-workership and co-workership development fall within the HR department's domain of responsibility. The HR department can be concerned with the development of co-workership in several ways. Co-workership can be a specialisation which a HR specialist can have particular responsibility for. HR specialists may be assigned to, or by their own initiative, develop co-workership in their organisation by means of special projects. What should one bear in mind when one is tasked with this assignment?

When one is to formulate the structure of a co-workership development pro-gramme for a large-scale implementation, then note that the structure should include those factors which have been shown to support co-workership devel-opment with respect to (i) local adaptation, (ii) the integration of co-workership development in the daily work, and (iii) securing the participation of the em-ployees. Furthermore, the provision of supporting materials and an overarching direction to the development work to be done should also be seen as being ben-eficial. However, one needs to allow for openness about how the co-workership development will take place at the local level, so that the development work that is to be done can be adapted to local needs and conditions.

'Co-workership' is a multifaceted and flexible concept. The actual content assigned to the concept, and the issues that are emphasised, can be different, depending on the perspective that the concept is viewed from. Research shows that there is a clear dividing line in interpretations of the concept, between the employer's perspective and the employee's perspective. To ensure that the notion of 'co-workership' gains a proper audience and is taken seriously, communication between the various levels within organisations about the content of 'co-workership' and its implementation must take place, and different vested interests and perspectives should be taken into account. Such communication and dis-cussions can create a common platform for co-workership development within an organisation. Doing so also allows for the thoughtful consideration of 'co-workership' as it is situated in the context of the organisation and the values that the organisation, the management, and the employees subscribe to. For this purpose (and the associated analysis that is to be done before and during the de-velopment work), the model in Figure 1.1, which summarises the areas of tension described earlier, can be used as a tool.

With respect to the area of tension between 'co-workership' as an individual versus a collective concept, the individual aspects are emphasised in the discourse. Primarily, focus has been placed on the individual's taking on responsibility and the individual's actions. A suitable space and support structure within one's environment is, however, needed to allow one to change oneself and one's actions. Thus the interaction between management and employees is important, as well as the support that is provided in the work team. The collective aspects of 'co-workership' should also be present and made clear during co-workership development.

The area of tension which includes how the idea of 'co-workership' is perceived to impact on the individual – whether it is perceived to be an opportunity for development and something which will strengthen the individual, or whether it is perceived to be something demanding and a source of stress – is also something which should be taken into consideration. What can be done to ensure that co-workership development is seen as something beneficial for the individual, and thus lead to more engaged employees? The creation of balance is one way to move forward; for example, create a balance between existing preconditions and the demands placed on the employee by providing the employees adequate resources in the form of time, competence, and a clear mandate to properly engage with the development work and to take responsibility for what is expected of them. Research has shown that it is necessary to adapt the level of responsibility and demands made on individuals according to the individual's willingness and ability (Hällstén, 2007; Hällstén & Tengblad, 2006). People find themselves in different life situations and have different ambitions. They do not always find themselves ready to engage themselves 100% in such development work. Everyone cannot be treated in the same way; one should be considerate but also encourage the engagement of individuals by taking into account their unique circumstances. The HR department has an important role in this regard to support managers in their local co-workership development work.

Leadership and co-workership are mutually dependent on each other. The way in which co-workership is practiced is dependent on leadership, and *vice versa*. If a co-workership development project is to give rise to the desired results, then the leadership within an organisation should be put on a course which is in agreement with the goals which one wishes to achieve with co-workership. Consequently, it may be appropriate to engage in parallel projects where both co-workership and leadership are developed, so that leaders can come to understand their role. It concerns both the management's daily behaviour and the way that they create opportunities for delegating responsibility and allowing for participation which characterises a developed co-workership.

Co-workership is fundamental to an organisation, just as leadership is, irrespective of whether the concept of 'co-workership' is used or not. Some form or another of co-workership is practiced in every organisation where we find employees. Focusing on 'co-workership' and its use can clarify how important employees are within, and for, an organisation. Such practices can form the basis for further development, which can lead to something beneficial for both the individual employees and for the organisation as a whole.

Co-workership builds on trust in the employees and their abilities. Consequently, the employees' participation in the formulation of the co-workership that is present within an organisation should be seen as granted. The employees' perspective must be taken into account and their knowledge properly curated. Implementing co-workership development only from the employer's perspective and according to the employer's conditions stands in opposition to the original conception of 'co-workership'. Influence, participation, and even respect and trust for the employee demand a mutual understanding where both parties perceive that they will benefit from this development.

Recommended reading

Kilhammar, Karin (2011), *Idén om medarbetarskap: En studie av en idés resa in i och genom två organisationer.* [The idea of Co-workership. A study of an idea's journey into and through two organizations]. English summary, pp. 235–251. Academic dissertation. Linköping: Linköping University. Department of Behavioural Science and Learning.
Kilhammar, Karin & Ellström, Eva (2015), Co-workership in practice: A study of two Swedish organizations. *Human Resource Development International, 18*(4), pp. 328–345.

Notes

1 The common features thus identified in the interpretation of 'co-workership' are based on previous research, how the concept has been used historically, and on the empirical data collected as part of my doctoral dissertation (Kilhammar, 2011).
2 A 'discourse' can be simply described as a public conversation about some phenomenon. A discourse is not limited to oral communication, but may include all forms of communication.
3 The 'employer's perspective' is represented by managers and the HR department, whilst employees and union representatives represented the 'employee's perspective'.
4 The classification of these two different perspectives is based on research of implementation (e.g., McLaughlin, 1976; Elmore, 1979/1980).

References

Boud, David (2006), Creating the space for reflection at work. In David Boud, Peter Cressey & Peter Docherty (eds.), *Productive reflection at work* (pp. 158–169). London: Routledge.
Czarniawska, Barbara & Joerges, Bernward (1996), Travels of ideas. In Barbara Czarniawska & Guje Sevón (eds.), *Translating organizational change* (pp. 13–48). Berlin: Walter de Gruyter.
Eklund, Jörgen (2003), Ledning genom styrning och genom participation. [Leadership by management and by participation.] In Per-Erik Ellström & Henrik Kock (eds.), *Ledarskap i teamorganiserad verksamhet: En antologi* [Leadership in business operations that are organised according to teams: An anthology] (pp. 148–158). CMTO Research Monographs No 2. Linköping: CMTO, Linköpings universitet.
Ellinger, Andrea D. & Bostrom, Robert P. (1999), Managerial coaching behaviors in learning organizations. *Journal of Management Development, 18*(9), pp. 752–771.

Ellström, Eva (2012), Managerial support for learning at work: A qualitative study of first-line managers in elder care. *Leadership in Health Science, 25*(4), pp. 278–287.

Ellström, Eva & Ellström, Per-Erik (2014), Learning outcomes of Work-Based Training Programme: The significance of managerial support. *European Journal of Training and Development, 38*(3), pp. 180–197.

Ellström, Per-Erik (1996), *Arbete och lärande: Förutsättningar och hinder för lärande i dagligt arbete.* [Work and learning: Facilitating and constraining factors for learning in daily work] Solna: Arbetslivsinstitutet.

Ellström, Per-Erik (2006a), Two logics of learning. In Elena Antonacopoulou, Peter Jarvis, Vibeke Andersen, Bente Elkjaer, & Steen Høyrup (eds.), *Learning, working and living. mapping the terrain of working life learning* (pp. 33–49). New York, NY: Palgrave Macmillan.

Ellström, Per-Erik (2006b), The meaning and role of reflection in informal learning at work. In David Boud, Peter Cressey, & Peter Docherty (eds.), *Productive reflection at work* (pp. 43–53). London: Routledge.

Elmore, Richard F. (1979/1980), Backward mapping: Implementation research and policy decisions. *Political Science Quarterly, 94*(4), pp. 601–616.

Goldstein, Irwin L. & Ford, Kevin (2002), *Training in organizations: Needs assessment, development, and evaluation* (4th edition). Belmont, CA: Wadsworth, Thomson Learning.

Hällstén, Freddy (2007), Medarbetarskap i praktiken – karta och kompass för förändring. [Co-workership in practice – Map and compass for change] In Stefan Tengblad, Freddy Hällstén, Christer Ackerman, & Johan Velten (eds.), *Medarbetarskap: Från ord till handling* [Co-workership – from words to action] (pp. 136–152). Malmö: Liber.

Hällstén, Freddy & Tengblad, Stefan (2006), Medarbetarskap i praktiken [Co-workership in practice]. In Freddy Hällstén & Stefan Tengblad (eds.), *Medarbetarskap i praktiken* [Co-workership in practice] (pp. 9–32). Lund: Studentlitteratur.

Jonsson, Karin (2003), *Från vision till verklighet?* [From vision to reality?] Master's dissertation no. 2003: 5. Uppsala: Pedagogiska institutionen, Uppsala universitet.

Kilhammar, Karin (2011), *Idén om medarbetarskap: En studie av en idés resa in i och genom två organisationer.* [The idea of Co-workership. A study of an idea's journey into and through two organizations] Academic dissertation. Linköping: Linköping University, Department of Behavioural Science and Learning.

Kilhammar, Karin & Ellström, Eva (2015), Co-workership in practice: A study of two Swedish organizations. *Human Resource Development International, 18*(4), pp. 328–345.

Mahon, Rianne (1994), Wage-earners and/or co-workers? Contested identities. *Economic and Industrial Democracy – An International Journal, 15*(3), pp. 355–383.

Majone, Giandomenico & Wildavsky, Aaron (1979/1984), Implementation as evolution. In Jeffrey L. Pressman & Aaron Wildavsky (eds.), *Implementation* (3rd edition, pp. 163–180). Berkley and Los Angeles: University of California Press.

McLaughlin, Milbrey W. (1976), Implementation as mutual adaptation: Change in classroom organization. In Walter Williams & Richard F. Elmore (eds.), *Social program implementation* (pp. 167–180). New York: Academic Press.

McLaughlin, Milbrey W. (1987), Learning from experience: Lessons from policy implementation. *Educational Evaluation and Policy Analysis, 9*(2), pp. 171–178.

Mezirow, Jack (1991), *Transformative dimensions of adult learning.* San Francisco, CA: Jossey Bass.

Sabatier, Paul A. (1986), Top–down and bottom–up: Approaches to implementation research: A critical analysis and suggested synthesis. *Journal of Public Policy, 6*(1), pp. 21–48.

Stråth, Bo (2000), *Mellan medbestämmande och medarbetare: Metall och samhällsutvecklingen 1957–1976.* [Between Co-determination and Co-worker: The Swedish Metal Workers' Federation and the transformation of society, 1957–1976]. Stockholm: Metall.

Stråth, Bo (2002), 1968: From co-determination to co-worker: The power of language. *Thesis Eleven, 68,* pp. 64–81.

Tengblad, Stefan (2011), *Medarbetarskap på 60 minuter.* [Co-workership in 60 minutes]. Skövde: Skövde högskola.

2

EFFECTIVE INTERACTION IN ORGANISATIONS

Annika Engström

The number of meetings that are held at the workplace is on the increase, despite the fact that many claim that such meetings are ineffective, irrelevant, and sometimes even a waste of time (Rogelberg, Leach, Warr & Burnfield, 2006; Rogelberg, Shanock & Scott, 2011). One strategic issue for the HR department in an organisation is to consider how different meetings (within the organisation) can be supported, organised, and managed so that they are effective. This chapter presents an in-depth discussion of this issue and challenges the rationalist approach towards effectiveness by presenting a more humanist approach, where learning and the complexity of human resources within an organisation are two very important aspects to take into consideration.

Most discussions about effectiveness in organisations make a distinction between *external effectiveness*, usually described as "doing the right thing" or "*what* is done", and *internal effectiveness* (*efficiency*), "doing things in the right way" or "*how* things are done". This distinction can be further elaborated on by defining *external effectiveness* in terms of how well the recipient's demands are met, thereby focussing on the results of a process. *Internal effectiveness* can be understood in terms of how well certain finite resources are used in the above-mentioned process, such that the maximum benefit is enjoyed from those resources. *Effectiveness* describes a system's ability to use resources to the best possible effect. Hackman (1987) claims, however, that it is not sufficient to merely measure effectiveness at an isolated point in time, using a rationalist approach only, for example, in economic terms or in terms of a number of goods produced. Instead, effectiveness must be considered over time and provided with a humanist dimension where human beings are included as part of the resource(s) being used. He claims that effectiveness is achieved (i) when groups of people complete their tasks and achieve the goals which have been established, (ii) when the group has learnt something and has improved its way of working, and (iii) when the individuals within the group are acknowledged and receive the support from within the group which is needed for their own work. Groups that consist of individuals who, for some time, are frustrated or display dissatisfaction cannot be considered to be effective, irrespective of how they achieve their goals.

Communication as part of the learning process

People are contradictory and complex beings in their nature and learn from their experiences in interaction with other people (Dewey, 2002). People often experience difficulty in confronting differences and things that deviate from what they consider to be 'normal' or what they habitually do, despite the fact that these are the very things which people need to be confronted with if they are to develop (Gantt & Agazarian, 2004). Human complexity sometimes gives rise to contradictions and conflict in organisations, something which researchers highlight as providing opportunities for learning and change. Even tensions in hierarchical structures and disruptions and a lack of consistency in organisations can be considered to be opportunities for change and development (Easterby-Smith & Lyles, 2003; Engeström, 2001; Seo & Creed, 2002; Weick, 1976). In this chapter, these discrepancies are identified and named and categorised as *triggers* in the context of 'organisational learning'. When these discrepancies are revealed and properly dealt with within an organisation, then they can be used to contribute positively to developmental work. However, if they are suppressed, left invisible, or left to operate in the background, there is the danger that they can retard the progress of the organisation (Engeström, 2014).

A challenge that is faced by many organisations is to find a balance between 'cost efficiency' and 'innovation', and the assignment of the time that is to be used in developmental activities. This is a difficult task, not least for small- and medium-sized companies (Ekberg, Eklund, Ellström & Johansson, 2006). The intense pursuit for efficiency may hamper innovation. Within an industry, the use of different management models and meetings for day-to-day management has shown some success in controlling the delivery of that which has already been planned for. The difficulty that arises during the same type of meetings is the proper exploitation of the innovation potential that exists within the organisation (Lovén, 2013). A similar challenge is faced by researchers when they consider learning in organisations and that difficult-to-find (but nonetheless necessary) balance between *learning to execute* and *learning to develop* (Ellström, 2010a; Engeström, 2014).

How well an organisation performs, as well as how effective it is, is dependent on the interaction that takes place within groups (Hackman & Morris, 1978) and between groups (McGrath & Tschan, 2004) when they execute a task. Edmondson (2012) argues that it is at the group level where organisational learning takes place. In today's workplace, work groups are not as static and tightly knit as they were previously; nowadays different constellations of groups continually intersect with each other, as they perform different tasks. Because of this, Edmondson argues that employees who are involved in such interaction need to be trained in *teaming* so that this important competence can be mastered. This entails rapidly establishing what is needed in relationships so that the group members feel secure, as they move on to quickly formulate a plan as to how the task on hand will be dealt with and how work tasks will be distributed within the group. It is this interaction which enables critical reflection over routines and work methods that develops the organisation's operations, which, in turn, allows important decisions and necessary prioritisations to be made. However, this interaction may also give rise to incorrect decisions being made, allowing groups to waste time and energy on conflicts and establishing norms at the workplace, which lead to passivity instead of activity (Hackman, 1990). An important area for interaction and learning in organisations are at different work meetings, where individuals who possess different professional functions and competencies communicate with each other about common tasks (Engström, 2014)

An organisation is identified by the assignments and tasks that it performs. It is also the nature of these tasks which creates the conditions for individual- and group learning, whilst these different tasks simultaneously allow us to presuppose that these individuals and groups possess the knowledge to perform these tasks correctly. We note that this is a mutual relationship. The degree of complexity in the work tasks results in different courses of action and places different demands on reflective practices. Simple tasks, for example, may be performed by following a previously given instruction or dealt with by following a routine. More complex tasks may need to be completed by using new ways of working. It is during the execution of these tasks, the so-called 'work processes', when learning in the organisation takes place.

Ellström (2010b) differentiates between expressed, visible, explicit work processes and tacit, invisible, implicit work processes. Explicit work processes include those assignments, tasks, and routines which are published in the organisation's documents like policies and in written instructions of various types. These may also include agreements of a less formal nature or even performance models which an organisation might use for quality assurance purposes. Explicit work processes establish the framework for the work that should take place. Such work processes are official, open to scrutiny, and quite easy to question or have opinions about. Implicit work processes are the interpretations and values which inform the employee how the work is actually performed. Power struggles, disagreements, and other divergent forces which lie beneath the surface may rise up and make themselves felt. That which is implicit, tacit, and not spoken of remains diffuse and obscure. The same work task can be completed in many different ways, despite the presence of explicit routines and instructions on how the task 'should' be performed. It is difficult to have opinions about or question such work processes because they are difficult to discern and interpret.

Ellström (2010b) argues that learning in an organisation takes place in the interaction between these two types of work process (see Figure 2.1), and that the tension that exists between these two processes gives rise to the discrepancies which were described in the introduction of this chapter. In the figure, note that

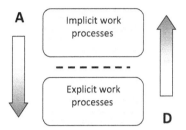

FIGURE 2.1 How learning takes place in organisations, in the interaction between explicit and implicit work processes. 'A' represents adaptive learning according to the logic of task execution, and 'D' represents developmental learning according to the logic of task development.

in the direction of arrow 'A', adaptive learning takes place, via instructions and regulations. Here, learning is focussed on the knowledge which is needed to complete and master a task. Problem-solving occurs, based on predefined knowledge, goals, concepts, regulations, and methods, and can be called the *logic of execution*. In the direction of the arrow marked 'D', developmental learning takes place, when that which occurs in the implicit processes is made visible and results in reflection and common agreement. In this process, innovation and enquiry are focussed on. Furthermore, central to this process is the questioning of established structures and routines, since the goal for such learning are formulated *post hoc*, as new ideas emerge and norms are tested. This is called *logic of development*.[1]

Research on communication in groups can be related to the logic discussed earlier, where a distinction between communication that is used to *explain* something and communication that is used to *explore* something is drawn (Agazaran & Gantt, 2000). The first mode of communication entails just reporting on something that is already known – existing knowledge, presented as factual constructions. The second mode of communication entails the search for answers to things that one does *not* know – new knowledge and experiences (primarily). In the explanatory approach, it is easy to be confronted with contradictions which do not lead to the solution of a problem. The conversation may primarily become an argument about who knows (or is thinking) correctly or incorrectly. This type of communication can lead to deadlocks which are sometimes difficult to extract oneself out from. It is not uncommon that such arguments end with some form of dismissal, including sarcasm, insult, or, at worst, a personal attack. In contrast, in the exploring mode of communication, the point of departure is to discover something new. Such a standpoint can give rise to a dialogue where it is possible to shift through ideas and new ways of understanding and solving problems.

In order to deal with differences of opinions in groups, Agazarian and Gantt (2000) developed a theory called functional subgrouping. They claim that different opinions need to be kept apart because, otherwise arguments and disagreements can easily develop into a struggle during the meeting, and constructive dialogue comes to a halt. These researchers suggest that such differences of opinion should be examined, each on their own, so that work can be done on finding common ground between opposing positions. Doing so will allow for the development of new solutions to problems, with people working in cooperation with each other.

Losada and Heaply (2004) present a comprehensive study of communication in different business teams. Sixty business teams were categorised in terms of efficiency (their level of performance) according to a number of different parameters, including customer satisfaction, profitability, and a 360-degree assessment.[2] The result of the categorisation process was as follows: 15 teams had 'high-level performance', 26 teams had 'medium-level performance', and 19 teams had 'low-level performance'. The researchers then observed the teams and recorded and coded the verbal communication that took place within the teams according to three dimensions as follows: (i) the content of the communication (positive or negative), (ii) the focus of the conversation (on the speaker or on someone else), and (iii) the mode of communication (explanatory or exploratory). The high-level performance teams scored highly with respect to the amount of positive content in their communication, and they showed a balance between focussing on others and themselves, and a balance between an exploratory mode of communication v. an explanatory mode of communication. The other teams which were observed were predominantly negative, focussed their interest on themselves, and mainly used an explanatory mode of communication.

Meetings at an industrial company

A qualitative field study (Engström, 2014) took place at a small industrial company between 2008 and 2010. The company manufactured and sold custom-made cabinets and sheet metal cladding to the building, transport, and marine sectors. The company had its head office in Småland (Sweden) and sales offices in Denmark and Norway. Since 2005, the company formed part of a group of companies, along with two other companies. From this time, the company underwent rapid expansion, large investments in new machinery were made, the planning department was enlarged, the fabricators worked more closely with the customers, and weekly staff meetings, every Friday, were established. During its peak years of 2007 and 2008, the company had a turnover of almost 9 million euro, 50 employees, plus an additional 18 agency workers on the production line. The financial crisis of 2008/2009 and the general decline of industrial work in Sweden had a severe impact on the company. Customer orders decreased; for example, one customer who usually ordered 50 cabinets cut their order in half. The turnover sank drastically during 2008 and 2009 and all of the agency workers' contracts were terminated. A number of other retrenchments were made at the time.

Within the framework set out for the field study, a sub-study of 12 work meetings was conducted. These meetings took place during a 6-week period, in three different groupings which were responsible for dealing with all of the processes within the business, from request to delivery. These meetings were observed and filmed. The content and the processes that took place during the meetings were analysed. When the analysis of the content of the meetings was complete, statements were made about *what* the groups had spoken about (the task). The interaction analysis captured *how* the groups discussed the different issues that were addressed during the meetings. Each content sequence was then analysed by focussing on how the communication developed and what it led up to. By doing this, it was possible at the next stage of the analysis to relate *content* and *process* with each other, thus enabling reasoning and arguments such as "During meeting A spoke of task B and conversed according to communicative pattern C". The next stage of the analysis was to establish links between certain communicative patterns and specific ways in which tasks were dealt with. The results are discussed in the following.[3]

More space is assigned to certain questions

A number of interesting phenomena were observed in the results of the study. When the different groups dealt with technical problems, then the dialogue, in the most part, moved forward and problems were solved. Knowledge was shared without prestige, routines and methods of working were questioned and challenged, and the groups were able to use their powers of exploring to solve problems. However, when it came to dealing with problems about organising the work, they found themselves on rocky ground. The meetings then fell silent, became somewhat sombre, and deadlocks arose. It sometimes seemed as if the tasks at hand were impossible to complete, and the same fundamental problems in the company came up during the meetings, over and over again, without being solved.

Another pattern which emerged was with respect to technical questions; there were forums for problems which needed to be solved for both in the short-term and for the long-term. The short-term problems entailed changes in some already-existing construction so as to more simply satisfy a customer's demands or to make the manufacturing process cheaper or faster. Other issues could involve finding a solution to a technical production problem, for example, by using a special welding technique or surface treatment to improve the quality of the product. This type of question was dealt with during the regular weekly meetings. For long-term problems, there was a forum for changes in design where more fundamental technical problems could be dealt with. In these forums, general design problems were discussed and debated, for example, decisions about what bolt sizes were to be considered as standard and how drawings and suggestions for improvements in the technical system should be dealt with. Topics were dealt with such as which design types should be promoted for the customers' attention, so that products could be made using more cost-efficient methods and materials. Issues of a technical character thus enjoyed dedicated forums, including the execution of manufacturing tasks, as well as the development of these tasks.

Certain simple work organisational questions and priorities were also addressed during the weekly meetings. This may have included a tender that should be prioritised, a change in the production flow, or the deployment of extra employees. The more fundamental problems and issues to do with work organisation lacked a forum for discussion. This type of question was addressed, however, during the weekly meetings (so-called 'execution meetings') where ongoing production projects and daily deliveries were to be discussed. Sometimes there was a flood of problems that had to be solved, some of them production problems, but also more fundamental issues for the company. When the groups (during their meetings) came up against a wall with regard to a project which needed to be prioritised or because an important customer had made a warranty claim, the groups responsible for production had problems in giving space to these issues. The company's customer centre, on many occasions, had accepted projects from customers with too short a delivery date, something which put the production group in a bind. An already very busy business was asked to deal with too many orders, and sometimes it seemed impossible to satisfy all the orders. A great deal of frustration was felt at these moments, and no solution was found during the meetings. Simply put, there was no forum for developmental questions concerning production at the factory.

Different patterns of interaction for execution and development

The communication in the meetings showed a different pattern, depending on whether execution or development issues were being dealt with. Even the management revealed different attitudes, depending on the issues that were being dealt with. Figure 2.2 presents the patterns which were observed.

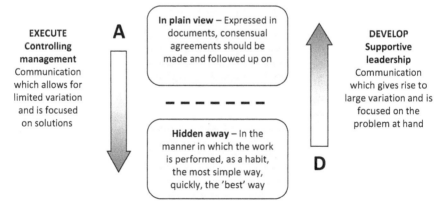

FIGURE 2.2 How different communicative patterns and management were related to the different forms of logic depending on whether execution or development issues were being dealt with.

Communication that was related to the execution of specific tasks was often short and consisted of instructions, orders, clarifications, and suggestions for solutions. The manager directed these conversations and kept everyone's attention focussed on the task at hand. Communication related to development was dominated by the participation of the other staff members at the meetings. The conversations consisted mainly of the generation of ideas, exploratory questions and answers, and the questioning of current work methods. In these instances, management was in the background and functioned more as a source of support for the ongoing dialogue.

A lack of interaction between groups

Another result of this research project concerned the interaction between groups. It was quite clear that certain groups were more effective than others in relation to the specific tasks that the group was responsible for. It also became apparent that the groups were dependent on each other because a large part of the production at the factory occurred as a constant flow where one person's work tasks were dependent on another person completing their tasks. In those cases where there was a 'human chain' that linked the groups' work together, the transfer of information worked properly. But when this condition was not present, the separate groups simply took on responsibility for their own tasks and did not really reflect over what consequences their work had for the other groups. This caused problems, and learning at the organisational level suffered because of this.

Some conclusions about effective teamwork

One conclusion that we draw from the examples given above is that groups who are expected to cooperate with each other on certain tasks should be given the possibility and the correct task(s) so that this actually occurs. This is a point raised in the previous chapter, where Karin Kilhammar describes the importance of people's participation and the interaction between employees and managers as a function of this. Another conclusion we can draw is that issues that are not brought to everyone's attention and issues that lack a dedicated forum where they can be addressed are a source of disruption for the organisation and decrease the organisation's effectiveness. This argument is developed further in the next chapter by Cecilia Bjursell and Dag Raudberget as they investigate the different tensions which can be found in organisations and highlight the importance of bringing tacit knowledge to the fore and making such knowledge available so that it can be shared within an organisation.

People who are frustrated experience difficulties in focussing on their work task, and a business that is under stress and fails to set aside time for critical reflection will experience difficulties in achieving effectiveness, in the long term. The results of the study reported on in this chapter (Engström, 2014) show that developmental forces that are left unchecked can cause frustration and disrupt execution. Execution and development are two different, but equally important, processes with their own distinct logic which should be kept apart. Integration of these two processes takes place when the same individuals and groups are involved in both processes and they are related to the same task. An additional conclusion is that execution and development meetings should be kept distinct from each other; in separate meetings where communication and management can be adapted to each purpose (see Figure 2.3).

Dedicated meetings for execution issues, where participants can communicate with each other about what they already know and can do, will stimulate adaptive learning in an organisation and its internal efficiency ('doing things the right way'). This will preserve and secure stability in the organisation. Meetings for development issues, on the other hand, where people can critically evaluate ideas and contribute new ideas, will stimulate developmental learning in the organisation and its external effectiveness ('doing the right things'). This is a source of transformation and ensures innovation in an organisation. Both of these logics are important, since they are the two sides of the same coin.

The chairperson, or other leading position, of a meeting needs to possess different actions for different situations; just as different individuals across the whole organisation need to develop their ability to communicate for effective interaction, according to the demands of the different meeting contexts and meeting logic. The HR department has an important role in sharing knowledge of the

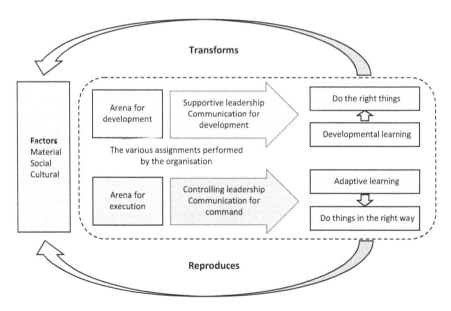

FIGURE 2.3 A dynamic model of effectiveness which shows how different tasks can be dealt with in parallel, in meetings for execution and development, respectively.

human forces that are at play in such situations, which is crucial for achieving effectiveness. Work meetings are necessary in organisations to stimulate learning and the exchange of knowledge, including both simple and complex tasks. What needs to be improved is the clarity of the purpose of the meeting, the ways in which communication takes place, and the way in which meetings are lead.

Some tips for efficient interaction

The models presented in this chapter are theoretical and should be translated into practice depending on the conditions that prevail in each organisation. The following includes a number of tips for those who work with learning in organisations and who are involved in work meetings:

- Map discrepancies within the organisation so that any potential development forces associated with these issues can be dealt with in a dedicated meeting forum.
- Assess the organisation's meeting structure and schedule so that each meeting is synchronised with the next and ensure that each meeting 'delivers' to the next.
- Ensure that there are 'human links' who have a clear assignment to transfer important information and feedback to different groups.
- Specify the purpose of each meeting. Differentiate between execution meetings and development meetings. Note that knowledge integration takes place between individuals and groups, and so the same people (as far as possible) should be involved in both processes.
- Ensure that the correct competencies are in attendance at the different meetings.
- Practice communication across the organisation.
- Train the meeting chairs or leaders to deal with different types of meetings in different ways.

Recommended reading

Argyris, Chris (2010), *Organizational Traps: Leadership, Culture, Organizational Design*. New York: Oxford University Press.
Benjamin, Ben E., Yeager, Amy & Simon, Anita (2012), *Conversation Transformation: Recognize and Overcome the 6 Most Destructive Communication Patterns*. New York: McGraw-Hill.
Edmondson, Amy (2012), *Teaming: How Organizations Learn, Innovate and Compete in the Knowledge Economy*. San Fransisco: Jossey-Bass.
Dewey, John (2002), *Human Nature and Conduct*. Dover Publications.

Notes

1 The two different logics of learning; 'adaptive learning' and 'developmental learning' can be compared with Argyris and Schön's (1978) terms of *single-loop learning*, where questions about the facts associated with a problem are asked and solutions

are discussed, and *double-loop learning*, where questions about causes and underlying factors to the problem are asked, respectively.
2 For example, a team member is evaluated by his superiors, peers, and subordinates.
3 A more comprehensive description of the study and the results can be found in Engström (2014).

References

Agazarian, Y. M., & Gantt, S. P. (2000). *Autobiography of a Theory. Developing a Theory of Living Human Systems and Its System-Centered Practice*. Philadelphia: Jessica Kingsley Publishers Ltd.

Dewey, J. (2002). *Human Nature and Conduct*. Dover Publications.

Easterby-Smith, M., & Lyles, M. A. (2003). *Handbook of Organizational Learning and Knowledge Management*. Malden, MA: Blackwell.

Edmondson, A. (2012). Teamwork on the Fly. *Harvard Business Review, 90*(4), 72–80.

Ekberg, K., Eklund, J., Ellström, P.-E., Johansson, S., & (Eds.). (2006). *Tid för utveckling?* [Time for development?] Lund Studentlitteratur.

Ellström, P.-E. (2010a). Organizational learning in P. L. Peterson, E. Baker & B. McGaw, (Eds.), *International Encyclopedia of Education* (Vol. 3rd Edition), 47–52. Amsterdam: Elsevier.

Ellström, P.-E. (2010b). Practice-based Innovation: A Learning Perspective. *Journal of Workplace Learning, 22*(1/2), 27.

Engeström, Y. (2001). Expansive Learning at Work: Toward an Activity Theoretical Reconceptualization. *Journal of Education and Work, 14*(1), 133–156. doi:10.1080/13639080020028747.

Engström, A. (2014). *Lärande samspel för effektivitet – en studie av arbetsgrupper i ett mindre industriföretag.* [Learning interactions for efficiency – a study of work teams in a small industrial company] (Fil dr), Linköpings Universitet, Linköping. (Linköping Studies in Behavioural Science No. 185)

Gantt, S. P., & Agazarian, Y. M. (2004). System-centered Emotional Intelligence: Beyond Individual Systems to Organizational Systems. *Organizational Analysis, 12*(2), 147–169.

Hackman, R. (Ed.) (1990). *Groups that Work (and those that don't)*. San Francisco: Jossey-Bass.

Hackman, R. (1987). The Design of Work Teams. In J. W. Lorsch (Ed.), *Handbook of Organizational Behavior* (pp. 315–342). Englewood Cliff: Prentice-Hall.

Hackman, R., & Morris, C. G. (Eds.). (1978). *Group Process and Group Effectiveness: A Reappraisal*. New York: Academic Press.

Losada, M., & Heaphy, E. (2004). The Role of Positivity and Connectivity in the Performance of Business Teams. *The American Behavioral Scientist, 47*(6), 740–765.

Lovén, E. (2013). Kreativitet, innovation och lean. [Creativity, innovation, and lean] In P. Sederblad (Ed.), *Lean i arbetslivet.* [Lean in the work-life] Stockholm: Liber.

McGrath, J. E., & Tschan, F. (2004). Dynamics in Groups and Teams. In M. S. Poole & A. H. Van de Ven (Eds.), *Handbook of Organizational Change and Innovation*. New York: Oxford University Press.

Rogelberg, S. G., Leach, D. J., Warr, P. B., & Burnfield, J. L. (2006). "Not Another Meeting!" Are Meeting Time Demands Related to Employee Well-Being? *Journal of Applied Psychology, 91*(1), 83–96. doi:10.1037/0021-9010.91.1.83.

Rogelberg, S. G., Shanock, L. R., & Scott, C. W. (2011). Wasted Time and Money in Meetings: Increasing Return on Investment. *Small Group Research*, *43*(2), 236–245. doi:10.1177/1046496411429170.

Seo, M.-G., & Creed, D. W. E. (2002). Institutional Contradictions, Praxis, and Institutional Change: A Dialectical Perspective. *The Academy of Management Review*, *27*(2), 222–247.

Weick, K. E. (1976). Educational Organizations as Loosely Coupled Systems. *Administrative Science Quarterly*, *21*(1), 1–19.

3

ORGANISING FOR KNOWLEDGE AND LEARNING – A BALANCING ACT BETWEEN DIVERGENT FORCES

Cecilia Bjursell and Dag Raudberget

Investment in knowledge management and knowledge systems are seen as key factors for today's business development, innovation potential, and general competitiveness. A strategic question for HR departments is how a number of different divergent forces within an organisation can be dealt with so as to best support knowledge and learning within the organisation. The discussion of the divergent forces, or oppositions, which are examined in this chapter is taken from a study of the organisation of knowledge and learning in the context of product development. When such oppositions and issues are made visible and highlighted, then they can actually contribute to an organisation's development work instead of hindering such development (Engström, 2014). In this chapter we examine a number of different oppositions which have been previously identified (at a technology firm) and discuss what they mean, and how they can be dealt with, so as to facilitate the transfer of knowledge between different projects and between departments. Finally, we ask a critical question: *What is the HR department's role in this work?*

Knowledge transfer

Many organisations wish to secure the knowledge that exists within the organisation because such knowledge is often key to the organisation's competitiveness, irrespective of which area the organisation operates in. Management is constantly in search for new ways to collect and use knowledge resources more efficiently, but such efforts only become meaningful if the knowledge that is collected is shared and integrated into the organisation through practical applications (Rozenfeld et al., 2009; Zahra et al., 2007). The mere identification and storage of knowledge is not sufficient to support the company's strategic work; such knowledge needs to be *put to use* if any effect is to be realised. There are many different definitions, perspectives, and theoretical models that describe knowledge and knowledge management (Small & Sage, 2006; Alavi & Leidner, 2001), but here we use the concept 'knowledge transfer' to emphasise the practice of knowledge collection, knowledge development, and the application of knowledge in an organisation.

Knowledge transfer is one method by which organisations can secure the knowledge and experience which exists in the organisation's employees. Interest in knowledge transfer has increased because there is a need to be part of the development of knowledge in many different areas. If this is not taken advantage of, then organisations run the risk of making the same mistakes over and over again. However, by transferring information and knowledge between different projects, departments, and generations of employees, this problem can be solved. Knowledge and learning processes need to be supported, and once this happens, the question arises: *Which systems and which organisational support exist so as to enable the success of these processes?* In the area of product development, there is a need to go beyond existing information- and knowledge systems, by working with new methods and tools so that the organisation can function successfully in a world that is culturally diverse, digitalised, and socially responsible (Bertoni m.fl., 2011). There is no easy trick to achieving effective knowledge transfer, since the sharing of knowledge demands a great deal of forethought if the desired effect is to be achieved. We also note that this is an area where work is organised in response to a number of oppositions, something which we will return to later.

Another reason why we refer to the concept of 'knowledge transfer' is to establish a link between two related areas, namely *knowledge management* and *organisational learning*. *Knowledge management* addresses how an organisation deals with and shares its knowledge, and tends to adopt a management perspective on this phenomenon. *Organisational learning* emphasises the learning processes between people who work together, as they develop their skills and abilities, in an organisational context. Thus they constitute two related, but not completely overlapping, areas of research and practice, which have grown independently of each other. The development of these two areas has, however, started to overlap (Jonsson, 2012); a welcome development because a combination of the two perspectives provides us with a better starting point in our understanding of the modern organisation (Bennet & Tomblin, 2006). This is the case because it is necessary to adopt a holistic perspective if we are to further develop our insights into what knowledge and learning in organisations actually means and entails. The major point which we take with us from the area of knowledge management is that management has the ultimate responsibility for knowledge as a point of strategic focus. Organisational learning, on the other hand, informs us that people and relationships are central to achieving the desired result(s).

A strategic perspective on knowledge transfer primarily entails adopting suitable and effective ways of supporting the flow of knowledge within an organisation. This includes adapting general ideas and solutions to specific situations. In our earlier study of how a technology firm managed its knowledge transfer processes (Raudberget & Bjursell, 2014), it became clear that there were several divergent forces at work within the organisation which had to be dealt with so as to facilitate the transfer of knowledge across projects and departments. The case study company and method of investigation are summarised below, and are followed by a description of the divergent forces (pairs of oppositions) which were identified during the study.

Case study company: Husqvarna AB

This chapter is based on material gathered in a study of professional development work at a research and development department at Husqvarna AB. This company employs more than 14,000 people globally, in 40 countries. The company has undergone many changes since its establishment in 1689. Originally it was a weapons factory and has since manufactured a variety of goods, including sewing machines, kitchen equipment, bicycles, motorcycles, lawnmowers, and chainsaws. Today, the company is a world-leading manufacturer of chainsaws, garden trimmers, robot lawnmowers, and garden tractors. Husqvarna traditionally produces such products for professional use. For example, in the chainsaw department, professional use criteria demand that the chainsaws that they produce are of a light weight because they are carried around the forest all day by loggers. Consequently, a great deal of product development work is directed at product weight reduction. Notwithstanding this, the machines also have to be durable and operate for a long time before being refuelled. Furthermore, each country where these products are manufactured or distributed has legislation concerning the operation of these machines which has to be satisfied. These legal criteria are also taken into account during the development and testing of prototype machines and in the end products.

As the product portfolio of the company changes (including an increasing use of their products by nonprofessional users), the product development process is influenced. Note that a range of products are offered to both private consumers and professional users. Since the company finds itself in a mature market, demand for their products is primarily driven by the economic growth of the target market: "The activity of single-family homes, their buying power, and consumer trust are important drivers of demand" (Husqvarna, 2016). Private consumption is very important for business and is one of the factors which influence professional development work, something which we will return to below.

The department that was studied is engaged in product development and consists of 250 employees. The material used in this chapter consists of 26 interviews which we conducted with engineers who held different positions in the department. Increasing competition on a global level increased the need for knowledge from different areas and the need to reuse the knowledge that had been developed in the organisation. This, in turn, has consequences for how knowledge transfer takes place within the organisation. In the study that was conducted, it was apparent that the organisation did not follow one specific way in its arrangements to organise knowledge and learning. Instead a balance was found between dualities. In this chapter, these dualities are termed *pairs of oppositions*, so as to highlight the fact that they belong together and that they represent different dimensions of a single question.

The balance between pairs of opposition

In this section, we present a number of pairs of opposition which were identified during the Husqvarna study (see Table 3.1). These pairs of opposition enable us to discuss how different areas can be dealt with so as to facilitate knowledge transfer between projects and between departments. In this context, the HR department is a partner in this process, as it offers up new knowledge, experience, and alternative perspectives. With respect to the different pairs of opposition, no unambiguous answer is provided; instead, it is up to each group or organisation to make the choices which suit the particular organisation best. These may change over time. Note too that the nature of the company's operations, in terms of their content, ways of working, and competitive conditions and strategies, determines what choices an organisation might make.

Written knowledge transfer – verbal knowledge transfer

Written v. verbal knowledge transfer illustrates an opposition between two ways of sharing knowledge. Written knowledge transfer entails the use of documentation, whilst verbal knowledge transfer takes place during conversations. Written knowledge transfer has its advantages in that which is written down persists though time and can be used to reach large numbers of recipients. The disadvantages with this type of transfer are that it might be difficult to express certain knowledge in writing and that documents might not be archived properly and reused. Verbal knowledge transfer can be used to share complex ideas in a short time and stimulate the development of new ideas. The social dimension associated with verbal communication is both an advantage and a disadvantage. Social

TABLE 3.1 Pairs of oppositions that organise knowledge and learning

Written knowledge transfer	*Verbal knowledge transfer*
Meetings take up time	Meetings save time
'Front-loading'	'Back-loading'
Space to make mistakes	Minimise repetition of the same mistake
Mastering a task	'Good enough'
Action	Reflection
One's own interests	The organisation's interests
Technical knowledge	Administrative knowledge
Global perspective	Local perspective

contact with others is something fundamentally good, but if such contact is problematic, then knowledge transfer becomes problematic too (Table 3.1).

At the case study company, they use a so-called 'design advice form' where knowledge about how specific parts of their machines should be designed is summarised in writing. The production of these documents is supported by the company's management team and is stored in a database. The problem is that it can sometimes be difficult to find these documents, and, furthermore, there exists an oral tradition concerning solving problems and transferring knowledge between the fabricators. Consequently, the design advice forms are not used to any great extent, despite the good intentions that lie behind them.

In brief: written knowledge transfer – verbal knowledge transfer

The task here is to find a balance between effective forms of written and verbal knowledge transfer in an organisation. To understand how they can complement each other, we must know the advantages and disadvantages associated with different modes of knowledge transfer.

Meetings take up time – meetings save time

The purpose of a meeting can be to coordinate, inform, discuss, and develop issues, and/or make decisions. This is done to save time, since the employees receive the information that they need and decisions are made as a unified group. Despite this, many people think that meetings are a waste of time. Such meetings use up a significant number of working hours and so incur a significant cost to the organisation. Different forms of meetings can be used to make decisions, place decisions on record, share information, and engage in learning. The purpose of the meeting will determine the type of meeting and who will participate in the meeting. Consequently, one should avoid organising every meeting in the same way. If the meeting's purpose is just to announce company reports, it is perhaps best that only those people who are immediately concerned with this information need attend the meeting, instead of every employee at the company. For coordination and information-sharing meetings, it may be the case that every employee should attend. However, in the product development and manufacturing industries, problem-solving meetings are most common. These meetings can be improved if pre-prepared materials that provide rich and varied information to the meeting participants are distributed before the meeting. For example, pictorial information in the form of images, videos, and physical details or a study visit can provide a holistic presentation of when, where, and how a certain problem arises. In the case study, it seemed that many of the meetings that were held had the same form, irrespective of their purpose. This resulted in ineffective meetings. On occasion, the engineers avoided attending meetings so that they could catch up on their work.

In brief: meetings take up time – meetings save time

Consideration must be made as to where a meeting needs to be called or not, and what the meeting should result in. This entails that careful thought should be given to the meeting's purpose, its form, and its execution.

'Front-loading' – 'back-loading'

Front-loading entails acting proactively by committing additional resources for analysis and evaluation in the beginning of a project, so as to capture the lessons learnt from previous projects. *Back-loading* refers to solving problems as they emerge during the course of the project. Both of these alternatives are costly, even if there exist indications that front-loading can be significantly more efficient (Morgan & Liker, 2006). The difficulty with front-loading lies with the fact that not all problems are known at the start of a project. Some important differences in these approaches are the time period during the project when the associated costs are incurred, and how they influence the time planning during a development project. Whilst there well may be certain advantages to be gained by incorporating previously learnt lessons early on in a project, there will always be areas where this is not possible or even preferable to plan for in advance because of the nature of development work. The case study company tended to use back-loading in this regard more frequently because it was deemed important to show that activity was taking place and they were moving forward quickly with the project planning work. Because of this, there was a sense of continually starting afresh with certain questions, instead of applying previous knowledge and experience.

In brief: 'front-loading' – 'back-loading'

The balance to be found here is to commit sufficient resources, early on in the project so as to avoid common mistakes, but also allowing the project to move forward. It is not possible to prepare oneself for all possible scenarios and contingencies that will appear along the way.

Space to make mistakes – minimise repetition of the same mistake

In discussions of business enterprise and innovation, it is often emphasised how important it is that there exists space for people to make mistakes because if one is not allowed to make a mistake, then one runs the risk of never producing anything. At a product development department, permission to experiment is very important. There thus must be space for mistakes to be made during the development process – it is part of the learning process during development and cannot be completely determined or controlled. However, frustration may result if the same mistakes are repeated over and over again, and it is noted that the development process could be improved by a more efficient system of recycling previously won knowledge, but that such a system may be lacking. To this, we must consider the financial aspects; mistakes that are made early on in a development process are often simpler and cheaper to correct than mistakes that are made in the later phases of a development project. The reason for this is that the later that a change is made, the more the value chain is influenced in the form of changes in production equipment, sales, and distribution. In the case study, a genuine interest in product development and becoming the best in their area was observed, so, in this context, a failure of some sort can provide important clues as to how one should proceed in product development in general. What was missing at the company were proper procedures to transfer what others had learnt during the process and procedures to other departments and projects.

In brief: space to make mistakes – minimise repetition of the same mistake

The balance to be found between this pair of oppositions lies in the creation of an environment where making mistakes is accepted because this is fundamental to the dynamic ability to innovate. At the same time, there should be structures and systems in place to record knowledge and experiences from previous learning contexts.

Mastering a task – 'good enough'

The goals for development work can be different, depending on who the target group is for the product. This should always be the basic starting point, but how much can the final touches to the product cost? When new target groups are included, then this may entail new ways of thinking about the product. If the product is solely aimed at professional users, then a single feature of the machine might be a deciding factor, and just this feature might become the subject of the product development department's attention. If a new target group consisting of private users is identified, then other features might play a bigger role in their decision to buy the product in comparison with professional users. For a technical company who works with product development, it can be tempting to set standards as high as possible; to always find the absolutely best solution to a problem from a technical perspective. In such cases, it might be difficult to stop at a point where the product is just 'good enough' or includes other criteria or values besides solely technical criteria. For consumer products, this may involve creating products that are not too expensive or that have a nice design, for example. Other features or properties that may differentiate products include their performance, weight, and durability.

Different types of competencies are involved in product development, and the choice of competencies that are deployed in the product development department is dependent on which features of the product are subject to development. One way of considering the pair of oppositions, *mastering a task – 'good enough'*, is to imagine that they represent two different perspectives towards product development. The one perspective aims to optimise development work with a professional enduser in mind; that is to say, to make the product as lightweight as possible, with an efficient use of fuel, and a high level of durability. The other perspective aims to develop a product which satisfies the expectations and needs of the private user, where other features are more relevant, such as design and price.

In brief: mastering a task – 'good enough'

Use the target group's expectations and needs to find a balance between which features the product needs, and use this to inform the amount of product development work that needs to be done, including the competencies that are needed for this work.

Action – reflection

The ability to take positive action differentiates successful companies from companies who are less successful. Those companies who wish to be successful must also spend some time with reflection. Reflection allows one to evaluate and analyse previous actions and may also be a moment when creative ideas are let loose. The tension between this pair of oppositions lies in the fact that action and reflection have different internal time frames. Action can identify with a particular forward movement, whilst reflection demands one to pause and absorb that which has taken place, that which is taking place, and that which will come to pass. From the company's perspective, the results of the project and the employee's efforts in developing the product are evaluated against the project's delivery. The project leader has thus the incentive to prioritise visible deliveries over personal reflection and learning. Consequently, reflection only takes place when there is time to do so, and on many occasions experiences which could have been added to the design advice database, and the like, remain undocumented and unavailable for use for future projects. In the case study, there was a lack of time, from a project management perspective and a high work tempo. One way of introducing learning and reflection into project development could be to make these activities more visible by scheduling time in the department's work calendar, for example, "every Tuesday, 15:00–17:00 learning and reflection concerning [insert project area]".

In brief: action – reflection

Consider how individuals are supported as they move between moments of activity and moments of reflection, and whether there is time in the project plan to include the setup time that is needed for the changeover between these two activities.

One's own interests – the organisation's interests

In all companies, many different interests coexist together. A common motivational factor at the product development department is the drive to develop good products, but this may agree with other driving forces too, including focus on cost reduction and global organisation. Product development, when all is said and done, is a fundamentally creative process. Designers are experts in their areas, and the whole development process is built on the desire to develop and master the designs. Organisational concerns, for example, demands for standardisation, can be seen as obstacles to development and innovation. It is possible for standardisation work to stifle product development if it goes too far. Each component in a machine needs to be integrated with other components during its production, in addition to demands made by the rest of the world, many of which are concerned with standardisation. Standardisation criteria can seem to be a hindrance to the development process, but they can be necessary to follow so as to reduce costs. However, note that certain standardised features or details may actually incur greater costs. The profit that one might gain from using a cheaper feature or detail can be lost to costs that may arise because of substandard performance or low quality.

Standardisation can also be understood as a way of working with knowledge transfer between projects and products by exploiting previous lessons and experiences which are 'built into' the standard.

The development department has the duty to maintain and develop specialist knowledge about product features which are unique. The individual employee's interest may lie with obtaining a good salary and self-development in a chosen career. In the case study, it was clear that most engineers wanted a variety of work assignments, which entailed that many individuals preferred to be involved in innovative work rather than standardisation work. One way to encourage this desire for development might be to allow an engineer who has made a plastic handle to make a metal engine part next time. Note that such variation in work tasks demands different competencies, something which attention must be paid to when such work assignments are distributed to the employees.

In brief: one's own interests – the organisation's interests

A balance has to be found between the individual's interests and the organisation's interests. By allowing individuals to develop their critical specialist knowledge further, and by creating good conditions for them so that they choose to remain with the company, then it is possible to combine the individual employee's interests with the organisation's interests.

Technical knowledge – administrative knowledge[1]

In any project, it is important that the levels of both technical and administrative knowledge domains are high. Technical knowledge directly concerns the product; its details and features and its fabrication. Administrative knowledge is primarily concerned with project management. The most common career path in the case study went from taking responsibility for technical matters to moving on to an administrative management position. Such management functions lead to higher salaries. A comparable salary increase was not available for those who merely developed specialist technical knowledge. For some, the career path from being responsible for certain details or features of a product to a more general responsibility for whole projects was a natural development and worked well in satisfying different wishes about the content of the work to be done during different phases of the individual's career. For other employees, they wished to continue with their specialisation in the technical field instead of taking on administrative roles because, they felt, this involved a different type of work assignment and different competencies. At the same time, individuals might wish to advance their career both in terms of salary and in terms of knowledge. (Cf. Chapter 4 and the different perspectives on career paths presented there.)

In brief: technical knowledge – administrative knowledge

A balance should be found so that career paths which support either a technical or administrative career can be implemented. Companies need technical expertise which develops over time, whilst project managers must be of a high level of competency so that they do not get bogged down by isolated details in the technical development without taking into consideration market demands.

Global perspective – local perspective

In a company which has factories and offices across the world, things can look quite different from different vantage points. At one location, there might be a team who has a holistic perspective and is good at dealing with everyday problems. If this self-directed project group is to transfer knowledge to a manufacturing unit which is managed by a traditional top-down hierarchy in a different country, then various difficulties may arise. Beyond these cultural differences, language barriers can hinder transfer of knowledge. Another obstacle may be caused by a factory which has a high level of employee turnover because the factory considers employees to be interchangeable. This may cause the factory to lose production speed and competence, and may be forced to start operations over and over again. A high level of employee turnover causes increased demands on documentation, but if one does not know *why* work is performed in a certain way, then it is difficult to produce the proper documentation. Problems on a global level may include different standards for measurements (metric v. imperial), different methods and material properties, different legislative requirements, and different perspectives on knowledge transfer. Furthermore, development processes often take place in close cooperation with suppliers, irrespective of their geographical location.

In brief: global perspective – local perspective

The balance to be found here is to determine whether it is profitable to integrate one's operations on a global level, or whether is it is more efficient to preserve local strengths and differences.

The responsibility for finding a balance between oppositions

The challenges which exist at Husqvarna AB with respect to supporting knowledge transfer in the organisation, as described above, demand that one finds a balance between a number of different pairs of opposition. These oppositions have the potential to contribute to the company, but, at the same time, they create tension because they can be seen to pull the company or its operations in different directions. It is easy to want to manage processes which pull in different directions, but the creative dimension demands a great deal of freedom so that innovation can take place. This is especially relevant for a product development department. This results in a lack of interest in drawing sharp distinctions between the oppositions. More important questions which should be addressed is how one relates to these oppositions and how will one continually evaluate and update one's activities in relation to the goals that one wishes to achieve.

We now ask: *How can the HR department contribute to a product development department?* The core HR assignment is related to issues about careers and the development of the employees. In the case study, the line managers were responsible for these issues and drove knowledge development forward. In the area of 'knowledge management' there is a certain apprehension that, as the HR department takes on responsibility for knowledge and learning, one runs the risk of ending up on a far too abstract system level which slows down the work rate and creates obstacles for the development and preservation of expert knowledge. HR probably does not have insight into which type of knowledge is needed. Those who oppose HR's engagement in this work claim, instead, that the responsibility for knowledge and learning processes should be with the line managers, who, in turn, should drive development forward on several different fronts.

What does a situation where knowledge transfer is a line manager's responsibility entail for the HR department? In the area of HR research, there are opinions that the more traditional HR work – administrative and operational work – should be assigned to line managers or some form or HR service centre, whilst the HR department proper is responsible for the organisation's strategic assignment (Becton & Schraeder, 2009). To be assigned with only the strategic assignment is very rare in practice, not least in small- and medium-sized companies which may find it difficult to justify a purely strategic function for the HR department. In this context, the question of how the responsibility for strategic planning should be distributed between top management and the HR department also raises its head. The strategies that are developed in the HR area of operations must be tightly connected to the overarching company strategies.

If questions about knowledge and learning are to be considered as strategic in an organisation, then the management should support this. In the next section, we provide a recommendation for how HR can operate in large organisations where the management considers knowledge development as a strategic area and where the line managers have an overarching responsibility for the content and development of knowledge and learning.

Support and strategies from HR

The HR department's role has changed over time. From being responsible for traditional personnel work, including salaries, business travel, time and personnel administration, HR has more and more begun to be involved in the strategic dimension. Nowadays, HR focuses on developing systems and strategies which support the organisation's long-term development. The case study shows, however, that there is a need for HR to combine long-term strategies with work that supports the day-to-day operations of the organisation (as informed by these strategies).

In Figure 3.1, we provide examples of strategies which the HR department can identify. These strategies are, in turn, linked to the management's overarching strategies for the company. When the strategies are identified, they are then handed over to the line managers, who take responsibility for them. The figure also illustrates how HR should provide operative support to the line managers,

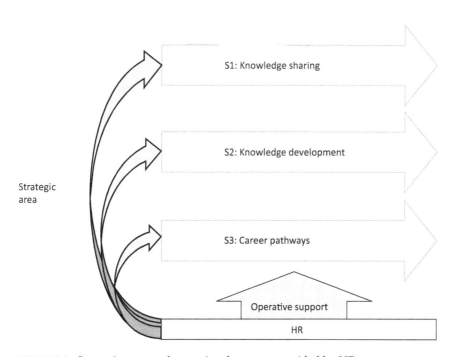

FIGURE 3.1 Strategic areas and operational support provided by HR.

as they work with these strategies. The operative support can consist of ongoing work with salaries, business travel, and time and personnel administration, but it may also include providing knowledge and competence for issues to do with the organisation, structures, and culture. Using the Husqvarna study and the pairs of oppositions presented in this chapter, we identify three possible strategic areas of interest: (i) knowledge transfer, (ii) knowledge development, and (iii) career paths.

In Table 3.2, a summary of the pairs of opposition, as they are present in the three strategic areas, is provided. These are also associated with example areas where HR can contribute with insights which should promote the work done in each strategic area. What the HR department thus contributes, irrespective of who is ultimately responsible, are insights into how work with knowledge and learning can be supported and systematised in an organisation.

The HR department can thus offer support and strategies with respect to the pairs of oppositions identified above. The strategic approach highlights a number of different areas which should be prioritised and then HR can provide operational support when this is needed on the line. This way of working also enables one to find a balance between another pair of oppositions (not mentioned previously in this chapter); namely, the opposition between *Freedom – Control*. To be subject to 'organisation', to be organised, entails that one sacrifices a certain amount of freedom, for the sake of control. However, it is not immediately clear where the border lies between Freedom and Control in this context. *Organisation* is sometimes interpreted as 'standardisation', 'control', and 'conformity', but *organisation* can equally be interpreted as providing the conditions and space for 'self-determination', 'the possibility of choice', and 'taking the initiative'. In response to the needs of the product development

TABLE 3.2 Strategic areas where HR can provide support (from the case study)

Strategic area	Oppositions that need to be balanced within each area	Areas where the HR department may have insight into
Knowledge transfer	Written knowledge transfer – Verbal knowledge transfer Meetings take time – Meetings save time 'Front-loading' – 'Back-loading'	Organising projects
Knowledge development	Space to make mistakes – Minimise repetition of the same mistake Action – Reflection Mastering a task – 'Good enough'	Culture and attitudes
Career pathways	One's own interests – The organisation's interests Technical knowledge – Administrative knowledge Global perspective – Local perspective	Career structure

department, the HR department's operational support should include features of the second interpretation; then the conditions that enable development and learning will be created.

Recommended reading

Becerra-Fernandez, Irma, & Sabherwal, Rajiv (2015), *Knowledge management: Systems and processes*. Routledge.

McElroy, Mark W (2003), *The new knowledge management: Complexity, learning, and sustainable innovation*. Routledge.

Jones, Nory B & Mahon, John F (2018), *Knowledge transfer and innovation*. Routledge.

References

Alavi, Maryam & Leidner, Dorothy E. (2001), Review: Knowledge management and knowledge management systems: Conceptual foundations and research issues. *MIS Quarterly, 25*(1), pp. 107–136.

Becton, J. Bret & Schraeder, Mike (2009), Strategic human resource management. Are we there yet? *The Journal for Quality & Participation, 31*(4), pp. 11–18.

Bennet, Alex & Tomblin, M. Shane (2006), A learning network framework for modern organizations: Organizational learning, knowledge management and ICT support. *VINE Journal of Information and Knowledge Management Systems, 36*(3), pp. 289–303.

Bertoni, Marco, Johansson, Christian & Larsson, Tobias (2011), Methods and tools for knowledge sharing in product development. In Monica Bordegoni & Caterina Rizzi (eds.), *Innovation in product design: From CAD to virtual prototyping* (pp. 37–53). London: Springer.

Engström, Annika (2014), *Lärande samspel för effektivitet: En studie av arbetsgrupper i ett mindre industriföretag.* [Interactive learning for efficacy: A study of work groups in a small industrial company]. Linköping Studies in Behavioural Science No 185. Linköping: Linköping University.

Husqvarna (2016), *Det här är vi.* [This is us]. A company brochure.

Jonsson, Anna (2012), *Kunskapsöverföring & knowledge management.* [Knowledge transfer and knowledge management]. Malmö: Liber.

Morgan, James M. & Liker, Jeffrey K. (2006), *The Toyota product development system: Integrating people, process, and technology.* New York: Productivity Press.

Raudberget, Dag & Bjursell, Cecilia (2014), A3 reports for knowledge codification, transfer and creation in research and development organisations. *International Journal of Product Development, 19*(5/6), pp. 413–431.

Rozenfeld, Henrique, Amaral, Creusa Sayuri Tahara, Da Costa, Janaina Mascarenhas Hornos & Jubileu, Andrea Padovan (2009), Knowledge-oriented process portal with BPM approach to leverage NPD management. *Knowledge and Process Management, 16*(3), pp. 134–145.

Small, Cynthia T. & Sage, Andrew P. (2006), Knowledge management and knowledge sharing: A review. *Information Knowledge Systems Management, 5*(3), pp. 153–169.

Zahra, Shaker A., Neubaum, Donald O. & Larrañeta, Bárbara (2007), Knowledge sharing and technological capabilities: The moderating role of family involvement. *Journal of Business Research, 60*(10), pp. 1070–1079.

4

'CAREER' FROM A PERSPECTIVE OF EFFORT AND REWARD

Ingela Bergmo-Prvulovic

What does a *career* refer to actually? Are we talking about the same thing when questions about *careers* are discussed at work? When *careers* is the topic of conversation, there seems to be a tacit agreement about what careers are; everyone knows what it means (Collin, 2007). People have everyday knowledge about careers, which allows them to talk about careers in their everyday life, without them having to define what they mean. People's everyday knowledge of a variety of things is formed by social interaction and communication. In a similar fashion, different professional groups who work with careers develop their professional point of view of what a career is (Bergmo-Prvulovic, 2015). We establish value systems, ideas, and practices which we use to construct the world we live in, as we believe it is, or should be. By appealing to these systems, we establish social order, enabling us to orientate ourselves in the world and control our environment. We establish particular symbols and codes so that we can speak of abstract ideas. We use such codes to communicate with each other, including things that concern us in our everyday life or is an issue in our professional practices.[1]

In our everyday speech, we conceptualise a *career* as 'climbing a ladder', which, according to Savickas (2008), has become the predominant metaphor that is used to speak of a career. This metaphor can serve as a symbol of what is understood as a 'traditional view on careers', which is formed in the development of hierarchical organisational structures, where each step up the ladder entails a new position, more responsibility, and a higher salary. This traditional view is based on how working life used to be. After the industrial revolution, a subsequent development and growth in national and multinational companies took place. New professions, possibilities for advancement, positions, and a gradual improvement in working conditions and social status were also introduced (Savickas, 2008). It was also during this period, and after the Second World War, that the development of theories about careers, career development, and career choice grew apace. Consequently, it can be stated that 'career', as a concept, is rooted in previously prevailing work conditions found in industrial societies with hierarchical structures, resulting in stable, transparent, and predictable organisational structures and career paths (Bergmo-Prvulovic, 2015).

Theories about careers have, in the meantime, been developed in different fields in parallel with each other, which has resulted in contrasting points of view on how one should view one's 'career'. Different fields emphasise different aspects of the concept (Arthur et al., 1989; Collin, 2007; Kidd, 2006). The labour market sector often emphasise *matching* as an important principle, based on the rationality of Taylorism and the notion of 'the right man in the right place', where people are viewed as objects which should primarily adapt to *society's* needs (Lovén, 2015). The 'career guidance and counselling field' is found in the area between the school system and work-life and is primarily driven according to the *individual's* needs, dreams, and goals, whilst in the organisational and business sectors, the development of human resources from the perspective of the *organisation's* needs is emphasised (cf. Bergmo-Prvulovc, 2015; McDonald & Hite, 2016). At the same time, there remains the everyday understanding of a career as 'climbing a ladder' (cf. Savickas, 2008) among people in working life (see Bergmo-Prvulovic, 2013). This state of affairs makes a common understanding of *career* somewhat difficult. Neither is the matter made any simpler by the fact that we currently find ourselves in a transition phase, as we now gradually move to an evermore knowledge-based society in a globalised economy.

The present chapter presents a discussion of *careers* in this transition period. I begin by discussing how careers have taken shape according to the conditions set by work-life, and how interpretations of this term are often taken for granted without actually being based on a common understanding of the term. In that section, I also demonstrate how trends which characterise and influence career questions, in conjunction with changes in work-life, are reflected in the research on careers. I also touch upon how different issues in HR work can affect one's understanding of what a career is.

After this overview, I present the results of a study where I asked people who found themselves in the middle of these changes, how they viewed the notion of a 'career'. The results of this study provided the reason why I discuss careers as an 'exchange game'; the stake in the game is made in terms of effort, and the outcome is the reward. However, a change in how people speak of careers has taken place; a movement from emphasis on external rewards (such as salary and status) to an emphasis on internal rewards, including personal development. Since my research results give reason to question this, I formulate my ideas about careers in terms of a perspective that is based on the notion of 'exchange'. An 'exchange perspective' includes the mutual exchange between employees and employers. This is based on the idea that both parties need each other and have something to offer to the other. Employees have their competencies and ability to work to offer in the performance of a specific job of work, an assignment, or task which the employer needs to have completed so as to achieve the goals of the organisation.

More generally, we note the exchange between the employee's effort and contributions at the workplace and the employer's ability and willingness to reward the employee. In the final section of this chapter, I discuss what consequences this veiwpoint can entail at the workplace and what challenges the HR department is faced with respect to future strategic career planning.

Career issues in a changing working life

The changeover to a knowledge-based, global society has brought with it new organisational trends, resulting in continual challenges to hierarchical organisational structures. This has entailed, in turn, that the concept of a 'career', which is rooted in earlier work-life conditions and structures, is also being challenged (Bergmo-Prvulovic, 2015). According to Collin (1998), the phenomenon and concept of 'career' entered into an 'uncomfortable phase' in pace with these changes, where new ways of talking about careers and new ways of trying to face changes at the workplace emerged, whilst old traditions and perspectives remained. Of late, organisations can be characterised by 'deregulation', 'decentralisation processes', 'flat organisations', and as 'goal directed' (see Ekstedt & Sundin, 2006). In this context, questions about careers have been toned down, to the benefit of questions of 'competence'. Globalisation has brought with it an emphasis on new concepts, including 'flexibility', 'fast changes', 'adaptation', and 'the ability to adapt', with respect to both organisations and individuals. Stable working conditions and employment conditions, and predictable, transparent career paths belong to the past (cf. Savickas et al., 2009). This has led to uncertainty and unclear career structures. In the last few decades, debates and social trends have dealt with the problem of *matching* on the labour market and the company's need to maintain/retain competence in its workforce. In an effort to deal with increased uncertainty in an environment of increasing global competition, organisations have implemented a number of different strategies. 'Validation and maintenance of competencies', 'competence development (professional development)', 'lifelong learning', 'workplace learning', and 'learning organisations' are typical examples of such strategies (Bergmo-Prvulovic, 2015).

During the 1990s, an increasing number of researchers became interested in what these changes in work-life would entail for 'careers'. Hall (1996) remarked on the double message associated with the changes in work-life with the following paradox: "The career is dead – long live the career!" (Hall, 1996: 8). It is somewhat ironic that interest in 'careers' has increased drastically since then, especially at the policy level. However, it is not possible to ignore the fact that, in the very middle of these trends and changes, we find people in work-life, doing their jobs, with their own ideas about their career; something which does not sit well with the career conditions which exist today (Bergmo-Prvulovic, 2015).

"We have to invent careers!" an HR specialist told me once. What the person was referring to was the observation that there were not enough traditional career paths within the specialist's organisation. The employees had the expectation, however, of being able to "make a career of it" in the traditional sense. Consequently the HR department created 'project leader' positions in the organisation.

To try and come to terms with this paradox – how careers are considered as something of the past, whilst seeming to be something more relevant than ever – it is useful to look back in history at the transition trends which have characterised the career field. In Bergmo-Prvulovic (2015: 23–27), it is shown how people involved in research and organisational management have tried to gradually broaden the understanding of what career is, moving away from traditional perspectives.

On the one hand, we note that there is an understanding of 'career' which emphasises the centrality of work (see, e.g., Nicholson & West, 1989; Thomas, 1989), even involving time outside work-time proper, other life roles, and other forms of gainful employment. Also demarcated by this central position is one's life before and after one's career, one's role as a student and as a pensioner, voluntary work and unpaid work (see, e.g., Richardson, 1993). Careers have moved on from being granted only to successful people to now include everyone who works, irrespective of their position, specific profession, or status (see, e.g., Blustein, 2001). To greater degrees, life itself is emphasised – even 'lifecareer' is suggested as a concept (Miller-Tiedeman, 1988; Miller-Tiedeman & Tiedeman, 1990). We also note a shift from careers being a goal in themselves to careers being viewed as continual processes, the journey itself being in focus.

On the other hand, a desire to replace the traditional perspective on careers can be observed because of challenging economic developments and changed circumstances which have resulted in fewer stable conditions. According to Inkson (2004), the use of different, influential academic concepts, expressed in terms of metaphors, have been promoted so that the meaning of *career* can be adapted to prevailing conditions. Amongst these terms we find *boundaryless careers* (Arthur & Rousseau, 1996), *protean careers* (Hall, 1996), and *career construction* (Savickas et al., 2009). The term *boundaryless careers* was launched as a new employment principle in a new organisational era, which is reflected in the trend of project hires and time-limited employment. Included in this is a certain mobility and changeability in organisations with respect to structure, work positions, assignments, and responsibility. That a career needs to be adaptive is revealed in policy documents and in the new way of reasoning about what people are expected to deal with in today's work-life. In addition to this, there is an increase in the amount of responsibility that individuals are burdened with, as per the rhetoric used in policy documents (Sparrhoff, 2016). This is expressed in European policy documents about the individual's own responsibility to direct and create one's own career, and to ensure that one is adaptable and employable (Bergmo-Prvulovic, 2012).

Inkson (2004) also highlights how an increasingly resource-based perspective on careers began to take form at the end of the 1990s, exemplified in the economic metaphor: *career as resource*. This perspective is clearly present within the framework of HR as a discipline and practice and is seen as fundamental to the creation of growth and prosperity (Pryor & Bright, 2011). According to Pryor and Bright (2011), a great deal of the literature on 'change management' is based on this point of view, with the purpose of exerting pressure on individuals so that they will accept the fact that they have to adapt to change. To view 'career' as resource in such a strategy is not completely unproblematic because the 're-source' (as intended) is for the use of the organisation, and the other party in the 'career relationship' runs the risk of being forgotten. Inkson (2004) also identifies a number of other problems associated with this perspective, since it can trans-form 'career' from being an individual's project to a mere good that is primarily meant to satisfy the organisation's purpose. To this we can add the observation made by Bergmo-Prvulovic (2012) that the fundamental perspective on careers in European policy documents for career guidance is primarily an *economic per-spective*, where 'careers' are seen as answers to market forces, followed by a *learning perspective* which is based on ideas about adaptation and change. Also noted in this context are perspectives which emphasise the individual's autonomy and self-responsibility. This message is communicated primarily in response to the organisation's needs, which prompts us to ask if peoples' careers are subordinated to market forces? (Bergmo-Prvulovic, 2012).

These trends, which attempt to transform the traditional view on *career* into a term which is in more agreement with today's work-life situation, are a re-sponse to the challenges that organisations and workplaces are faced with in a global, competitive, and changeable work-life. In an attempt to deal with these challenges, companies have begun to take more interest in organisational man-agement that is more market-directed (Dalsvall & Lindström, 2012). Thus, in a manner similar to the transition trends that have been identified in the career field, organisations have also tried to confront and manage the changes that take place in work-life. These changes are clearly observable in the contexts of work-place education and professional development. In these contexts, people's careers are influenced by the organisation's strategies and needs and are also thus influ-enced by HR strategies (Bergmo-Prvulovic, 2015).

According to an early definition of *human resource management* (HRM), HRM is concerned with every decision in an organisation which influences the rela-tionship between the organisation and the employees (Beer et al., 1984). Ellström (2010) claims, however, that a developmental dimension in HRM was introduced in the 2000s and has become more popular, such that HRM is more frequently described as a strategy (i) to develop competitive advantages via a competent and engaged workforce (Bratton & Gold, 2007) and (ii) to develop organisational performance and abilities in order to develop and survive in the long term (Boselie et al., 2005). Ellström (2010) further observes that HRM and skills development thus overlap with each other and emphasises the claim that skills development should be viewed as part of HRM. The question we may ask now is: *How do career issues stand within an organisation, when these issues are related in this manner to HRM?*

Looking back to the early 1900s, we note how different trends informed HR's development and growth (Söderström & Lindström, 1994). Initially, the personnel profession was characterised as a 'vocation' or a 'passion'. This was followed by a period of tension between socially oriented personnel work, on the one side, and, on the other side, a desire to integrate personnel issues into the organisation's administrative organisational function. During the 1970s, personnel work was influenced by democratic reforms, and in the 1980s, personnel work was relabelled 'Human Resource Management' and became more business and competence directed under the prevailing management perspective of the time (Söderström & Lindström, 1994).

Söderström (1997) further illustrates how HR issues have changed in their focus over time. Initially, the individual employee was the centre of focus, followed by the organisation. Later, this was followed by a mutual focus on both the individual and the organisation. From the end of the 1980s, focus is placed only on the organisation. Since then, the emphasis of HR-related issues has moved from a mutual and relational focus between the individual and the organisation to an interest in what benefits the organisation and its competitiveness. It is possible that this is related to the current perspectives that are trending in HRM at the moment. These perspectives are described by Tengblad (2000), who approaches HRM partly by using the Michigan model (see Tichy, Fombrun & Devanna, 1982; Fombrun, Tichy & Devanna, 1984) and partly by using the Harvard model (see Walton, 1985; Beer et al., 1984). The Michigan model is stated to be the 'hard' version of HRM, where focus is placed only on the organisation, and any benefits that are enjoyed by the individual are merely side effects of this. The Harvard model is described as the 'soft' model, where the interaction between individuals and the organisation is more clearly emphasised. Consequently, a focus on only the organisation that is too one sided (as described by the Michigan model) may well effect which perspective on careers will prevail in an organisation and how career questions are dealt with (Bergmo-Prvulovic, 2015). The 'softer' perspective in HRM on careers, with a relational focus and a mutual exchange between the individual and the organisation, is at risk of being overshadowed by an increasing focus on the organisation. Because of this, uncertainty about *for whom* the 'career' actually is for has emerged in today's work-life.

A study of perspectives on careers

Because the concept of 'career' is in a somewhat uncomfortable transition phase (Collin, 1998), it is of interest to examine what meaning is ascribed to the concept of 'career' by people who find themselves in the middle of this change in work-life. Bergmo-Prvulovic (2013) reports on the thoughts and perspectives on 'careers' of a group of people who, at the time of the study, stated that they were undergoing or had just undergone work-related changes of various forms.[2] The groups of people consisted of 21 participants who were asked to free-associate to three phrases related to careers: *career, career development*, and *work situation in change*. The first two phrases established the key concepts, and the last phrase was intended to prompt the participants' thoughts about changes in work situations.

The participants wrote down their spontaneous, free associations to each of the phrases in two columns. These free associations were then analysed by using a qualitative content analysis method, based on social representation theory as the theoretical framework. The results of the analysis show that the concept 'career' is viewed from two stable social representations and from two dynamic social representations.[3]

The two stable social representations are clearly related to an established, taken-for-granted system, which is informed by previously relevant work conditions. 'Career' is associated with a *personal meaning*, such as expressed as an *individual project* and *self-realisation*. In addition to this, 'career' is endowed with a *social meaning* in terms of *social/hierarchical climbing*. The personal meaning emphasises the realisation of personal dreams, whilst the social meaning emphasises upward mobility, achieving higher positions, roles, status, and management functions. 'Success' in this context is related to status and is evaluated by others. Such success, however, can be seen as either positive or negative. It may be judged as positive if the success results in higher positions, more responsibility, and authority. But in some cases, it can be regarded as something bad to climb the ladder and something bad to have ambition and drive (Bergmo-Prvulovic, 2013).

The dynamic social representations, on the other hand, reveal how people reason with themselves about the content of the concept 'career', by thinking in terms of opposites.[4] In the first dynamic social representation, i.e., simplified as a system of thought, a 'career' is viewed as a *game of exchange*, as revealed in terms of thoughts and ideas about *expected effort* versus *expected outcome*. Education is considered to be an expected effort in this context, and a career is viewed the outcome of this effort. Other expected efforts include hard work, ability to handle relationships, experience, loyalty, good performance and taking on greater responsibility. Career development is the expected outcome of these efforts, in addition to new and better work assignments, challenges, and delegation of more responsibility. Responsibility thus emerges as both an effort and the outcome of effort. These efforts are also expected to result in rewards, including *internal rewards* and *external rewards*. Internal rewards are associated with the personal content of one's career (as per the above). However, external rewards receive more emphasis. Financial rewards, higher social ranking, and acknowledgement in terms of higher status and higher positions are key words in this context. A certain ambiguity also emerges in (i) whether it is the individual who creates the desired results or are they offered up to the individual, (ii) who it is who actually determines the value of the individual's efforts, and (iii) whether the career benefits the individual or the organisation.

In the second dynamic, social representation, 'career' is viewed as an *uncertain outcome*. In this system of thought, a 'career' is conceptualised as an *uncertain outcome*, and the thought show uncertainty because of changing conditions; on the one side caused by the environment, and on the other side, caused by the individual's powerlessness. Changing conditions are related to external conditions such as profitability, competitiveness, a focus on costs, outsourcing, technical developments, and the effects of globalisation. The demand for constant change makes the work demanding, challenging, and exhausting (in cases), all whilst the individual views himself or herself as powerless. Other types of oppositional reasoning are concerned with the need for security, predictability, and transparency, especially in situations which are insecure and unpredictable. In this context, notions of 'control' and a 'lack of control' also emerge.

Consequently, it can thus be stated that the concept of 'career' is viewed as containing both *personal meaning* and *social meaning*, as expressed in terms of a game of exchange between the individual and the organisation (Bergmo-Prvulovic, 2013). The conditions and the outcomes, however, seem to be uncertain and changeable. A comparison can be made with a board game: the players play the game by using their experience and knowledge and the rules of the game. At the same time, the game has developed and changed since it was first sold at the shop, but not all of the players know this. The players have their own ideas about what the current rules of the game are, and so naturally there are moments where there is confusion when it is shown that new rules apply. In the best case scenario, the new rules to the game are written down somewhere, and the players can read them at their leisure and then play the game together on an equal footing. In the worst case scenario, the new rules are not sufficiently clear, have not been written down, or have changed whilst the game is being played. Under such conditions, we can easily imagine that playing this game would be far from pleasant.

In conjunction with the transitional trends which have taken place in the area of careers (the development of new strategies by organisations and new management procedures to deal with new challenges in the work-life, along with the gradual shift from traditional viewpoints to a broader vision on careers), it can thus be claimed that a process of transformation is occurring. 'Career', as a phenomenon, finds itself on the border between the old and the new; where traditional points of view have, to a certain degree, become fossilised and taken for granted, whilst new points of view are emergent.

This development indicates that the mutual exchange model between the employer and employee is at risk of being put out of balance, and that the organisation will benefit more so than the employee. Unclear structures create frustration and dissatisfaction when employees cannot see what the exchange of additional effort (on their part) will result in. The career trends of late have emphasised the individual's own efforts and input, adaptability, and ability to manage and even continually reconstruct his or her career. At the same time, organisations seem to have toned down their role in this exchange model. In the following discussion, I thus examine career issues in a changeable work-life context from an *exchange perspective*. The challenge for organisations is to compose structures that allow for balanced interactions in the relationships between employees and employers from an *effort v. reward perspective*. So as to be able to achieve this, we need to speak very clearly about career and its meaning. There exists a palpable risk that we think that we are talking about the same thing and that we are in agreement with each other, when perhaps this is not the case. Notwithstanding this, when the outcome is not what either party thought it would be (according to their respective ideas about what a career is about), then dissatisfaction and misunderstanding between the parties might occur.

Career from an exchange perspective

As discussed above, people view a 'career' as containing a personal and a social dimension of meaning (Bergmo-Prvulovic, 2013). It is important to highlight that, for each individual, the emphasis on which dimension of meaning is more important depends on, and may vary, according to the person's life situation, the stage in life that they are in, and the context that they find themselves in. We thus note that the concept of 'career' seems to consist of both of these dimensions of meaning in people's system of thought, with, to some part, a personal meaning, and to some other part, with social meaning. This admixture of parts forms the basis for how people reason and think when they speak about careers.

The claim that the concept of 'career' contains two components, the one addressing subjective issues and the other objective issues, has been noted by several researchers. According to Kidd (2006), 'career' can be objectively described as consisting of observable outcomes, for example, a position in a hierarchy, status, salary, work-related abilities, and social reputation. From a subjective stance, 'career' is interpreted in terms of the individual's values (Kidd, 2006). Both of these viewpoints on 'career' were identified by Hughes in the 1950s (Hughes, 1958) and have prompted a debate ever since on whether one notion of 'career' is superior to the other (Hall & Chandler, 2005; Nicholson & de Waal-Andrews, 2005). Different areas in the 'career' field have emphasised one or the other perspective, which, to some degree, has divided up this field into different specialisations. Practitioners in the field of 'career guidance' have primarily emphasised the subjective aspects of 'career'; the personal meaning of the concept. The traditional perspective on 'careers', originating in previous conceptions of organisational structures, has, instead, focussed on the objective aspects of the concept; namely, its social meaning.

In connection with trends that intend to widen perspectives on 'career', beyond traditional perspectives, the concept of 'psychological success' has been introduced (Hall & Chandler, 2005; Hall & Mirvis, 1996). Psychological success emphasises the subjective aspects of 'careers' even within the organisational sphere. What appears to have happened is that there has been a toning down, or de-emphasis, of the objective aspects of 'career' in conjunction with a number of observable outcomes in the organisational context, which are taken as a direct result of work-life transformations. These trends have entailed that emphasis is placed on the individual's self-management of their career, their personal development, and their continuous learning. Is this, however, enough in exchange for the employee's efforts and input, and their investment in professional development and their performance? Is personal and/or professional development *in itself* sufficient reward? Are people satisfied with the fact that the exchange primarily consists of their own inner developmental journey at the workplace?

Examining the results of Bergmo-Prvulovic (2013), it can be clearly noted that people who find themselves in work-related situations of change have two stable systems of thoughts to appeal to which are based on personal and social meaning (where a career is seen as a mutual exchange). Consequently, I am doubtful that people are satisfied with what is offered to them in this context. Thus, I argue that a 'career', in the context of the organisation, must be seen as relational, and that within this relationship it is necessary to consider career from an effort v. reward perspective, where both personal and social meaning are included. Consequently, it can be noted that the personal and social meaning of the concept of 'career' interact with each other. When one deals with career issues with employees, one is not faced with a choice between either personal *or* social meaning, but rather, *both*. A 'career' is thus a relational phenomenon, partly because both meanings interact with each other in people's thoughts and actions as they follow a career, and partly because a career is a relational issue between the employee and the employee's workplace.

Career issues are naturally relational because 'career', as a phenomenon at the workplace, exists between the individual employee and the hiring organisation. Thus, I present the following description, based on the Harvard model on HRM, developed by Richard Walton (1985) and colleagues in the Harvard research team (Beer et al., 1984), noted by Tengblad as the 'soft' perspective on HRM (2000).

The concept of 'career' is intertwined with several other HR issues. The recruitment process serves as a good example (see Chapter 6). What is it actually that leads to recruitment? Who is involved in the recruitment process? It is the organisation' need for employees that leads to initiating the recruitment process, whether this is to perform certain tasks or to fill a certain post. Job advertisements are formulated in terms of competencies and abilities that the organisation hopes that an employee candidate will bring to the organisation. The employer thus desires that candidate employees have something which they can satisfy the needs that the organisation may have. The employer desires these competencies and abilities in exchange for the job on offer and for the salary that is paid to the employee in the execution of his or her work. The candidate employee, in turn, searches for a position which he or she considers himself or herself to possess the desired competencies and abilities. The employee thereby desires to obtain the position and a salary in form of exchange for his or her efforts within the organisation.

It is thus clear that, already during the recruitment process, there are two parties involved in the process who both desire an exchange in the relationship that they wish to establish. Thus an exchange perspective is naturally integrated into this process, which also includes both parties' perspectives on, and thoughts about, careers. It is not immediately apparent, however, that these thoughts are *shared* between the parties involved, or even explored in a discussion. During the establishment of a relationship between an employer and an employee, each other's expectations with respect to the other party forms part of the process.

This is illustrated by the respondents' thoughts about expected effort and expected outcomes from these efforts in the context of a career (Bergmo-Prvulovic, 2013). The employer also has expectations of the employee, which are usually announced in the job description (cf. Chapter 6). This exchange which the employer provides to the employee at the start of the relationship includes the appointment itself and a salary.

Once the employment has begun and the employee continually performs his or her work, it is not 100% clear what is given in exchange. What exactly is the nature of the exchange when employees are constantly faced with new demands for competence development, new or changeable work assignments, or changed work conditions? Because transparent and predictable career paths have gradually disappeared and current trends emphasise employees managing themselves and their career in accordance with the organisation's goals (Bergmo-Prvulovic, 2013), it is no longer obvious what possible career changes are offered by organisations to their employees in response to their efforts. Noting that both parties need each other (the Harvard model's soft perspective on HRM; cf. Tengblad, 2000), careers should be dealt with from a mutual exchange perspective. This informs us that both parties need to be clear about what expectations they have for each other with respect to careers, and what opportunities are on offer.

This issue is of particular importance during times of change, when the conditions in the relationship between the parties change and the new conditions are less transparent. From a relational exchange perspective, it is important that the organisation take into consideration the other party in the relationship, the employee, and thus clarify what the employee's work effort and degree of engagement can lead to for that person, in terms of both the personal implications and the social implications of the career.

Challenges for future strategic careers planning

How can we plan for careers in a work-life which cannot be planned for? Can we even talk about 'a career' which can be planned for? The answers to these questions depend on how we view careers; as either a goal or as a continual process, or as both. In pace with the gradual change in organisational structure from a hierarchy to a horizontal structure, there are positions which can be more readily reached on the horizontal level. It is no longer self-evident what 'having a career' actually means. Traditional perspectives on careers were clear on which goals an employee could achieve, for example, a higher position and new authority in the organisation. With clear goals and career pathways which can be mapped, it is easier to plan one's journey to a specific destination. With this current emphasis on careers as a continual personal development process, it becomes less clear for the employee what reward the employee is due for his or her effort and contribution to the organisation. When the employee is confronted with structures in the organisation and work-life that are not transparent, then the employee will have difficulty in planning a career. One might say that the employee is tasked to drive the train and lay the tracks at the same time, using the employee's flexibility, adaptability, and engagement in continuous learning.

How then can an organisation enable success which satisfies the employee's ideas about a career in terms of both the personal and social meaning of a career? How can we develop an interplay perspective on questions about careers, in future HR strategies?

First, it is important to make it quite clear what is intended when the concept of 'career' is spoken of in the organisation, and which basic view prevails of what a career is. Is the organisation's reasoning about careers solely focussed on achieving the organisation's goals or is there a more relational perspective within the organisation where both the organisation and the individual employee are viewed as partners with respect to careers? Second, it is important to reflect over what the organisation's attitude is and how it deals with situations where other points of view on careers exists, for example, if the employee's view on careers is not in alignment with the organisation's point of view. It is also important that the 'rules of the game' are made clear to both parties. Third, it is important to clarify how the organisation works to achieve a balance and a state of mutual exchange between the employer and employee. Organisations and their HR departments need to re-examine their understanding of what career means within their own organisation and revise how they actually enable a career structure for the employees, in a context that is becoming more and more unpredictable.

Discussions should be held about what such new career structures should look like; structures which are adapted to the changeability and flexibility which is demanded in a globalised and competitive work-life. By using new ways of talking about careers, where the responsibility is primarily placed on individuals to create and drive forward their own career, it is this very flexibility, ability for continuous learning, and adaptability that is shown by the individual that is emphasised. It is, however, important that the organisation takes on its part of the responsibility of dealing with career questions, from a relational perspective. A relationship involved, by definition, at least two parties, both of whom are responsible for nurturing the relationship.

The following questions should be asked and reflected over if a HR department is to work in a strategic way with career questions in the organisation:

- How is an employee's inner career development rewarded, in cases where a career is considered to be more of a process and less of a destination (in the form of clear goals which are to be achieved)?
- Does the organisation reward the employees with more educational opportunities which are supposed to stimulate personal development?
- Does the organisation take into consideration the fact that employees expect some form of exchange for their efforts? How does the organisation respond to and satisfy these expectations?

The challenge facing today's globalised and changeable organisations is to develop transparent structures, even in 'flat' organisations. These structures do not need to be hierarchical in the traditional sense of the word (and in many cases they are not), but organisations do need to define how interaction and exchange is to take place between the employer and employee. It is probable that employers need to develop new systems so as to show acknowledgement to employees for their efforts and competencies and to value them within the organisation's flat structure. Using an interplay and an exchange perspective on career-related questions, the organisation can lay the foundation for a mutual exchange where the organisation, as well as the individual employee, is provided with the opportunity to clarify their expectations of each other and create the conditions where both parties can satisfy their needs and achieve their goals.

Recommended reading

Readers who may wish to read more about how our everyday knowledge about 'careers' has been formed and challenged in a changeable work-life, and how different parties who have different interests in career questions have created different viewpoints of the concept 'career', depending on their role in work-life are referred to Bergmo-Prvulovic (2015). Further reading on the theory of social representations can be found in Moscovici (2008). Other work which provide further discussion of different conceptualisations of 'career' and associated metaphors include Arthur and Rousseau (1996), Collin (2007), Hall (1996), Hall and Mirvis (1996), Inkson (2004), and Savickas et al. (2009). These sources are all listed in the References.

Notes

1 The argument above is based on a theory of social representations, originally presented by Serge Moscovici (1961, 1973, and 2008). For further information about his theory of social representations in relation to 'careers' as a phenomenon, the reader is referred to Bergmo-Prvulovic (2015: 42–57).
2 These changes included organisational changes, reorganisations caused by various factors within or without the organisation, changes in competitiveness, or changes which influenced the work situation, the work assignment, or the job position either positively or negatively.
3 The concept of 'social representations' was used in the study referred to above. In this chapter, the term *system of thought* is used in parts of the text as a simplified explanation of the content of this concept.
4 For a more complete overview of the opposites that are discussed above, the reader is referred to Table 1 in Bergmo-Prvulovic (2013).

References

Arthur, Michael B., Hall, Douglas T. & Lawrence, Barbara S. (1989), Generating new directions in career theory: The case for a transdisciplinary approach. In Michael B. Arthur, Douglas T. Hall & Barbara S. Lawrence (eds.), *Handbook of career theory* (pp. 7–25). Cambridge: Cambridge University Press.

Arthur, Michael B. & Rousseau, Denise M. (1996), *The boundaryless career: A new employment principle for a new organizational era.* New York: Oxford University Press.

Beer, Michael, Spector, Bert, Lawrence, Paul R., Quinn, Mills D. & Walton, Richard E. (1984), *Managing human assets.* New York: The Free Press.

Bergmo-Prvulovic, Ingela (2012), Subordinating careers to market forces? A critical analysis of European career guidance policy. *European Journal for Research on the Education and Learning of Adults, 3*(2), pp. 155–170.

Bergmo-Prvulovic, Ingela (2013), Social representations of career: Anchored in the past, conflicting with the future. *Papers on Social Representations, 22*(1), pp. 14.11–14.27.

Bergmo-Prvulovic, Ingela (2014), Is career guidance for the individual or for the market? Implications of EU policy for career guidance. *International Journal of Lifelong Education, 33*(3), pp. 376–392.

Bergmo-Prvulovic, Ingela (2015), *Social representations of career and career guidance in the changing world of working life.* Jönköping: School of Education and Communication, Jönköping University.

Blustein, D. L. (2001). Extending the reach of vocational psychology: Toward an inclusive and integrative psychology of working. *Journal of Vocational Behavior, 59*(2), pp. 171–182.

Boselie, Paul, Dietz, Graham & Boon, Corine (2005), Commonalities and contradictions in HRM and performance research. *Human Resource Management Journal, 13*(3), pp. 67–94.

Bratton, John & Gold, Jeff (2007), *Human resource management: Theory and practice.* London: Palgrave.

Collin, Audrey (1998), New challenges in the study of career. *Personnel Review, 27*(5), pp. 412–425.

Collin, Audrey (2007), The meanings of career. In Hugh P. Gunz & Maury Peiperl (eds.), *Handbook of career studies* (pp. 558–565). Thousand Oaks, CA: Sage.

Dalsvall, Magnus & Lindström, Kjell (2012), *Bortom tankefällan: Om organisatoriska landskap, ledarskap och personalarbete i framtiden.* [Beyond the thought trap. The organizational landscape, leadership, and personnel work of the future]. Uppsala: Noden AB.

Ekstedt, Eskil & Sundin, Elisabeth (eds.) (2006), *Den nya arbetsdelningen: Arbets- och näringslivets organisatoriska omvandling i tid, rum och tal.* [The new division of labour: The transformation of working life and business in time, place, and speech]. Vol. 2006:11. Stockholm: Arbetslivsinstitutet.

Ellström, Per-Erik (2010), Forskning om kompetensutveckling i företag och organisationer. [Research on professional development in companies and organisations] In Henrik Kock (ed.), *Arbetsplatslärande: Att leda och organisera kompetensutveckling* [Workplace learning: Leading and organising professional development] (pp. 21–48). Lund: Studentlitteratur.

Fombrun, C., Tichy, N., & Devanna, M. A. (1984). *Strategic human resource management.* New York: John Wiley & Sons.

Hall, Douglas T. (1996), Protean careers of the 21st century. *Academy of Management Executive, 10*(4), pp. 8–16.

Hall, Douglas T. & Chandler, D. E. (2005), Psychological success: When the career is a calling. *Journal of Organizational Behavior, 26*, pp. 155–176.

Hall, Douglas T. & Mirvis, Philip H. (1996), The new protean career: Psychological success and the path with a heart. In Douglas T. Hall & Associates (eds.), *The career is dead – long live the career: A relational approach to careers* (pp. 15–45). San Francisco: Jossey Bass.

Hughes, Everett C. (1958), *Men and their work*. London: The Free Press of Glencoe, Collier-Macmillan Limited

Inkson, Kerr (2004), Images of career: Nine key metaphors. *Journal of Vocational Behavior*, 65, pp. 96–111.

Kidd, Jennifer M. (2006), *Understanding career counselling: Theory, research and practice*. London: Sage.

Lovén, Anders (2015), Teorier inom vägledningsfältet. [Theories within the guidance and counselling field]. In Anders Lovén (ed.), *Karriärvägledning: En forskningsöversikt* (pp. 63–99). [Career Guidance: a research overview]. Lund: Studentlitteratur AB.

McDonald, Kimberly & Hite, Linda (2016), *Career development: A human resource development perspective*. New York & London: Routledge, Taylor & Francis Group.

Miller-Tiedeman, Anna (1988), *Lifecareer: The quantum leap into a process theory of career*. Vista, CA: Lifecareer Foundation.

Miller-Tiedeman, Anna & Tiedeman, David Valentine (1990), Career decision making: An individualistic perspective. In Duane Brown & Linda Brooks (eds.), *Career choice and development: Applying contemporary theories to practice* (pp. 308–338). San Francisco: Jossey-Bass.

Moscovici, Serge (1961), *La psychanalyse, son image et son public*. [Psychoanalysis: Its image and its public]. Paris: Sorbonne.

Moscovici, Serge (1973), Foreword (D. Graham, Trans.). In Claudine Herzlich (ed.), *Health and illness: A social psychological analysis*. London: Published in cooperation with the European Association of Experimental Social Psychology by Academic Press Inc. Ltd.

Moscovici, Serge (2008), *Psychoanalysis: Its image and its public*. Cambridge, UK: Polity Press.

Nicholson, Nigel & de Waal-Andrews, Wendy (2005), Playing to win: Biological imperatives, self-regulation, and trade-offs in the game of career success. *Journal of Organizational Behavior*, 26, pp. 137–154.

Nicholson, Nigel & West, Michael (1989). Transitions, work histories, and careers. In Michael B. Arthur, Douglas. T. Hall & Barbara S. Lawrence (eds.), *Handbook of career theory*. Cambridge: Cambridge University.

Pryor, Robert & Bright, Jim (2011), *The chaos theory of careers: A new perspective on working in the twenty-first century*. New York: Routledge, Taylor & Francis Group.

Richardson, M. S. (1993). Work in people's lives: A location for counselling psychologists. *Journal of Counseling Psychology*, 40(4), pp. 423–433.

Savickas, Mark L. (2008), Helping people choose jobs: A history of the guidance profession. In James A. Athanasou & Raoul Van Esbroeck (eds.), *International handbook of career guidance* (pp. 97–113). Dordrecht: Springer Science and Business Media.

Savickas, Mark L., Nota, Laura, Rossier, Jerome, Dauwalder, Jean-Pierre., Duarte, Maria E., Guichard, Jean, Soresi, Salvatore, Van Esbroeck, Raoul & van Vianen, Annelies E. M. (2009), Life-designing: A paradigm for career construction in the 21st century. *Journal of Vocational Behavior*, 75, pp. 239–250.

Söderström, Magnus & Lindström, Kjell (1994), *Från IR till HRM: Två synsätt på personalarbete*. [From IR to HRM: Two perspectives on personnel work]. Uppsala: Institutet för personal & företagsutveckling.

Söderström, Magnus (1997), HRM in Sweden: A strategic challenge or a struggle for survival? In Shaun Tyson (ed.), *The practice of human resource strategy* (pp. 325–339). London: Pitman.

Sparrhoff, Gun (2016), Anställningsbarhet: Ett tecken i tiden. [Employability: a sign of the times]. In Gun Sparrhoff & Andreas Fejes (red.), *Anställningsbarhet: Perspektiv från utbildning och arbetsliv* (pp. 25–36) [Employability: perspectives from education and work]. Lund: Studentlitteratur.

Tengblad, Stefan (2000), Vad innebär human resource management? [What does human resource management entail?] In Ola Bergström & Mette Sandoff (eds.), *Handla med människor: Perspektiv på human resource management.* [Managing people: Perspectives on human resource management]. Lund: Academia Acta.

Thomas, Robert J. (1989). Blue-collar careers: Meaning and choice in a world of constraints. In Michael B., Arthur, Douglas T. Hall & Barbara S. Lawrence (eds.), *Handbook of career theory.* Cambridge: Cambridge University Press.

Tichy, N., Fombrun, C., & Devanna, M. A. (1982). Strategic human resource management. *Sloan Management Review, 23*(2), pp. 47–61.

Walton, R. (1985, March–April). From control to commitment. *Harvard Business Review,* pp. 77–84.

5

CREATIVITY AT THE WORKPLACE

Ylva Lindberg

Rapid developments in technology and a globalised economy have brought with them a high rate of change in today's world. One characteristic that is most desired at the workplace, as a response to this rate of change, is 'creativity'. In Chapter 14, Persson and Aktas discuss what organisations can do to attract and retain particularly creative employees or 'talents'. In this chapter, I examine what an organisation can do to facilitate creative processes and innovative thought for all employees. The assumption is that every employee can make important, creative contributions to the organisation, irrespective of the work that they do or the position that they hold. Even in routine assignments there exists opportunity for re-evaluation and improvement.

There is no simple definition of *creativity*, something which may depend on the fact that it is a characteristic which describes someone who creates something new. Someone who does something considered to be creative is also considered to be a creative person. It is possible to study the "new", i.e., that which is created; whilst the characteristic is more elusive. Therefore, amongst the attempts to define *creativity*, researchers have focused on the thing produced, the result of the creative process (which may involve a number of different people). *Creativity* is thus isolated in terms of two factors (Glăveanu, 2014):

- the product's innovation and originality;
- the product's value, benefit, meaningfulness, and suitability.

The term *product* should not be interpreted literally. A product may also include a new service, or a new way of organising things, for example, by packing furniture in flat boxes so as to save on transport and storage costs. Stein (1953: 311) claims in his definition of *creativity* that the creative work is a novel work that is accepted as tenable or useful or satisfying by a group in some point in time.

Note that Stein claims that that which is created is not original, new, or useful if it is not accepted as such by other people, in a specific context, at a specific point in time. The social aspect of creativity is thus shown to be central (Glăveanu, 2010, 2014; Rhodes, 1961).

In what follows, the importance of the social dimension of creativity will be emphasised, not least for organisations, public and private, since they are, by definition, 'social organisations'. Whilst it might be the case that the creative genius works best without explicit management and control (Ivancevic & Dunning, 2001; Lackner 2012; see also Chapter 14), an organisation brings with it the necessary management and control systems so that it may achieve its goals. 'Organisation' sets conditions on the creative process by setting limits and providing opportunities for creativity. Too much management and control smothers creativity. Just the right amount of management can provide exciting challenges and stimulate creativity. However, 'just the right amount' does not mean the same thing for every employee; a certain degree of adaptability on behalf of the employer may be needed. Establishing a creative climate can thus be described as a balancing act between opposite pairs, for example, finding the balance between freedom and control.

This chapter does not aspire to present an exhaustive account of the conditions for creativity in organisations. However, I will share a number of practical experiences from work-life and a number of practical arrangements which should stimulate creativity. Reference is also made to the results of previous research on creative processes in organisations. This will allow me to describe some approaches to when, where, and how creativity can be encouraged at the workplace and what effects these approaches may have.

I begin by reporting on four different cases and discussing (i) the balance between freedom and control that needs to be evaluated to suit both the workplace and the employees and (ii) the fact that creativity may need to be stimulated. Next, I explain how one can encourage the emergence of creative practices, not least by allowing playfulness at the workplace. This is followed by a discussion of whether creativity is encouraged by group work or not, and whether creativity is aided by a safe work climate. The section that follows this discussion addresses management's role in the creative process. The chapter ends with a description of several opposite pairs that need to be balanced against each other so as to promote creativity at the workplace.

The right balance between freedom and control

The American psychologist Rollo May (1975/1994: 113) argues that "*creativity itself requires limits*, for the creative act arises out of the struggle of human beings with and against that which limits them". All creative acts demand some restrictive mould which establishes necessary limits and structure for an end product. It is thus important to consider which limits and structures exist at the workplace, and at which level(s) in the organisation these limits are to be found. These instantiate the conditions under which the collective creativity in the organisation has to operate under.

Leif Denti (2013), the author of a dissertation on how management and organisational structures can promote creativity and innovation in the business world, claims that a balance must be found between freedom, on the one side, and detailed instructions, on the other. To this should be added the ability to listen to and understand other people. The following case studies, conducted at two different workplaces, provide us with everyday examples of frameworks that are too strict (or limiting) *versus* too much freedom. In both cases, a lack of responsiveness is made apparent.

Case 1

The magazine section at a university department employed an apprentice who was asked to create searchable digital posts for all the editions of the physical magazines that were available in the library. Immediately after starting, the apprentice noticed that the existing digital posts did not follow the same format as the new digital posts. The apprentice went to the library director to report on the problem and the apprentice offered to correct the existing posts in parallel with the work to be done in the creation of the new posts. The library director turned this offer down immediately, arguing that this was not what was initially asked of the employee.

The employee had identified a problem and also saw an opportunity to make the job assignment more stimulating, and to make a more efficient system. The employee's behaviour can thus be described as 'creative' because it demonstrated a willingness to perform improvement work and development work. The employee's ideas were thrown away, without due reflection.

Case 2

At a research institute, a researcher in sociology hired a research assistant who was tasked to perform a study into the number of distance-learning courses offered by the French education system which could be searched for on the internet. The research assistant was assigned to work on this task one day per week, for three months. This work resulted in a written report, including a presentation of the different categories of distance-learning courses on offer. The research leader was unhappy with this result, since the information that had been collected was not sufficient and the categories could not be used.

A timely examination of the work should have identified some fundamental problems in the structure and the layout of the work. An employee who works once a week at a workplace, on a specific project, does not have the same opportunity to engage in the purpose and goals of the work in the same way that full-time employees have. Furthermore, this case suggests that the time schedule for the assignment was not realistic or achievable. One might ask whether the research assistant understood which part of the puzzle her contribution made to the larger picture. Unclear communication of this type may indicate too much freedom and insufficient instructions, and even too high demands, with respect to the structure of the assignment.

Both of the cases referred to above provide us with snapshots of how creative ability and innovation can be snatched away from an employee in just a moment; for the one employee because they did not respond exactly to the task given, and for the other, because they were not sufficiently informed of the purpose of the task. In both cases, trust was an important factor. In the first case, one might think that the library director did not trust, or have faith in, the apprentice, whilst in the second case, the manager had far too much faith in the assistant's ability, and perhaps in the assistant's previous knowledge and skills. We note that such trust should not be indiscriminately given to employees. Instead, the awarding of trust (in this context) must be in agreement with an evaluation of what one can generally expect of a person in relation to the person's employment status, education, qualifications, and personality.

Denti (2013) claims that creativity is promoted at the workplace if the HR department has the ability to recruit highly skilled and motivated people in different competence areas. This type of 'elite' employees who Denti refers to expect a larger amount of freedom and trust with respect to their work, than compared with other employees. Notwithstanding this, both types of employees need to be managed by people who can support and channel each individual's creativity. The provision of support to the organisation's management team for this task is a big challenge for the whole HR department. Both cases described above clearly demonstrate the importance of a management team who can judiciously balance freedom against control. The balance between these two opposites creates a space within which creativity can flourish.

Creativity may need to be stimulated

In the fields of business economics and organisational research, the term *innovation* is often preferred over *creativity*. It is claimed that *innovation* is the practical application of *creative* ideas (Westwood & Low, 2003). Those who make a distinction between these terms argue that *innovation* is the process of realising a product, and that *creativity* refers to the thought processes and ideas behind the process of realising a product. However, the terms are often used as if they were synonyms. Swedish county councils (SKL) have initiated a project to increase creativity and the innovation ability in those organisations which the counties are responsible for. Their report shows that most people have a common need to "be able to contribute to positive results for those one serves, to be acknowledged, and to receive recognition for what one does" (Jansson, 2015:7, author's translation). This can be a great challenge for rule-governed, bureaucratic, administrative organisations where employees are traditionally expected to follow rules, instead of being creative. This national project encouraged municipalities to establish an 'innovation prize'. This was a success.

According to SKL's report, organisations can influence support for creativity and innovation on different levels. The project led to personal development, the development of the organisation, and to useful products. Cooperative and networking practices were also developed. The innovation project at the municipalities demonstrated how self-actualisation and benefiting society goes hand in hand. This is a lesson which can be shared at the workplace (Jansson, 2015).

Despite these positive effects, the report clearly states that a creative climate is not achieved over night; several methodical steps must be taken towards this goal so that "renewal becomes a natural part of the job" (Jansson, 2015: 16–17, author's translation). One of the first steps that needs to be taken is the creation of an open climate, where the identity of every employee can be seen and heard (Sanchez-Burks et al., 2015). The question to ask is: *How can such an open climate be established?*

What follows are two examples from two different municipalities in Sweden, where different types of activities contributed to creating an open climate.

Case 3

A section leader at an ER department suggested that they organise an arts and crafts exhibition where the 150-odd employees could display whatever they made in their time off from work. The initiative was well received, and the doctors, nurses, secretaries, and receptionists participated by producing arts and crafts items that were displayed in the staff conference room. The items included water-coloured paintings, scrapbooks, photographs, ceramics, clay sculptures, glass paintings, steel wire art, and designer children's clothes. One doctor stated that the event had changed his view of the secretaries and receptionists, who, during the working day, were merely anonymous faces who functioned as an information exchange. Now suddenly the doctor saw the person wearing the white overcoat. Another doctor admitted that it was "shocking" to discover all the skills that existed in the group and that so much creative power was enjoyed by certain colleagues. Other colleagues were positively surprised by a male doctor who created heart-shaped candlestick holders as a hobby.

Case 4

At the food health and safety inspectorate in one municipality, the employees felt that the work climate was somewhat dull, bureaucratic, and impersonal. The department consisted of 30-odd employees. Some of the younger employees made a suggestion that each week should have a theme which should be connected to a particular employee. In the first week, the theme was 'Norrland' (the northern part of Sweden). The employees learnt several surprising facts about the area. The climax of the themed week was reached when the only Norrlander person who was employed at the office offered *pitepalt* (a traditional potato dish) to everyone to eat. This new playful addition to the work environment did not only make work more fun, but as one employee stated, it also had a positive effect on the daily work. The employees felt that it had become easier to say what was on their mind and to share new ideas with each other.

They also began to reflect over their work methods. Every year, the inspectors went out into the community and inspected a number of foodstuff environments, according to a list stored in an MSExcel workbook. However, these inspections were never completed because nobody was particularly motivated to perform this assignment. The group leader for the inspectors began a dialogue with the employees where they agreed to a routine where one or more inspectors were chosen to organise the inspections according to thematic categories which the inspectors had chosen themselves. Thus, the work was made more efficient, whilst the employees were forced to reflect over and consider their clients and their work in a new, playful, and more thoughtful way.

Both of the above cases demonstrate the importance of being personable without being private. Both initiatives encouraged the emergence of the unique character of each person, and not just the limited job role. Personal relationships improved and made the work week more interesting and fun. The activities introduced an element of creativity without a clear purpose or goal for the actual business on hand. These improvised and voluntary activities, performed without thought of reward, created opportunities for the employees to interact with each other in a new way, giving rise to new ways of thinking.

Play and the importance of the social context for creativity

In the examples described above, it appears that it is important that one 'has a little bit of fun' at work. Samuel West (2015), in his dissertation *Playing at work*, investigates whether, and how, play influences creativity at work. West's study demonstrates that play at work has a great potential to increase motivation and establish good relationships between employees. However, explicit permission to play should be given, and note that one cannot force employees to engage in an activity that is supposed to be fun, especially if the stress levels at the workplace are high. Play must be based on voluntary participation. If the work climate allows for it, then play can get us to forget about goal-driven work tasks and open our minds and intellect to new impressions and ideas.

Mainemelis and Ronson (2006) identify five features of play, which they claim are of importance to the emergence of creative ability.

i Experience of crossing boundaries. Play allows participants to find themselves between opposites, including new and old, true and false, and internal and external.

ii Time frames and spatial limits. Play is enclosed by time and spatial limits, which separate it from everyday life. Because of this, play can reveal patterns, roles, and behaviour that are usually suppressed and considered undesirable.
iii Uncertainty and freedom from compulsion. All play entails discovery and some form of uncertainty about undefined possibilities.
iv Flexibility and freedom with respect to ways of playing and the goal for the play activity. There is no rational goal behind playing or methodical way in which play is performed. The manner and goal fall out, after the event.
v Positive feelings. Play involves positive feelings. The intensity and complexity of these feelings may vary depending on the play activity and the participants. The results of playing are often some form of happiness, pleasure, and emotional relief.

Play at the workplace remains a relatively unexplored field. It is only in the last few years that methodical and systematic research has been conducted in this area. The acceptance of play at the workplace is steadily increasing at companies and other organisations. If play was previously considered to be illegitimate and aberrational behaviour, it is now seen, to an increasing extent, as a desirable behaviour (Mainemelis & Dionysiou, 2015).

Group dynamics at various stages of creativity

'Brainstorming' is a method similar to play, which can be used to create an open and creative climate. During brainstorming, one works together with others to generate many ideas or solutions to a problem. Brainstorming was a successful method used by the advertising agent Alex Osborn (1957) and continues to exist in different forms in the work-life. This method has, however, been shown to have its limitations. The fact remains that people who work in a group seldom have better ideas or think of more solutions than if they work alone. In fact, it is the case that individual contemplation is more creative (Furnham, 2000). Brainstorming can, however, work in a group where everyone has a relevant role, can contribute to the discussion with specific competencies, and is motivated to do so; although this can be difficult to achieve (Paulus & Nijstad, 2003). One alternative is to engage in brainstorming alone, and then meet with one's colleagues later to share and evaluate ideas together (Furnham, 2000). The choice of working method is dependent on where one is in the creative work process and what the result of the creative work is intended to be (West, 2014). Consequently, it is necessary to take into consideration the different stages in creative work.

In the 1920s, Graham Wallas formulated a psychodynamic model to describe the inner creative process (Wallas, 1926/2014). The creative process is divided into four stages, which include an interface between consciousness and the unconscious where one continually is trying to move across this interface. The *preparatory stage* is when one gathers knowledge of the area in which one is to work. This is followed by the *incubation stage*, where one processes the information that was gathered during the preparatory stage. This is not always done consciously; it is a process which occurs in different daily situations, even whilst one is asleep. It is as if one 'broods' over an idea, like an egg that is incubated. This stage is followed by the experience that one has discovered something new; the *illumination stage*. The majority of one's ideas are cast to the wayside, but some of them bear fruit. These ideas are worthy of advancing to the *verification stage*, where these ideas are tested. The creative process thus described is for individuals, where a single person runs the course of the process.

Companies and other organisations wish to understand and apply the creative process in *groups* of employees. Per Kristensson's (2003) dissertation on group creativity in IT laboratories and IT companies demonstrates that it is not a simple task to manage the first stages in this process because they do not follow clear rules. In the preparatory and incubation stages, it is thus of importance that opportunities to share information and experience are provided. One does not necessarily need to work with other people, but those who are involved in the process should receive a rich description of the problem area. According to Kristensson, it has been fruitful to include clients in this stage, since they may offer up unexpected suggestions and ideas which the employees may not have been able to come up with by themselves. This may prevent the employees from being 'locked in' a particular perspective or mindset about what is to be created.

The studies that Kristensson (2003) builds upon demonstrate how different groups of people and different employees come together in the process, all the way to product delivery. The process encourages (i) flexibility in interpersonal relationships, (ii) respect for one's colleagues, and (iii) respect for one's colleagues' need for fellowship at work and for their (occasional) desire to work alone. Note that people change jobs more frequently now than before, and employees also often change their membership with different workgroups within the organisation. The human resources that are 'on the move' also function as information exchanges and brokers of knowledge, practices, opinions, and ideas across different workgroups (Lave & Wenger, 1991; Wenger, 1998). In contexts where creativity is elevated to being one of the most valuable resources needed for success, then these knowledge brokers become important pieces of the puzzle which can stimulate the business and provide valuable 'input'. However, common experience informs us that groups usually tend to 'school' new members to the group in a common, already-established, prevailing practice, instead of listening to what the new members might be able to teach the old members about a different work culture. A creative climate is promoted if the employer can make employees conscious of this tendency and stimulate and motivate learning between and across different groups.

Creativity benefits from a safe and friendly work atmosphere

One can imagine that the combination of social fellowship at work *and* the possibility of working alone should have a good effect on creativity, but research in this area remains somewhat sparse (Gilson et al., 2015). Google conducted an empirical study with its employees in an attempt to discover what the secret was with certain especially productive work teams. The results of their study showed that these teams did not include the 'smartest' employees. The success factor was simply how the employees interacted with each other. In the groups where respect was shown for each other's feelings and everyone could speak their opinions as equals, an open atmosphere and a generous culture was established which promoted creativity and productivity (Mohdin, 2016).

This study confirms Edmondson's results on the importance of psychological security at the workplace in building effective teams (Edmondson, 1999). She demonstrates that there is a connection between daring to expose oneself within a group, efficiency, learning, and productivity. The connection between creativity and the social environment is an area in the research field on creativity which originally was identified by Amabile (1983, 1996) in her research. In the Google study, the interpersonal perspective was discovered to be more important to the collective creativity in the organisation than the creative abilities of individuals (Glăveanu & Clapp, 2018; Sawyer, 2007). Consequently, since their study, Google works according to the mantra: 'The key to good teamwork is being nice' (Mohdin, 2016).

Research on creativity and group composition partly contradict Google's investigation. According to Baer et al. (2008), Somech and Drach-Zahavy (2013), and Gilson et al. (2015), certain characteristics of the members of a group can influence, either positively or negatively, the group's creativity. Research does clearly indicate, however, that diversity in a group can stimulate creativity if the different competencies and areas of expertise can be gathered around a common perspective or a common issue or area of enquiry. This is difficult to achieve, but it does allow for different abilities to be used and integrated so as to develop ideas and realise them.

Creative leadership and participation

The literature on 'creativity' highlights the value of developing creativity both for individuals and in groups and organisations (Rasulzada & Brodin, 2014). Leadership and management which stimulates creativity can take on different forms, including (i) supporting leadership (Scott & Bruce, 1994), (ii) empowering leadership (Zhang & Bartol, 2010), and (iii) transformational leadership (Shin & Zhou, 2003). However, there is no consensus in the literature on how leadership influences creativity. Notwithstanding this, certain tendencies can be identified. A boss who behaves in a controlling manner and excessively monitors the employees can inhibit creativity (Rasulzada & Brodin, 2014). Creative behaviour is promoted by leadership which consciously supports the employees and ensures that information circulates within the organisation (Scott & Bruce, 1994). Motivation levels are raised in organisations where the leadership reinforces the employees' power over their work; for example, by emphasising the importance of the employees' efforts and by encouraging independence in the employees (Zhang & Bartol, 2010).

Transformational leadership is more complex and consists of inspiring and motivating others, as well as stimulating others intellectually (Shin & Zhou, 2003). This entails continually searching for change and having high expectations of one's employees, whilst reinforcing their abilities and providing space for work that is done alone and for playfulness (Shin, 2015). The aim is to create an environment where the employees can improve on themselves. Such transformational leaders emphasise the importance of cooperation between employees, who are treated as "individuals by the manager who cares about their thoughts and feelings, and tries to satisfy their needs" (Rasulzada & Brodin, 2014: 379, author's translation). To be a creative leader, even more is demanded; for example, such a leader should possess visionary ideas, flexibility, an ability to make connections and associations, be able to take risks, engage in critical thinking and the generation of new ideas, and the ability to bring projects to fruition.

The question to ask is whether the organisation needs a creative leader or whether it needs a leader who facilitates creativity. Creative leaders do not always influence the work atmosphere in a positive way, since they are often strong and stubborn personalities, with fixed opinions which do not tolerate contradiction (Rasulzada & Brodin, 2014). This can stifle the collective creative potential in the rest of the employees. The transformational leader who facilitates creativity in others is less concerned with his or her own creativity than the engagement of everyone else in the creative work. This may include introducing improvements and more effective systems, but even radically different ideas. Different work groups and different work assignments demand different types of leadership if they are to be innovative. Flexibility of leadership facilitates management of the creative process, which is characterised by uncertainty and surprises (Komporozos-Athanasiou & Fotaki, 2015).

The ideal leadership style for the promotion of creativity can be summarised as the ability to connect together three different dimensions. The first dimension is one's own capacity to be creative in one's leadership role, and to dare to think and act outside the frameworks and rule systems which govern the business. The second dimension is one's competence to create the conditions necessary for creative ideas and actions for different groups at the workplace. The third dimension includes how the two previous dimensions can be made to match the employees' level of motivation and their ability to express their creativity (Rasulzada & Brodin, 2014). It is not merely sufficient to be the boss; one must lead with enthusiasm and with one's own active participation if one is to bring these three dimensions together.

The consequences for HR work

This chapter has argued that creativity benefits from stimulation. In our current 'information society', creativity is a force that one works at together, to research and promote at all levels. This becomes crucially important at a time when "the demands to be flexible, efficient, and possess the competence to change are continually on the increase" (Rasulzada, 2014: 418, author's translation). The demands placed on leadership also have developed in this context, towards a clearer participation in the organisation and paying more attention to individual employees and to group dynamics. In the examples which have been presented so far, it is revealed that creativity can be initiated if the leader creates space in which the employees can 'manoeuvre' themselves. In the next section, the central ideas of this chapter are summarised in terms of five tools which can be used to (i) control this space for manoeuvre and (ii) promote creativity at the workplace.

The balance between freedom and control

Structure, limits, and control are necessary things if one is to manage an organisation in such a way that its goals are achieved. Employees also need to know that they are wanted at the workplace because of their qualifications and their ability to deliver on what is asked of them. Limiting structures, for example, extremely frequent reporting cycles and strict reporting templates, should not dominate the workplace. The freedom to independently take the initiative and take control of the work methods should be cherished and protected so that creativity can take its place at work. Undoubtedly, employees need a framework which they should follow, but there should also exist certain opportunities and trust in the employees as they create their own work situation. There is, however, no universal recipe for this – the balance between freedom and control will be found at different points for different organisations, people, and professional roles.

The balance between playfulness and seriousness

One should be able to work efficiently under time pressure and in competition with others. Professional situations are thus taken to be serious situations. It is important that one is serious about what one does. This does not pose as an obstacle to the promotion of an open climate at the workplace. An open climate entails that the employees can accept new ideas and practices and also rely on the fact that their own ideas and suggestions are desired and welcomed – even as one needs to be prepared to take risks and sometimes fail. This open climate is promoted by introducing playful elements and ensuring that opportunities exist where one can be personal without being private. Motivation and good relationships are reinforced by playfulness, which in turn, benefits creativity.

The balance between social fellowship and being alone

The workplace is a social environment which includes several people who are involved in the creation of a product. The promotion of creativity in cooperation with each other is thus important. However, people need to know that at some stages in the creative process employees need to be left alone, whilst at other stages group work may be more appropriate. In general, solitary thought generates the largest number of and the most original ideas. However, groups can work together if each member of the group has a specific role and is just as motivated as the others to achieve a common goal. The group is also needed to test and evaluate ideas. One condition for well-functioning group work is mutual respect by the participants. The employer also needs to create an environment where it is possible both to work alone and in social fellowship with others.

The balance between different employee profiles

One cannot be certain that an organisation will be more productive and in-novative just because it has hired particularly creative employees. The process from idea to product demands a cohesive team, including highly creative people and also people who can realise these ideas. Creative people often have strong personalities with fixed opinions. This can have a negative effect on group dynamics, even as they provide new ideas, as requested. Thus, a balance needs to be found between people who have different personality profiles.

The balance between stability and change

Fear does not promote creativity. Employees need to feel safe and secure at the workplace. Security does not mean 'being content and satisfied', but rather, that there is an open-minded and easy-going attitude at the workplace which allows for the expression of different ideas from all employees. Respect and kind behaviour displayed by the employees is important. However, creativity also demands uncertainty and the possibility to conduct experiments. The act of creation is by nature uncertain and holds the potential to surprise. Thus, risk-taking should also be supported.

Recommended reading

Collister, Patrick (2017), *How to: Use innovation and creativity in the workplace*. London: Pan Macmillan.
Garud, Raghu, Simpson, Barbara, Langley, Ann, & Tsoukas, Haridimos (eds.) (2015), *The emergence of novelty in organizations*. Oxford: Oxford University Press.
Reiter-Palmon, Roni (ed.) (2017), *Team creativity and innovation*. New York, NY: Oxford University Press.
Škerlavaj, Miha, Cerne, Matej, Dysvik, Anders, & Carlsen, Arne (eds.) (2016), *Capitalizing on creativity at work*. Northampton, MA: Edward Elgar Pub.

References

Amabile, Teresa M. (1983), *The social psychology of creativity*. New York: Springer.
Amabile, Teresa M. (1996), *Creativity in context: Update to "the social psychology of creativity"*. Oxford: Westview.
Baer, Markus, Oldham, Greg R., Jacobsohn, Gwendolyn Costa, & Hollingshead, Andrea B. (2008), The personality composition of teams and creativity: The moderating role of team creative confidence. *Fourth Quarter, 44*(4), pp. 255–282.

Denti, Leif (2013), *Leadership and innovation in R&D teams.* Dissertation. Göteborg: Psykologiska institutionen, Göteborgs universitet.

Edmondson, Amy (1999), Psychological safety and learning behavior in work teams. *Administrative Science Quarterly, 44*(1999), pp. 350–383.

Furnham, Adrian (2000), The brainstorming myth. *Business Strategy Review, 11*(4), pp. 21–28.

Gilson, Lucy L., Sook Lim, Hyoun, Litchfield, Robert C., & Gilson, Paul W. (2015), Creativity in teams: A key building block for innovation and entrepreneurship. In Christina Shalley, Michael A. Hitt & Jing Zhou (eds.), *The Oxford handbook of creativity, innovation, and entrepreneurship* (pp. 177–204). New York: Oxford University Press.

Glăveanu, Vlad P. (2010), Paradigms in the study of creativity: Introducing the perspective of cultural psychology. *New Ideas in Psychology, 28*(1), pp. 79–93.

Glăveanu, Vlad P. (2014), The psychology of creativity: A critical reading. *Creativity: Theories – Research – Applications, 1*(1), pp. 10–32.

Glăveanu, Vlad P. & Clapp, Edward P. (2018), Distributed and participatory creativity as a form of cultural empowerment: The role of alterity, difference and collaboration. In Angela Uchoa Branco & Maria Cláudia Lopes-de-Oliveira (eds.), *Alterity, values, and socialization* (pp. 51–63). Cultural Psychology of Education, vol. 6. Cham: Springer.

Ivancevic, John M. & Dunning, Thomas N. (2001), *Managing Einsteins: Leading high-tech workers in the digital age.* New York: McGraw-Hill.

Jansson, Anette (2015), *Medarbetarkraft: Insatser för kreativitet och nytänkande.* [Cooperative power: Creativity and innovation] Stockholm: Sveriges kommuner och landsting.

Komporozos-Athanasiou, Aris & Fotaki, Marianna (2015), Imagination in organizational creativity. In Raghu Garud, Barbara Simpson, Ann Langley, & Haridimos Tsoukas (eds.), *The emergence of novelty in organizations* (pp. 80–102). Oxford: Oxford University Press.

Kristensson, Per (2003), *Creativity in applied enterprise: Bringing impetus to innovation.* Dissertation. Göteborg: Psykologiska institutionen, Göteborgs universitet.

Lackner, Maximilian (2012), *Talent-Management spezial: Hochbegabte, Forscher und Künstler erfolgreich führen.* Wiesbaden: Gabler.

Lave, Jean & Wenger, Etienne (1991), *Situated learning: Legitimate peripheral participation.* Cambridge: Cambridge University Press.

Mainemelis, Charalampos & Dionysiou, Dionysios D. (2015), Play, flow and timelessness. In Christina Shalley, Michael A. Hitt, & Jing Zhou (eds.), *The Oxford handbook of creativity, innovation, and entrepreneurship* (pp. 121–140). Oxford & New York: Oxford University Press.

Mainemelis, Charalampos & Ronson, Sarah (2006), Ideas are born in fields of play: Towards a theory of play and creativity in organizational settings. *Research in Organizational Behavior, 27*, pp. 81–138.

May, Rollo (1994 [1975]), *The courage to create.* New York: W.W. Norton.

Mohdin, Aamna (2016), Imagine that after years of intensive analysis, Google discovers the key to good teamwork is being nice. *Quartz,* 26 Feb. Retrieved from http://qz.com [2016-04-06].

Osborn, Alex F. (1957), *Applied imagination: Principles and procedures of creative thinking* (revised edition). New York: Charles Scribner's Sons.

Paulus, Paul B. & Nijstad, Bernard, A. (eds.) (2003), *Group creativity: Innovation through collaboration.* Oxford: Oxford University Press.

Rasulzada, Farida (2014), Är kreativitet organisationens lyckopiller? [Is creativity an organisation's magic pill?] In Eva Brodin, Ingegerd Carlsson, Eva Hoff, & Farida

Rasulzada (eds.), *Kreativitet: Teori och praktik ur psykologiska perspektiv* [Creativity: Theory and practice from a psychological perspective] (pp. 416–435). Stockholm: Liber.

Rasulzada, Farida & Brodin, Eva (2014), Utmaning på topp: Kreativitetsfrämjande ledarskap. [Challenges from the top: Leadership that promotes creativity] In Eva Brodin, Ingegerd Carlsson, Eva Hoff, & Farida Rasulzada (eds.), *Kreativitet: Teori och praktik ur psykologiska perspektiv* [Creativity: Theory and practice from a psychological perspective] (pp. 370–394). Stockholm: Liber.

Rhodes, Mel (1961), An analysis of creativity. *The Phi Delta Kappan*, *42*(7), pp. 305–310.

Sanchez-Burks, Jeffrey, Karlesky, Matthew J., & Lee, Fiona (2015), Psychological bricolage: Integrating social identities to produce creative solutions. In Christina Shalley, Michael A. Hitt, & Jing Zhou (eds.), *The Oxford handbook of creativity, innovation, and entrepreneurship* (pp. 93–102). Oxford, New York: Oxford University Press.

Sawyer, Keith (2007), *Group genius*. New York: Basic Books.

Scott, Susanne G. & Bruce, Reginald A. (1994), Determinants of innovative behavior: A path model of individual innovation in the workplace. *Academy of Management Journal*, *37*(3), pp. 580–607.

Shin, Shung Jae (2015), Leadership and creativity: The mechanism perspective. In Christina Shalley, Michael A. Hitt, & Jing Zhou (eds.), *The Oxford handbook of creativity, innovation, and entrepreneurship* (pp. 17–30). Oxford, New York: Oxford University Press.

Shin, Shung Jae & Zhou, Jing (2003), Transformational leadership, conservation, and creativity: Evidence from Korea. *Academy of Management Journal*, *46*(6), pp. 703–714.

Somech, Anit & Drach-Zahavy, Anat (2013), Translating team creativity to innovation implementation: The role of team composition and climate for innovation. *Journal of Management*, *39*(3), pp. 684–708.

Stein, Morris (1953), Creativity and culture. *Journal of Psychology*, *36*, pp. 311–322.

Wallas, Graham (1926/2014). *The art of thought*. Kent, England: Solis Press.

Wenger, Etienne (1998), *Communities of practice: Learning, meaning, and identity*. Cambridge: Cambridge University Press.

West, Samuel (2014), Mer än brainstorming: Metoder för att öka kreativitet. [More than brainstorming: Methods to increase creativity] In Eva Brodin, Ingegerd Carlsson, Eva Hoff, & Farida Rasulzada (eds.), *Kreativitet: Teori och praktik ur psykologiska perspektiv* [Creativity: Theory and practice from a psychological perspective] (pp. 523–532). Stockholm: Liber.

West, Samuel (2015), *Playing at work: Organizational play as a facilitator of creativity*. Dissertation. Lund: Lunds universitet.

Westwood, Robert & Low, David (2003), The multicultural muse: Culture, creativity and innovation. *International Management of Cross-Cultural Management*, *3*(2), pp. 235–259.

Zhang, Xiaomeng & Bartol, Katheryn A. (2010), Linking empowering leadership and employee creativity: The influence of psychological empowerment, intrinsic motivation, and creative process engagement. *Academy of Management Journal*, *53*(1), pp. 107–128.

6

RECRUITMENT MISTAKES, FUTURE EMPLOYEES, AND FABULOUS FANTASIES

The market's need of magical qualities

Roland S. Persson

Are you, by any chance, a person who is structured, independent, not egotistical, able to take the initiative, responsible, extroverted, positive, service-minded, flexible, sales-driven, able to deal with stress, pedagogic, enthusiastic, analytic, able to communicate well, creative, disciplined, goal-directed, have an eye for small details, and competitive? If you are, then you have it made on the employment market, with the condition that you have enough experience and the right qualifications. In fact, you satisfy 20 of the most frequently asked for character traits or personality qualities on the Swedish labour market, as per published job advertisements (SAPLO/Monster, 2009).

There is a serious problem with the above list of desired character traits and personality features, however. We wonder whether a person who satisfies these criteria actually exists! The world of job advertisements is hardly the forum to look to when in search for what is real or possible. Job advertisements, instead, describe the needs the company or other organisation has. If the employer has a limited budget for a planned recruitment drive, and perhaps intends to increase efficiency by decreasing the number of employees, then it is easy for the employer to try to place all of the needs that they have into a single employment position, without actually thinking whether all of these needs can be satisfied by a single new employee (Terpstra, 1996). It is almost like the employer is in search for an 'organisational chameleon'; someone who can embody everything that the company wants and values (Ferris et al., 1991).

The descriptions of ideal candidates for vacant positions also have a tendency to contradict themselves. Belin and Hsin-Wang (2010) found in their study of how Swedish companies advertise positions that contradictory wishes were not uncommon. For example, employers were in need of "independent team players" and "calm but enthusiastic employees". Similar contradictions can be found at the world's most popular workplace, Google, which is continually on the search for creative, highly gifted employees with a penchant for working in a team. This wishful thinking is completely independent of the fact that the more extreme a person's giftedness is, the more probable that such a person works best alone. No one becomes more productive or innovative by participating in intensive brainstorming, even if this takes place in the company of other highly gifted individuals (see the previous chapter). This is a method which research has shown to be somewhat pointless if one is in search for new ideas. Companies which continue to routinely subject their employees to this exercise usually do so, and quite unconsciously, for reasons other than to produce creative ideas; namely, brainstorming is simply more fun and less serious than a traditional, more formal work meeting (Furnham, 2000).

Predictions from lax administrations

When an organisation plans for a recruitment drive, it does not always possess enough ability to decide how the recruitment for a specific post should take place or how it might best describe the person who the organisation wishes to employ, despite the fact that many larger organisations now have their own HR department. Even if knowledge and levels of experience are on the increase because of the labour market's rapid and continual restructuring, it is not currently self-evident in Europe that organisations actually understand *talent management* and thereby efficiently implement such strategies and methods of candidate selection in practice (see Ewerlin & Süss, 2016: Chapter 14 for a detailed description of *talent management*). Instead, organisations hire different types of external consultants and inform them of their recruitment needs and the role the person will have in the company.

Consultants have different backgrounds, different ideas, and use different methods and approaches in their search to find suitable candidates. More importantly, they rely on the results of what many years of academic research and evaluation has to say about different selection instruments and their reliability problems (Furnham, 2008). The most common situation is that recruitment consultants use established or patented, in-house *psychometric tests* and *batteries of tests* in their selection work. One might assume that such an approach is relatively objective and possibly more just, practical, and somewhat manageable. But this is true only under the assumption that the instruments that are used in the selection of candidates actually measure what they are intended to measure. Is this really the case? The answer to this question is fundamental to many test consultancies' business model.

This issue has a long history. At the beginning of the 1900s, the US authorities on New York's Ellis Island tested all arriving immigrants using an IQ test which was linguistically and culturally foreign to the majority of them. Goddard (1917) was primarily responsible for these tests. He claimed that the test results showed that 80% of all arrivals were "mentally retarded". These unfortunate souls were then sent back to their countries of origin as undesirables. But there was nothing wrong with their mental capacities. Immigrants from all over the world just did not understand the questions or the situation in which they found themselves, as created by Goddard and the American immigration authorities. Undeniably, this was a dark period in the history of psychometric testing. However, this demonstrates the problems that test users and commercial producers of these tests still face, in terms of what is ethically defensible, how well these tests work, and the purposes to which the test results are used (Samuda, 1998; Toomela & Valsiner, 2010; van de Vijver & Leung, 1996).

Researchers and psychologists now have sufficient experience to know whether these tests actually work or not. The difficulty remains, however, how well constructs on which psychological tests are based do actually work? A 'construct' is a concept of which psychologists avail themselves to describe different aspects which are assumed to be fundamental to certain measurable behaviours. 'Motivation' is such an aspect, as well as 'introversion', 'competitiveness', and 'easily stressed'.

Two American researchers, Frank L. Schmidt and John E. Hunter (1998), have investigated some of the scales which are frequently used during recruitment selections and how these scales relate to the successful candidates' work performance. These scales included 'general intellectual ability', 'tests of work performance', 'integrity', 'sense of purpose', 'structured and unstructured interviews', 'knowledge of the job applied for', 'probation period', 'colleagues' opinions', 'references', 'work experience', 'personal details', 'number of years of formal education', 'general interests', 'graphological tests', and 'age'. (See Table 6.1.)

TABLE 6.1 Predictive validity of a selection of frequently used variables during recruitment

Variable	Correlation*
'General intellectual ability'	0.51
'Tests of work performance'	0.54
'Integrity'	0.41
'Sense of purpose'	0.31
'Structured interviews'	0.51
'Unstructured interviews	0.38
'Knowledge of the job applied for'	0.48
'Probation period'	0.44
'Colleagues' opinions of the applicant'	0.49
'References'	0.26
'Work experience'	0.18
'Personal details'	0.35
'Number of years of formal education'	0.10
'General interests'	0.10
'Graphological tests'	0.02
'Age'	0.01

*Correlation is expressed in terms of a correlation coefficient (r), where a coefficient of 0.0 indicates that a variable does not, in any way, provide an accurate description of work performance in a future work situation. A coefficient of 1.0 indicates that the variable is extremely reliable, relevant, and is a scale which can be used to good effect in predicting future work performance.

Adapted from Schmidt and Hunter (1998).

Somewhat surprising is to note that an applicant's previous work experience and references have hardly any worth at all in the context of recruitment. More remarkable is that graphology is included as an accepted method for finding the right person for a certain job. In Northern Europe, this is a very unusual method, but in Continental Europe, graphological analysis is more the rule than the exception (Clark, 1992). The candidate is asked to submit examples of their handwriting, which is then inspected and analysed. Afterwards, the employer is informed of which personal and 'hidden' qualities the candidate's handwriting has revealed (Clark, 1992). That this is nonsense is not only shown in Table 6.1 but other research has also stated that graphological analysis, like brainstorming, does not at all provide the information that it is intended to (Furnham & Barrie, 1987).

Of course, each person is free to establish where the limit lies between valuable constructs, less valuable constructs, and constructs that are completely unusable. But it is hardly credible to use instruments during recruitment that have but negligible predictive validity. *Predictive validity* is the measure of a variable which it is said to reliably predict the value of another variable. The correlation between the two is described in terms of a correlation coefficient (r), which indicates the strength of the correlation. By using the coefficient value, one can predict whether a correlation exists. Table 6.2 shows the way in which the coefficient can be interpreted.

By consulting the values shown in Table 6.2, we note that only the variables 'general intellectual ability' (often understood as an IQ score), 'tests of work performance', and 'structured interviews' in Schmidt and Hunter's (1998) analysis achieve just a 'moderate' correlation. The variables that touch on the candidate's personality, 'integrity' and 'sense of purpose', which so often appear in job advertisements, show only a 'weak' to 'negligible' correlation. It thus seems difficult to reliably capture a candidate's personal qualities with psychometric tests. It is a challenge even for the work psychologist test consultant to inform the employer that a particular candidate, in the future, will be communicative, creative, disciplined, goal directed, meticulous, and competitive (to mention just a few of the examples given in the introduction of this chapter of the personal qualities that are most frequently mentioned in Swedish job advertisements (see also Blinkhorn & Johnson, 1990; Pittenger, 2005).

Investigations have been made how even the most acknowledged instruments that are used to profile different types of personality can be related to certain desired qualities for certain work categories. Barrick and Mount (1991) compared the

TABLE 6.2 Interpretive norms for the coefficient of correlation (r) according to Hinkle et al. (2003)

Very strong	Moderately strong	Moderate	Weak	Negligible
1.00–0.90	0.90–0.70	0.70–0.50	0.50–0.30	0.30–0.00

Note: The values in the table indicate the strength of an alleged correlation between variables; i.e., the degree to which measurable variables influence, or are dependent on, each other.

different dimensions included in the so-called 'Big Five' battery – 'Neuroticism', 'Extraversion', 'Openness to experience', 'Agreeableness', and 'Conscientiousness' (Costa & McCrae, 1992) with the work performance of civil servants, police, managers, sales people, and industrial workers. The researchers found only negligible correlations; r measured between 0.09 and 0.23. 'Conscientiousness' was the dimension that had the highest validity. All of the job categories that were compared could, to a limited degree, be described in terms of 'Conscientiousness' ($r = 0.20–0.23$), which, in short, indicates that a person tends to be meticulous, attentive, observant, efficient, and possesses a desire to do the job well; qualities that would benefit *any* employer. There is a statistically significant correlation between work performance and 'Conscientiousness', but one cannot ignore the fact that the correlation is so weak that it is actually negligible. Is it really worth the trouble, under such circumstances, to use such an instrument in the recruitment and selection process? (see Murphy Paul, 2005; Salgado et al., 2003). Opinions are divided and one receives different answers to this question depending on who one asks. This is an inevitable and significant problem for recruitment staff, work psychology consultants, and HR departments who place a great deal of value on recruiting people who possess specific personal characteristics.

Gilded statistical correlations

One cannot ignore the fact that the production of tests and work psychology consultancy constitutes a very lucrative business. Just in the United States, since the 1990s, this business brought in 5 billion SEK per year, and in the United Kingdom during the 2000s this business turned over 280 million SEK per year (Harper, 2008; Koocher & Rey Casserly, 2003). For comparison, one British pound (GBP) is in time of writing the equivalent of about 12 Swedish crowns (SEK). Work psychological testing is well on its way to becoming an industry worthy of investment, even in Sweden: seven out of ten Swedish companies use psychometric tests in their recruitment process (Chef, 2011). Given these facts, there is reason to issue a warning, since this market attracts some less than scrupulous players. This problem has prompted Koocher and Rey Cassidy (2003) to provide a description of how such unscrupulous people market their services, in the hope that businesses and HR departments who are looking for expert assistance in their recruitment work will avoid them. Koocher and Rey Cassidy (2003) make the following observations:

> They seldom speak of the qualifications they have which allows them to conduct psychometric tests.
>
> Companies who want to buy their services seldom have access to a psychometric evaluation of the tests that are being sold.
>
> The primary marketing strategy, which is supposed to suggest some quality assurance, is to provide a list of well-renowned clients that they have worked with.

The higher one goes in an organisation's hierarchy, the more usual it is that an external recruitment consultant is hired, and the less transparent the methods that are used by the consultancies are (Clark, 1992). It is also of interest to note that whilst the number of administered psychometric tests (in the context of recruitment) has increased in Sweden, the proportion of successful instances of recruitment has decreased from 47% to 35%. Furthermore, the proportion of less successful instances of recruitment has increased from 10% to 15% in the Swedish business sector, according to Poolia's 'competence indicators' (Schartau, 2011).

This is hardly good news for employers who risk losing a million SEK because the newly recruited manager does not live up to expectations (Poolia, n.d.), despite the fact that he or she (according to the selection instruments that were used in the recruitment process) was shown to be 'independent', 'able to take the initiative', 'can deal with stress', is 'enthusiastic', 'communicative', 'creative', 'competitive', and 'goal-driven'.

The figures are even more dismal outside Sweden. An American Gallup poll showed that 82% of all American directors and managers at different levels can be seen as incorrectly recruited, and this costs their employers huge amounts of money. The reason for this, claim Randall J. Beck and Jim Harper (2014), both employees of Gallup, is that American business people often award managerial positions to those who *deserve* to be the boss, instead of awarding this position to individuals who possess the requirements and the inherent talent to be the boss. One finds inherent talent, argue Beck and Harper, by using *scientific* methods of predictive analysis. They claim that the problem with incorrect recruitment can be alleviated if the selection process takes place with the help of carefully conducted psychometric testing. However, as discussed above, this is not necessarily a solution to the problem.

It is uncommon for consultants and recruitment experts to question the instruments that they use in their operations. Criticising one's own business and one's own services is hardly effective marketing in a world where all profit-driven companies try to exceed one another by maximising profits and winning market shares (Schmidt, 1995). Marketing something as 'scientific' lends a certain *cachet* of legitimacy and trustworthiness for one's own business and for the tools that are used to select candidates. Psychometric testing, depending on how and what is being measured, can be a useful resource if it is used in conjunction with several other selection tools (Furnham, 2005). It is of course possible that successful recruitment events take place when psychometric testing has been used. Consultants who are scientifically 'sound', self-critical, and experienced have several ways of deploying psychometric instruments and have taught themselves to understand who the candidate is and what he or she is capable of (Lindelöw, 2003). However, there is a risk that an instance of incorrect recruitment may well be the result of an uncritical, exaggerated belief in what psychometric recruitment methods can provide (Chamorro-Premuzic & Furnham, 2003). Regardless of who is doing the recruiting, there is always the danger that, after a person gains employment, the company or organisation is left standing with a hole in its budget and an important position that is filled by an incorrect candidate.

In addition to the problem of interpreting statistical correlations, a possible lack of marketing ethics, and a possible over-reliance on psychometric testing, there is a further important, and often ignored, aspect which dampens the reliability of personality profiling, namely, the successful research performed in the areas of genetics and evolution dynamics in the last few years. When such a well-established and widely accepted instrument as the *Big Five* is shown to have almost no validity – and when advanced and properly thought through recruitment strategies with candidate selection being informed by competent work psychological testing still fails to recruit the right people – then it is quite obvious that one has should suspect that one has overlooked something of importance in understanding how people actually function, both at work and in their everyday lives.

Here today, gone tomorrow!

Psychometric research and the use of psychometric tests, in themselves, constitute a welcome and useful addition to the arsenal of behavioural science methods. However, two very important aspects of human behaviour have not been included in the context of recruitment until quite recently in the history of psychology; namely, (i) general cultural differences (Chakraborty, 1991; Howitt & Owusu-Bempah, 1994; Norenzayan & Heine, 2005) and (ii) people's individual capacity to change their behaviour because of the specific cultural context in which they find themselves (Buss, 2001; Simonton, 2005; Tooby & Cosmides, 1990).

It is difficult to imagine how a psychometric test can be completely free from cultural influences. Despite this, there are widely used and acknowledged batteries of tests which actually claim to be culturally independent (see Cronbach, 1990 for an overview of this position). A rule of thumb for the use of any type of behaviour construct in research or in work psychological testing is to note that the more dependent a psychometric instrument is on biological factors, then the less probable it is influenced by cultural conditions, and vice versa. It is thus very difficult, if not impossible, to use the test outside its original cultural context (Persson, 2012).

The *Big Five* is generally considered to be an instrument which describes universal dimensions of a person's personality (McCrae & Costa, 1997), but this position should be put into contrast with the observation that personal characteristics (estimated over large populations) have been shown to be *inherited* 30%–60% of the time, depending on which characteristic is considered. This means that 40%–70% of that which is called *personality* is influenced and determined by the cultural context and possibly by other factors which are not genetically determined (Plomin et al., 2013). The importance of this research into behavioural genetics is considerable for our psychometric understanding of human behaviour from a scientific perspective and thus also is relevant to work-related psychological testing, irrespective of who conducts the tests and why the tests are conducted. Despite the fact that certain behaviours have a demonstrable genetic basis and can be considered to be universal, the influence of a person's environment is considerable. Consequently, the search for a personality trait that is desirable in a selection situation is, in principle, *unpredictable*.

In addition to the well-known problem of demarcating statistical limits to how well, or how poorly, a certain test can predict future character traits or the performance of an employee in a certain position, we are also faced with the problem of the presumptive *stability* of these character traits over time. In the beginning, it may be the case that the candidate who was awarded the job, to some degree, does display the personal characteristics that the test predicted that the candidate would have. However, after some time, the conditions at work, at home, or in the profession may change, causing the employee to also change in response to his or her environment in such a manner that is not necessarily predictable. It is human nature to either adapt to the prevailing conditions or to try to adapt the prevailing conditions to suit oneself (Ceci, 1996; Sternberg, 1988).

Investigations have been made to ascertain whether personality is something that remains stable over time, or is changeable. It has been shown that personality does change over time (Costa & McCrae, 2006). Personality can also change in pace with changes in one's social role, status, health, motivation, and work (Helson & Soto, 2005), and to some degree, people believe that they can change their personality when it suits them (Hudson & Fraley, 2015). A unique longitudinal study spanning 40 years has followed a large group of people in an attempt to ascertain whether the different dimensions included in the *Big Five* have changed. The conclusion of this study is that the *Big Five* lacks stability over such a long time period (Hampson & Goldberg, 2006). 'Extraversion', 'Conscientiousness', and 'Openness to experience' show a statistically significant, albeit very weak, stability ($r = 0.16-0.29$), whilst 'Agreeableness' and 'Neurotism' reveal themselves to be particularly transient characteristics.

There are a multitude of theories about what personality is and how it is constructed, but a common main thesis in many of these theories that has persisted for a long time is that 'personality' – in contrast to situation-based behaviour – contains an identifiable pattern of behaviour for each individual that remains stable over long periods of time (Ardelt, 2000). In the light of evolutionary, epigenetic, and behaviour-genetic research, it has been shown that this is an incorrect assumption. Personality is not what people *have*, but rather, personality is an evolutionary function which enables us to function in a social context. It is quite clear that the manner in which we currently understand personality is undergoing radical change and probably constitutes a somewhat unwelcome message for work psychology consultants and experts from all different camps who base part of their business on different types of personality profiles in the hope that these will sift out the most suitable salesperson, boss, administrator, data technician, and so on, as the best investment for the employer using the consultant's services.

Recruitment magic and the fourth industrial revolution

As early as the 1980s and the nascent third industrial revolution, people were completely aware that a company's profit margins and its survival rose and fell with the quality of its human capital (Plumbley, 1974). During this time, the use of computers became widespread. The Internet became the new meeting place, and information technology established itself as one of the most important industries for the world economy (Rifkin, 2011). Globalisation took off, more companies became international companies, and subsequently became increasingly more aware of different cultures and the changeable conditions and characteristics in the labour market in different countries. Education systems changed and prioritised technology, science, and mathematics over social studies and the humanities, since these subject areas were seen as less relevant to economic growth (Powell & Snellman, 2004; Tijssen, 2003).

In the fourth industrial revolution, declared to have begun by the World Economic Forum in Davos in 2015, it should be the case that a company's profit margins and success is now even more dependent on what the company's employees know, their efficiency, and how well they execute their work tasks. The global fight over attracting the most creative, innovative, and entrepreneurial human capital has become quite more aggressive, quite rapidly. In addition to having the desirable personal characteristics, now talented people often decide how they want to work and under which conditions. Employers now have to adjust to their employees' desires more so than previously (Dewhurst et al., 2012; Robertson & Abby, 2003). The new industrial revolution is assumed to focus on automation, artificial intelligence, flexibility, speed, and the Internet of things; i.e., more and more technical products in our everyday life are connected to the Internet via cloud services. Everything is accessible, everywhere, and people are becoming, step by step, members of the global *infosphere* (Floridi, 2014; Schwab, 2016).

This revolution (as with previous revolutions) entails that the labour market undergoes radical change. New types of jobs are created and other jobs become unimportant. As far as we concern ourselves with Sweden, in 2003, 53% of today's recognised job categories will no longer exist (Swedish foundation for strategic research, 2014). Primarily, jobs which can be automated in some way will disappear. The remaining job opportunities are predicted to fall under the following three, somewhat hierarchical, categories (Nonaka & Takeuchi, 1995):

- *knowledge practitioners* – an organisation's doers: experts, craftsmen, and scientific personnel.
- *knowledge engineers* – management roles who are responsible for how theory and practice interact in a knowledge economy. To be able to optimise this function, organisations must allow these employees to have a great deal of influence in the organisation and on its structure.
- *knowledge administrators* – the highest level of leadership in each company and organisation. These people set the framework and the goals for the organisation.

TABLE 6.3 Personal qualities and attributes which should characterise every employee in the global knowledge economy (according to Nonaka & Takeuchi, 1995), and whether it is possible for every employee to possess these qualities in the light of established behavioural science research

Desired attribute	Is it possible that every employee possesses this attribute?
1 Excellent education and experience	Yes
2 Ability to take responsibility for oneself and show initiative	Doubtful
3 Self-reliant	Doubtful
4 Flexibility	No
5 Lifelong, uninterrupted learning	Doubtful
6 Search for meaning and independence	No
7 Possesses an inner driving force/motivation	Doubtful
8 Keen to always learn something new	Doubtful

Being well acquainted with which type of services and industries are currently undergoing growth, Nonaka and Takeuchi speculate about which characteristics these globally orientated business men and women should possess in the global knowledge economy's labour market (see Table 6.3).

Compare Table 6.3 with the qualities listed below, which the German union of engineers demand that its members possess; namely, that in the fourth industrial revolution, their members must

- be highly motivated and show leadership,
- have a mind for business and a desire to put this into practice,
- be able to skilfully plan and lead projects,
- work alone in an organised and structured manner,
- be skilful communicators and be willing to communicate with others,
- be creative and able to have innovative thoughts,
- be internationally orientated and in their work demonstrate intercultural competence,
- be able to work and act with self-reliance,
- be convincing and capable of finishing what they have begun,
- be flexible and always willing and prepared to learn new things.

This list (reproduced from Lackner, 2012) is very similar to the wish list that appears in the introduction of this chapter.

The new industrial age is assumed to be characterised by somewhat more spectacular and perhaps somewhat unexpected qualities in its workforce. Besides 'speed', 'high levels of performance', 'creativity', and 'inventiveness' as important qualities, the World Economic Forum (WEF) (lead by Klaus Schwab (2016)) advocates that employees must learn how (i) to better manage their sleep, (ii) to better exploit their power of memorisation, (iii) to develop their ability to deal with anxiety, (iv) to develop their powers of resistance, (v) to become more tolerant of stress, and (vi) to learn how to cope with change, so as to maintain the employee's health and well-being. Paradoxically, it is predicted that future employees will have a good amount of time to enjoy their free time too (see Amanda Huffington's report on Davos, 2016, and Susskind & Susskind, 2015).

It seems, however, as if the fourth industrial revolution, despite several visionaries' assurances of the opposite, is hardly about adapting the global knowledge economy to society's needs and welfare, but rather it is about adapting society and the world's population to fit in with the world economy and its need for continual growth (Chomsky, 1999; Luyendijk, 2015; Mazlish, 2009). Alec Ross (2016), another visionary in this context, and previously former head of the Department of State Hillary Clinton's closest advisor on innovation issues, speaks of a future *human machine* and how gene technology will revolutionise humanity and future business opportunities. Unfortunately, it will be only through genetic manipulation and a dash of magic that the long wish lists of the desired qualities and characteristics of future human capital will be satisfied.

Examining Nonaka and Takeuchi's (1995) description of personal qualities and attributes above, we note that only two of them are generally applicable and with a certain amount of confidence can be used in a recruitment drive; namely, whether a candidate has undergone a suitable and proper education and whether the candidate has sufficient experience. The other items on their list lack validity because they are either culture-bound characteristics, inherited, or are based on a lack of understanding of how social beings actually function and normally behave.

As an employer, one might naturally wish that one's employees should possess all of these attractive and somewhat fabulous qualities, but one cannot take it for granted that these qualities will be possessed by every candidate or that all of these qualities will be possessed by even a single individual. Whether the battle for talented employees, which has started and now characterises the fourth industrial revolution – *the war for talent*, as it has been called (Michaels et al., 2001) – is to provide us with opportunities (or no opportunities at all) as long as we employ people instead of machines, this remains an open question. The lack of a suitable workforce, as described above, is already making itself felt. In Sweden, 39% of all companies and organisations are now experiencing difficulties in finding the desired type of workforce in the new labour market. In the European Union, the average figure is 33%, and across the whole world it is 38%. The problem is the worst in Japan, where 83% of companies find it difficult to find the right employees, whilst in Ireland this figure is a mere 11% – the best figure of all of the countries that were included in the review (Manpower Group, 2015).

With both feet on the ground – a final comment

It is a truism to say that recruitment is important. But how this should proceed is not at all obvious. The consultants who defend and market their business practices as being 'scientific' are not necessarily more accurate with respect to the final selection of candidates than the consultants who care a little less about academic traditions, ethics, and an understanding of the research on the matter. However, it is important to highlight the fact that incorrect recruitment does not necessarily depend on the shortcomings of different work psychology consultants. Even the organisation who gives the order to start a recruitment drive can be the source of the problem when they give the consultants impossible assignments. As I have demonstrated above, the wish list of qualities that the candidate is supposed to possess is both too long and too fantastic. These lists seem to get more advanced and unrealistic the more we enter the fourth industrial revolution. Humanity and the visionaries who claim to prophesise about the future often base their claims on the idea that the future can be controlled to high degree. But, as the growing body of scientific literature shows, *Homo sapiens*, as a species, can develop and change its environment very quickly and without much thought, and not always to everyone's advantage.

It seems to me that the most important future assignment for HR departments and the consultants who they hire to help with recruitment is to inform their principals (i.e., the director or boss of the organisation) about what is possible to achieve, what is probable, and what is mere wishful thinking. I am sure that this will not be a simple task to perform because our current visionaries seem to find it difficult to not to see people as merely invested capital whose quality and performance can be raised so as to achieve a continual profitability by suitable, lifelong learning only (Schultz, 1981). The underlying assumption is that every person can do anything; they just need the opportunity, support, incitement, and, most importantly, the right education. Thus, a population can be adapted through political management, so that it will fit into the planned, future social structure. Such reasoning, however, hides a very difficult problem; not every person can learn everything, irrespective of how hard they might try, and how much support, education, and motivation is offered to them (Mosing et al., 2014; Plomin et al., 2014). And perhaps more important to humanity's well-being in general is that everyone does not want to learn everything. There are studies which show that the European citizenry who are part of the knowledge economy's rapid advancement suffer from stress are depressed and suffer from identity problems in the wake knowledge economy's forward progress (Verhaeghe, 2014). Even politicians are faced with a dilemma when they try to reform each education system according to the OECD's guidelines (Nusche et al., 2011) so that schools are adapted to suit the future demands of the labour market. It is unrealistic to assume that every school student is capable of, or even enjoys, studying science, technology, and mathematics; the subjects which seem to be key to the surge of innovation which they hope will drive economic growth.

Against a background where leading economists and politicians plan for the developments discussed above, it is not a simple task for the employee at an HR department to indicate to his or her boss what is possible and what is impossible in a recruitment situation. Scientific facts do not always coincide with politicians' and economic visionaries' development strategies (Charlton, 2012; Fredriksson & Vlachos, 2011).

At the end of the day, it is in both the employer and the employee's interests to try and keep reality and fantasy apart. No one has anything to win by trying to achieve impossible goals. If one were to do so, then incorrect recruitment would be the rule instead of the exception, and the number of people recruited incorrectly (and the associated money wasted) would increase.

In conclusion, in the light of the above discussion, the following summary advice can be given to prospective HR employees:

> Write job advertisements in a way that corresponds to reality and in accordance with what newly-employed staff members can cope with. Do not describe the ideal candidate for the job solely in terms of the company's needs and its (perhaps) unrealistic desires.
>
> Avoid referring to personality variables in the advertisement and even later in the recruitment process. The person who is appointed to a job because he or she has certain personal attribute can very well change after some time, especially if the work conditions or context change.
>
> Remember that an incorrect recruitment may occur because of at least one of the following reasons: (i) One may have tried to recruit a person with qualities which cannot exist in one and the same person (an assignment error). (ii) One did not take into consideration the fact that people actually change over time and in a manner which is not always possible to predict (a knowledge error). Or, (iii) the selection for a certain post was perhaps done by using psychometric instruments which gave results which were over-interpreted, or based on doubtful constructs without taking into consideration the situation and/or the candidate's cultural membership (a system error). Irrespective of how advanced your selection strategy is and how expensive your consultant's fee might be, there are no absolute guarantees for a successful recruitment. If one does not do the selection oneself, then a cheap consultancy fee compared to an expensive one has no relevance to the outcome; given that both consultants are competent and serious about what they are doing. The cost is not necessarily an indication of quality or success.
>
> Considering the dire need of talent in the fourth industrial revolution, do not forget that talent is statistically distributed according to the standard normal curve. Consequently, the number of extremely skilful and/or creative people is limited. The battle to acquire talented people is very real and will surely intensify. Unfortunately, what many politicians and large cross sections of the labour market often claim is not true; everyone cannot know everything, even if they are provided support and incitement in their efforts to learn.
>
> Do not be deceived into thinking that something is good and free from problems just because it is marketed as 'scientific'. As a HR professional,

one must be somewhat experienced and possess sufficient scientific knowledge to make one's own evaluations about quality, even if this is knowledge is merely used to evaluate and choose a suitable consultancy, as need arises. HR professionals in the fourth industrial revolution must be well-educated and well-versed in behavioural science issues. It is hardly possible any longer to perform a HR job without a solid academic education.

Recommended reading

Furnham, Adrian (2004), *Management and myths: Challenging business fads, fallacies and fashions.* Houndmills, UK: Palgrave MacMillan.
Murphy Paul, Annie (2005), *The cult of personality testing.* New York: Free Press.
Schwab, Klaus (2016), *The fourth industrial revolution.* Geneva, Switzerland: World Economic Forum.
Susskind, Richard & Susskind, Daniel (2015), *The future of the professions: How technology will transform the world of human experts.* Oxford, UK: Oxford University Press.
Wyer, Robert S., Chiu, Chi-Ye & Hong, Ying-yi (eds.) (2009), *Understanding culture: Theory, research, and application.* New York: Psychology Press.

References

Ardelt, Monika (2000), Still stable after all these years? Personality stability theory revisited. *School Psychology Quarterly, 63*(4), pp. 392–405.
Barrick, Murray R. & Mount, Michael K. (1991), The Big Five personality dimensions and job performance: A meta-analysis. *Personnel Psychology, 44*, pp. 1–26.
Beck, Randall J. & Harper, Jim (2014), Managing people: Why good managers are so rare? *Harvard Business Review.* Retrieved from hbr.org.
Belin, Kirsten & Hsin Wang, Yi (2010), *Job adverts à la 2010: A study of content, style, recommendations and students' thoughts and perceptions.* Master's dissertation. Örebro: Handelshögskolan vid Örebro universitet.
Blinkhorn, Steve F. & Johnson, Charles E. (1990), The insignificance of personality testing. *Nature, 348*, pp. 671–672.
Buss, David M. (2001), Human nature and culture: An evolutionary psychological perspective. *Journal of Personality, 69*(6), pp. 955–978.
Ceci, Stephen J. (1996), *On intelligence: A bioecological treatise on intellectual development.* Cambridge, MA: Harvard University Press.
Chakraborty, Ajita (1991), Culture, colonialism, and psychiatry. *Lancet, 337*, pp. 1204–1207.
Chamorro-Premuzic, Tomas & Furnham, Adrian (2003), Personality traits and academic examination performance. *European Journal of Personality, 17*, pp. 237–250.
Charlton, Bruce G. (2012), *Not even trying: The corruption of real science.* Buckingham: University of Buckingham Press.
Chef (2011), Sju av tio företag gör psykologiska tester. [Seven out of 10 businesses use psychological tests] Retrieved from http://chef.se [2016-02-10].
Chomsky, Noam (1999), *Profit over people: Neoliberalism and global order.* New York: Seven Stories Press.
Clark, Timothy (1992), Management selection by executive recruitment consultancies: A survey and explanation of methods. *Journal of Managerial Psychology, 3*(1), pp. 9–15.

Costa, Paul T. Jr. & McCrae, Robert R. (1992), *Revised NEO personality inventory (NEO-PI-R) and NEO five-factor inventory (NEO-FFI) manual*. Odessa, FL: Psychological Assessment Resources.

Costa, Paul T. Jr. & McCrae, Robert R. (2006), Age changes in personality and their origins: Comments on Roberts, Walton, and Viechtbauer (2006). *Psychological Bulletin, 132*(1), pp. 26–28.

Cronbach, Lee J. (1990), *Essentials of psychological testing*. New York: HarperCollins.

Dewhurst, Martin, Pettigrew, Matthew & Srinivasan, Ramesh (2012), How multinationals can attract the talent they need. *McKinsey Quarterly*, pp. 1–8. Retrieved from www.mckinsey.com [2016-02-14].

Ewerlin, Denise & Süss, Stefan (2016), Dissemination of talent management in Germany: Myth, facade or economic necessity. *Personnel Review, 45*(1), pp. 142–160.

Ferris, Gerald, King, Thomas, Judge, Timothy & Kacmar, K. Michele (1991), The management of shared meaning in organisations: Opportunism in the reflection of attitudes, beliefs and values. In Robert Giacalone & Paul Rosenfeld (eds.), *Applied impression management: How image-making affects managerial decisions* (pp. 124–147). London: Sage.

Floridi, Luciano (2014), *The 4th revolution: How the infosphere is reshaping human reality*. Oxford: Oxford University Press.

Fredriksson, Peter & Vlachos, Jonas (2011), *Reformer och resultat: Kommer regeringens utbildningsreformer att ha någon betydelse?* [Reforms and results: Will the govenment's educational reforms have any effect?] Rapport till Finanspolitiska rådet nr 3. Stockholm: Finanspolitiska rådet.

Furnham, Adrian (2000), The brainstorming myth. *Business Strategy Review, 11*(4), pp. 21–28.

Furnham, Adrian (2005), *The psychology of behaviour at work*. Hove: Psychology Press.

Furnham, Adrian (2008), *Personality and intelligence at work: Exploring and explaining individual differences at work*. London: Routledge.

Furnham, Adrian & Barrie, Gunter (1987), Graphology and personality: Another failure to validate graphological analysis. *Personality and Individual Differences, 8*(3), pp. 433–435.

Goddard, Henry H. (1917), Mental tests and the immigrants. *Journal of Deliquency, 2*, pp. 241–277.

Hampson, Sarah E. & Goldberg, Lewis R. (2006), A first large-cohort study of personality-trait stability over 40 years between elementary school and midlife. *Journal of Personality and Social Psychology, 91*(4), pp. 763–779.

Harper, Annabel (2008), Psychometric tests are now a multi-million-pound business: What lies behind a coach's decision to use them? *International Journal of Evidence Based Coaching and Mentoring, 2* (special issue), pp. 40–51.

Helson, Ravenna & Soto, Christopher J. (2005), Up and down in middle age: Monotonic and nonmonotonic changes in roles, status, and personality. *Journal of Personality and Social Psychology, 89*(2), pp. 194–204.

Hinkle, Dennis E., Wiersma, William & Jurs, Stephen G. (2003), *Applied statistics for the behavioral sciences*. Boston, MA: Houghton Mifflin.

Howitt, Dennis & Owusu-Bempah, J. (1994), *The racism of psychology: Time for change*. New York: Harvester Wheatsheaf.

Hudson, Nathan W. & Fraley, R. Chris (2015), Personality traits change: Can people choose to change their personality traits? *Journal of Personality and Social Psychology, 109*(3), pp. 490–507.

Huffington, Amanda (2016), The fourth industrial revolution meets the sleep revolution. *The Huffington Post*. Retrieved from www.huffingtonpost.com [2016-02-14].

Koocher, Gerald P. & Rey Casserly, Celiane M. (2003), Ethical issues in psychological assessment. In John R. Graham, Jack A. Naglieri & Irwing B. Weiner (eds.), *Handbook of psychology. Volume 10: Assessment Psychology* (pp. 165–180). New York: John Wiley.

Lackner, Maximilian (2012), *Talent-Management spezial: Hochbegabte, Forscher, Künstler ... erfolgreich führen*. Wiesbaden: Gabler.

Lindelöw, Malin (2003), *Kompetensbaserad rekrytering, intervjuteknik och testning*. Stockholm: Natur och Kultur.

Luyendijk, Joris (2015), *Swimming with sharks: My journey into the world of bankers*. London: Faber & Faber.

Manpower Group (2015), *Talent shortage survey 2015*. Milwaukee, WI: ManpowerGroup. Retrieved from www.manpowergroup.com [2016-02-14].

Mazlish, Bruce (2009), *The idea of humanity in a global era*. New York: Palgrave MacMillan.

McCrae, Robert R. & Costa, Paul T. (1997), Personality structure as a human universal. *American Psychologist, 52*(5), pp. 509–516.

Michaels, Ed, Handfield-Jones, Helene & Axelrod, Beth (2001), *The war for talent*. Cambridge, MA: Harvard Business Review Press.

Mosing, Miriam A., Madison, Guy, Pederson, Nancy L., Kuja-Halkola, Ralf & Ullén, Fredrik (2014), Practice does not make perfect: No causal effect of music practice on music ability. *Psychological Science, 25*(9), pp. 1795–1803.

Murphy Paul, Annie (2005), *The cult of personality testing*. New York: Free Press.

Nonaka, Ikujiro & Takeuchi, Horitaka (1995), *The knowledge creating company: How Japanese companies create the dynamics of innovation*. New York: Oxford University Press.

Norenzayan, Ara & Heine, Stephen J. (2005), Psychological universals: What are they and how can we know? *Psychological Bulletin, 131*(5), pp. 763–784.

Nusche, Deborah, Halász, Gabor, Looney, Janet, Santiago, Paulo & Shewbridge, Claire (2011), *OECD reviews of evaluation and assessment in education: Sweden*. Paris: OECD. Retrieved from www.oecd.org/sweden [2016-02-14].

Persson, Roland P. (2012), Cultural variation and dominance in a globalised knowledge-economy: Towards a culture-sensitive research paradigm in the science of giftedness. *Gifted and Talented International, 27*(1), special issue, pp. 15–48.

Pittenger, David J. (2005), Cautionary comments regarding the Myers-Briggs Type Indicator. *Consulting Psycholohy Journal: Practice and Research, 57*(3), pp. 210–221.

Plomin, Robert, DeFries, John C., Knopik, Valerie S. & Neiderhiser, Jenae M. (2013), *Behavioral genetics*. New York: Worth.

Plomin, Robert, Shakeshaft, Nicholas G., MacMillan, Andrew & Trzaskowski, Maciej (2014), Nature, nurture, and expertise. *Intelligence, 45*, pp. 46–59.

Plumbley, Philip (1974), *Recruitment and selection*. London: Institute of Personnel Management.

Poolia (n.d.), *Whitepaper: 7 steg mot framgångsrik rekrytering*. [Whitepaper: 7 steps for successful recruitment] Stockholm: Poolia. Retrieved from www.poolia.se [2016-02-13].

Powell, Walter W. & Snellman, Kaisa (2004), The knowledge economy. *Annual Review of Sociology, 30*, pp. 199–230.

Rifkin, Jeremy (2011), *The third industrial revolution: How lateral power is transforming energy, the economy and the world*. New York: Palgrave Macmillan.

Robertson, Alan & Abbey, Graham (2003), *Managing talented people: Getting on with – and getting the best from – your top talent*. Harlow: Pearson Education.

Ross, Alec (2016), *The industries of the future*. London: Simon & Schuster.

Salgado, Jesús F., Anderson, Neil, Moscoso, Silvia, Bertua, Cristina, de Fruyt, Filip & Rolland, Jean P. (2003), A meta-analytic study of general mental ability validity for different occupations in the European community. *Journal of Applied Psychology, 88,* pp. 1068–1081.

Samuda, Ronald J. (1998). *Psychological testing of American minorities: Issues and consequences.* London: Sage.

SAPLO/Monster (2009), *Viktigaste egenskaperna hos anställda 2009.* [The most important employee qualities] Retrieved from http://blog.saplo.com [2016-02-09].

Schartau, Fredrika (2011), *Pressmeddelande: Antalet misslyckade rekryteringar ökar.* [News report: Number of failed recruitments on the increase] Retrieved from www.mynews-desk.com [2016-02-10].

Schmidt, Frank L. & Hunter, John E. (1998), The validity and utility of selection methods in personnel psychology: Practical and theoretical implications of 85 years of research findings. *Psychological Bulletin, 124,* pp. 262–274.

Schmidt, Jeffrey B. (1995), New product myopia. *Journal of Business & Industrial Marketing, 10*(1), pp. 23–33.

Schultz, Theodore W. (1981), *Investing in people: The economics of population quality.* Berkley, CA: The University of California Press.

Schwab, Klaus (2016), *The fourth industrial revolution.* Geneva: World Economic Forum.

Simonton, Dean Keith (2005), Giftedness and genetics: The emergenic-epigenetic model and its implications. *Journal for the Education of the Gifted, 28*(3/4), pp. 270–286.

Sternberg, Robert J. (1988), *The triarchic mind: A new theory of human intelligence.* New York: Penguin Books.

Susskind, Richard & Susskind, Daniel (2015), *The future of the professions: How technology will transform the world of human experts.* Oxford: Oxford University Press.

Swedish foundation for strategic research (2014), *Vartannat jobb automatiseras inom 20 år: Utmaningar inom 20 år.* [Every other job will be automated in 20 years: Challenges in the next 20 years] Stockholm: Swedish Foundation for Strategic Research. Retrieved from www.stratresearch.se [2016-02-14].

Terpstra, David (1996), The search for effective methods (employee recruitment and selection). *HR Focus, 17*(5), pp. 16–18.

Tijssen, Robert J. W. (2003), Scoreboards of research excellence. *Research Evaluation, 12*(2), pp. 91–103.

Tooby, John & Cosmides, Leda (1990), On the universality of human nature and the uniqueness of the individual: The role of genetics and adaptation. *Journal of Personality, 58*(1), pp. 17–67.

Toomela, Aaro & Valsiner, Jaan (eds.) (2010), *Methodological thinking in psychology: 60 years gone astray?* Charlotte, NC: Information Age Publishing.

Verhaeghe, Paul (2014), *What about me? The struggle for identity in a market-based society.* Brunswick, VIC: Scribe.

van de Vijver, Fons J. R. & Leung, Kwok (1996), Methods and data analysis of comparative research. In John W. Berry, Ype H. Poortinga & Janak Pandey (eds.), *Handbook of cross-cultural psychology. Volume 1: Theory and method* (pp. 257–300). Boston, MA: Allyn & Bacon.

PART II
Diversity and inclusion

7

THE EQUALITY WORK THAT NEEDS TO BE DONE

Helene Ahl

Gender inequality can still be found in today's workplaces, and something must be done about it. Gender inequality gives rise to negative consequences, both for individuals and for organisations. In many countries, we find legislation that places a special responsibility on the shoulders of employers, and, by implication, on the shoulders of managers and HR specialists. Notwithstanding this, opposing opinions and interests concerning gender equality prevail in the domain of the HR specialist's professional responsibility. If the HR specialist is to actively drive gender equality initiatives forward, then the specialist must be provided with the relevant knowledge and tools for the job.

This chapter deals with the identification of inequalities at the workplace and the examination of the following questions: Why are gender inequalities a problem? Why should we do something about these inequalities? What practical arrangements can we implement to address gender inequalities? But first we ask: What does gender equality entail?

In essence, gender equality is a human rights issue. The Council of Europe (2016) establishes gender equality as a "principle of human rights and women's human rights as an inalienable, integral and indivisible part of universal human rights". Gender equality is "a requirement for the achievement of social justice and a sine qua non of democracy" (ibid).

Gender equality is thus typically defined in terms of women and men having the same opportunities, rights, and responsibilities within all areas of life. It includes, according to the World Health Organization (WHO, 2011), "equal chances or opportunities for groups of women and men to access and control social, economic and political resources, including protection under the law". UNESCO (2003) defines it as the condition where "[...] women and men have equal conditions for realising their full human rights and for contributing to, and benefiting from, economic, social, cultural and political development".

Such definitions indicate that *gender equality* is a condition what we should all aspire for, and, to that aim, the term is also used to present strategies that we can employ to achieve this state; for example, "to change the structures in society which contribute to maintaining the unequal power relationships between women and men, and to reach a better balance in the various female and male values and priorities" (Council of Europe, 2016). Some people prefer to use the term *gender equity* to refer to the strategies that are used to achieve gender equality. The term recognises differences between men and women's conditions and preferences and introduces the notion that, sometimes, unequal treatment may be necessary to achieve gender equality. Others have objected to the use of the term since interpretations of what are "men and women's preferences" are often based on, or informed by custom, tradition, or religion. In such cases, these interpretations are often to the detriment of women, and so, somewhat ironically, gender equity may actually *reinforce* women's subordination to men. At the 1995 Beijing UN conference, it was therefore agreed that the term *gender equality* be used (UN Women, 2011). The term used to refer to strategies that can be employed to achieve gender equality is thus simply *gender equality work*.

Finally, we should note that the term *gender mainstreaming* is a term that has been embraced by policymakers and refers to "the integration of a gender perspective into the preparation, design, implementation, monitoring and evaluation of policies, regulatory measures and spending programmes, with a view to promoting equality between women and men, and combating discrimination" (EIGE, 2018). Thus we observe that gender equality work should not be merely considered as a woman's issue that is to be treated on the side of mainstream policy, but, rather, it should be integrated into *all* policy areas. The same approach may be applied to policies and procedures that are implemented at businesses and other organisations.

The definitions presented above should allow the reader to understand that gender equality is not a natural state of affairs or condition that arises in and of itself, merely given the passing of time. Quite the contrary; just as in the case of Justice, Equality, or Democracy, gender equality is a political and moral ideal which people have to agree on for it to exist. Thus, gender equality has to be created and maintained. This entails continuous effort.

Work in the area of gender equality in the Scandinavian countries has been particularly successful, not least in Sweden. The feminist movement of the 1900s in Sweden resulted in women gaining the right to vote in 1919, majority was granted to married women in 1921, and equal state pensions were awarded in 1935 for both men and women. In 1960, legislation was passed mandating that men and women receive equal pay for equal work, and in 1971 separate taxation was introduced. All types of job were opened up to women in 1989. As late as in 2001, a law was passed which prescribed equal treatment of male and female students at university. From an international perspective, Sweden is somewhat unique in terms of its Family Law which specifies generous terms and conditions for maternity and paternity leave and the provision of childcare, which makes it possible for men and women to engage in family life and work-life under equal conditions. Current legislation, together with the fact that women are well represented in the Swedish government and parliament, explains why Sweden is often ranked very high in international gender equality indexes (UNdata, 2012).

Despite the above, a great deal of work remains to be done, not least in the area of gender equality in the work-life. For example, women remain under-represented at the management level, in Sweden, and in the rest of the word. The labour market remains strictly segregated by gender, and careers which have been traditionally 'female', even including those which demand a prolonged educational qualification to perform, are lower paid than traditionally 'male' careers. Women are still paid less than men for equal work. Women still take on the main responsibility for running the home and family even when they are gainfully employed outside the home; that is to say, they maintain *two* jobs. This fact is reflected in the higher rate of sick leave for women. An investigation by the Swedish National Social Security Office found that fathers who increased their participation levels in caring for their young children also signed off as sick in equal measure as women did who had a similar work load (Försäkringskassans nyhetsbrev, 2015).

Organisational theory invokes the concepts of 'horizontal gender segregation', 'internal gender segregation', and 'vertical gender segregation' in descriptions of the state of gender equality on the labour market. *Horizontal gender segregation* highlights the fact that men and women do different things, even if they find themselves at the same hierarchical level within an organisation. For example, it is more common for nurses to be female, whilst medical technicians are more frequently male. Most assistant nurses are female, and most builders are male. Thus we note that, even in Sweden, most people work in quite obviously gender segregated jobs. Only three of the thirty largest jobs (in terms of employment numbers) showed an equal gender distribution in 2012, where 'equal gender distribution' is interpreted in cases where at least 40% of the under-represented gender is employed in the particular job (SCB, 2014).

The three jobs which showed equal gender distribution were cooks, physicians, and university and university college lecturers. However, in these job positions we often find *internal gender segregation* – a situation where we find that men and women do different things, even if they hold comparable positions, i.e., they have the same job. For example, it is more common that men teach prospective engineers, whilst it is more common to find females teaching candidate teachers. Female cooks are more frequently found in the school dinner hall, whilst head chefs are more frequently male. Even in the medical field, we find gender-typical specialisations; for example, most surgeons are male, whilst paediatric physicians are more frequently women.

Vertical gender segregation refers to situations where we note that men are over-represented at the management levels, in both public and private sector organisations. In many organisations, there is an invisible *glass ceiling* which retards many women's progression upwards in the hierarchy. According to 2016s EU statistics, the rate of representation of women on the boards of companies listed on the stock market in the EU member states ranged between 5% and 37%, with an average rate of female representation on the boards being of 23%. Only 1 in every 14 boards had a female chairperson, and women CEOs were even fewer – only 5.1% of the largest listed companies in Europe had a woman CEO (EC Fact Sheet, 2016).

Male-dominated jobs are typically higher paid than female-dominated jobs. In 2012, women earned, on average 86%, of what men earned in Sweden. If one takes into account differences between men and women in age distribution, education, working hours, and job sectors, then women earned 94% of what men did (SCB, 2016). This calculation reveals an unmotivated difference in salaries of 6% between men and women. Statistics from the European Union showed an unadjusted pay gap between men and women in 2015 that ranged between 5.5% in Italy and Luxembourg to 26.9% in Estonia (Eurostat, 2017).

Furthermore, we note that it is more common for women to work part-time than men. Women spend more time doing unpaid housework than men. Traditional gender roles play a part in this discrepancy, but so does the structure of the current welfare system. In many countries, it is too expensive for many households to pay for child day-care services (kindergarten, and the like) for it to be worthwhile for the other parent to be gainfully employed outside the home. Traditional gender roles, in combination with the fact that the man of the house most often earns the higher salary, results in situations where it is more common that the mother takes care of the children. Even in countries where access to Social Security or the Social Welfare system is structured so that either of the parents can continue with paid employment, it is more often the case that the mother takes on the larger part of caring for the family's child(ren). Sweden is a telling example of this: the country provides a system of very generous parental allowances, including 18 months of paid parental leave. Three months are reserved for the mother and three months are reserved for the father's exclusive use. The remaining 12 months can be used by either the mother or the father. Despite the possible equal distribution of parental leave between the parents, women still account for 75% of the use of the parental leave allowance (SCB, 2014). One result of this is that employers are often less willing to offer a job to a woman than they are to a man. This has the knock-on effect of reducing the life-time income of many women and thus a concomitant reduction in their pension benefits.

The statistics which are presented above quite clearly demonstrate that an equal work-life has not been achieved. In many countries across the world, there exists legislation against gender discrimination at the workplace. There are compulsory EU directives which state that member states must pass laws that prevent discrimination on the grounds of sex, racial or ethnic origin, religion or belief, disability, age, or sexual orientation. These laws are, however, different in each of the different countries. To demonstrate how one EU directive can be translated into actual law, we provide a discussion of the Swedish law against gender discrimination, and we encourage the reader to compare this with their own country's legislation in this area.

The Swedish law against gender discrimination

Swedish employers are legally obligated to work towards establishing and maintaining places of work that are gender equal. This is legislated for in the *Discrimination Act* (SFS, 2016: 828). The first paragraph informs us that the purpose of the act is:

> ... to combat discrimination and in other ways promote equal rights and opportunities for people, irrespective of their sex, transgender identity or expression, ethnicity, religion or other belief system, disability, sexual orientation, or age.

We thus note that, besides gender, there are many other grounds on which someone might be subject to discrimination. Since the term *gender equality* only refers to a person's sex, I will focus on what the law covers with respect to discrimination and the work to be done for equal rights and opportunities in the context of sex. Note too that the law covers aspects of discrimination in various areas of public life, but in this chapter I will only discuss a number of areas that are relevant to HR work.

The law against discrimination contains both prohibitions and obligations. For example, it is prohibited for an employer to discriminate against an employee or someone who is in search of employment (or an apprentice or intern position) or someone who has been hired or borrowed from another company to do a job. *Direct discrimination* entails that a person is put at a disadvantage or treated in a manner that is worse than someone else because of that person's sex. For example, consider the case of where a woman who is well qualified to do a job, and has applied for the job, is not invited to an interview. According to the law, such a person has the right to ask the employer information about the merits which the successful applicant actually possesses. Without access to this information, it is obviously quite difficult to claim that sex discrimination has taken place.

Indirect discrimination refers to situations where someone is put at a disadvantage or treated unfairly via the implementation of a decision or a course of action which may, at first glance, seem to be neutral, but can actually put people of a certain sex at a disadvantage. The Labour Court employment tribunal, for instance, found that a car manufacture's demand that an operator be of a certain minimum height to be an example of indirect discrimination which put women at a disadvantage, and consequently the tribunal awarded damages to the claimant (Arbetsdomstolen, 2005).

Bullying, sexual harassment, and instructions to discriminate against others are also prohibited. If an employer is aware that harassment has taken place at the workplace, it is the employer's duty to investigate it and take preventative action. Similarly, an employer may not subject an employee to reprisals if the employee has claimed that the employer has broken the law, or if the employee has rejected, or even complied with, the employer's harassment, be it sexual or any other form of harassment. The employer can be ordered to pay compensation to an employee who has been subject to bullying or harassment based on the employee's sex, or for with any reprisal action that the employer may have taken in conjunction with this.

After examining a small number of prohibitions, we now turn to the obligations that the employer is subject to, in cooperation with the employee, where they have to work in an *active* and *goal-directed* manner to counteract discrimination and to achieve equal rights and opportunities for everyone at the workplace. Particular emphasis is placed on the obligation to pay equal salaries for equal work, to prevent harassment, and to facilitate the conditions where both men and women can combine their work-life and parenthood. Furthermore, employers should aim to achieve an equal distribution of men and women in various job positions for different categories of employees. Active measures in this area include investigating whether there is any danger that discrimination may occur, to analyse the causes behind any obstacles or dangers relevant to this, to take preventative steps against the possibility of discrimination, and to follow up on and evaluate the work that is done in this area. Such work has to be documented, too.

Each year, employers are also tasked to examine and analyse their policies for setting salaries, so as to discover whether there are any pay differences between male and female employees who do the same kind of work. The employer must also analyse any differences in salary at the group level, i.e., between employees who perform traditionally female-dominated work and employees who perform work which is not considered to be traditionally female dominated but are awarded with higher salaries, despite the fact that the requirements to perform such work may be lower. The work described above must be done in cooperation with a workers' union. Employers who employ more than nine employees must document the work they do on such salary surveys on a yearly basis in a gender equality plan.

Are the tools provided by anti-discrimination legislation sufficient?

The tools that are provided for in the Swedish *Law against Discrimination* are excellent. However, not everyone is in agreement with this claim. A not uncommon opinion (extract below) was shared with the readers of the editorial of a Swedish daily newspaper, the *Östgötakorrespondenten*, in response to the discrimination ombudsman's (DO) plans to inspect the gender equality plans of 200 randomly selected companies.

> Discrimination based on a person's gender – or for any other reason – is dangerous and unworthy of a modern society. It is important to receive support if one feels that one has been discriminated against. In the present case, however, the DO is on a fishing expedition and is exercising the power of the office against small employers who have done nothing wrong.

To accommodate this authority, they are forced to spend time and effort on empty talk – which, in a best case scenario, just causes irritation and additional costs. In the worst case, it can become a paper tiger, which seems counterproductive.

(Corren.se, 2015-02-13)

'Empty talk' and 'paper tigers'. 'Irritation' and 'additional costs'. Surely, these are hardly the things which the legislator had in mind when drafting the law. Gender equality plans are supposed to aid the furtherance of gender equality work, not the opposite. If gender equality work is to be seen as meaningful and to have good effect, then the duty-bound completion of formulating a plan, i.e., 'going through the motions', is not enough; one must possess knowledge of why there exists inequalities in the work-life of many people and what the consequences of these inequalities are. It is also helpful to recognise and be able to evaluate the different types of arguments for equality. Of course, a positive stance *for* equality is also necessary. Only once these things are in place can one expect commitment to gender equality work. This knowledge should also be possessed by the organisation's HR department, as well as the organisation's management. Without management's whole-hearted support, successful gender equality work is not possible to be achieved.

Common arguments that are used in the gender equality debate

There exist, of course, many explanations as to why we find a lack of gender equality in today's work-life, including aspects such as (i) the male domination of senior positions, (ii) different salaries for equal work, (iii) different salary scales for male- and female-dominated job types, and (iv) the fact that women more frequently take on the main responsibility for unpaid childcare and household chores. Sometimes the explanations for these states of affairs compete with each other. Consequently, there are different opinions about what one should do about establishing gender equality. In the following sections, I address a number of fundamental issues in this debate.

Inheritance or environment?

It is a common conception that it is 'natural' for women to take up careers in (health)care provision and to take on the main responsibility for childcare and running the home because of the assumption that they possess qualities which makes them more suited for these activities. Some might say that males have qualities that suit them to be the boss. If one accepts this line of argument, then one assumes that men and women have different qualities, values, interests, and attitudes. This reasoning is based on an *essential* view of gender. *Essence*, in this case, refers to 'the innermost nature' or 'intrinsic to' a person. According to this view, certain qualities or characteristics of a person are determined by the person's biological sex. Once such a view is adopted, however, there is no real reason to try and influence the choices that men and women make, in one way or the other. Although it may be possible to hold this view and still argue for a change in the salary structure in female-dominated careers.

Feminists have reacted to the fact that injustices or inequalities are far too often legitimised by the claim that such injustices are 'natural'. Hirdman (1992) informs us, for example, about the Swedish member of parliament, Mr Bergquist, who in 1938 claimed that female teachers should continue to receive lower salaries than their male counterparts because, notwithstanding the fact that they did the same work, women had more sensitive nerves and less muscle power than men, and so could not do the work as well as a man could. A more recent example can be found in a 2001 Swedish court ruling where a midwife and a medical technician's work were considered to be equal. However, despite this, the court ruled that the employer had not broken the law when the midwife was paid less than the medical technician because the market price for medical technicians was higher (Arbetsdomstolen, 2001). In this case, we note how the 'market' has replaced the notion of 'nature' in the argument. In actuality, there are very few, if any, differences between men and women which have necessary social consequences. Each individual person possesses different qualities and characteristics, but these differences are not *necessarily* linked to the person's physical sex – a man can be just as caring for his family or career-driven as a woman (Doyle & Paludi, 1998).

So as to enable the discussion about women's conditions without invoking notions of women's 'qualities' or 'characteristics', the term *gender* has been coined. Whilst the distinction between sex and *gender* has become blurred, *gender*, properly used, refers to what is constructed socially and culturally, covering what people usually call *masculine* or *feminine*. In contrast to the term *sex* (which covers two possibilities), there are, in principle, an infinite number of ways in which a person can be masculine or feminine – it completely depends on what a particular society defines as 'masculine' or 'feminine', at a particular time and place. Historically, this has undergone a great deal of variation.

Gender is not something that one is born with, but rather, it is learnt and is something that one does. "One is not born a woman, one becomes one," claimed Simone de Beauvoir (1953). One has to learn what it means to be a socially accepted man or woman from one's parents, role models, friends, one's schooling, teachers, and the media. One also learns one's gender role by being subject to correction if one does something 'wrong'. Because, despite the fact that gender can vary greatly, it is the case that the accepted ways of being male or female in a particular place and time are often very strictly limited, and limiting. This is the reason why men and women enter careers which are deemed socially acceptable for each sex, and it is also the reason why men and women who go against these norms, for example, a female soldier, are subject to bullying and harassment. This also explains why either sex prefers contexts where the same sex can be found; something called *homosociality* or *homosocial reproduction*. This is true even in contexts where money and power are to be found, for example, in the boardroom. This line of argument can be used to explain why it is so difficult to break the male dominance found at the top management level (Ibarra, 1992; Kanter, 1977).

Even if it is the case that what we refer to as masculine and feminine is variable, the *gender order* does not change. That which is labelled as 'male/masculine' is often more highly valued than that which is 'female/feminine' (Hirdman, 1990). The purpose behind making the distinction between *gender* and *sex* is to facilitate one's interrogation and questioning of the gender ranking. Gender and gender ranking are more easily subject to negotiation than a person's sex is, for example. If society has agreed that something should *be* in a certain way, it is then also possible to come to agreement that the same thing could *be* in some other way.

The individual or structure?

The early women's movement of the 1900s was, fundamentally, a liberal movement. According to liberal feminist theory, women and men share exactly same intellectual and other preconditions. From this perspective, the only reason why women fail to achieve the same levels of success as men is because discriminatory structures hinder their advancement or because individual women are subject to direct discrimination. If women were provided with the same conditions as men are, then they would make rational choices which would result in them catching up with the men, it was said. Thus, structural obstacles were removed – women were granted the right to vote, the right to receive an education, the right to all different types of jobs, and the 'special' women's salaries were abolished. Parental benefits and public childcare were legislated for. With all these done, this issue should have just vanished.

But that did not happen. A great deal changed, but women continued to take on the main responsibility for the family's home life, and they continued to choose careers which paid less than 'male' careers. Employers continued to prefer to hire men in certain jobs and promote them to certain positions. Now we have a dividing line between those who wish to continue with removing structural obstacles and implementing different structural arrangements, on the one side, and those who claim that one should respect people's free will and their right to choose, on the other side. The same dividing line can be found between those who believe that the state and politicians should arrange things for society (Hirdman, 1998) and those who believe that the state should limit its involvement in such things as much as possible.

This dividing line is not consistently respected by the usual Left v. Right political spectrum, but if one simplifies one's analysis somewhat, then one could say that the conservative approach and/or a belief in market forces and the individual's power of free choice would reject the state's involvement in such social issues. Parents, for example, would be granted the freedom to choose for themselves how they would like to divide up their parental leave benefits, and they would object to the state's imposition of a quota of female positions on company boards. The conservative approach would claim that this is something that the owners of the company should decide. It has even been suggested that such quotas run the risk of forcing incompetent candidates into such positions. Conservatives also claim that, for a long time now, women are, on average, more educated than men, even at the tertiary level and start businesses at an ever increasing rate, thereby suggesting that gender equality will be gradually realised in the future, without the need for external interference by the state. It may be possible to stimulate development in this area with certain arrangements, for example, in the form of a bonus to fathers who choose to use a larger proportion of their parental leave benefit, but changes in the areas of life and work relevant to gender equality should not be *forced* upon people.

However, there are people who believe that the establishment of gender equality proper is taking far too much time and they promote an approach to the problem which is diametrically opposed to the conservative approach described above. Such people claim that parental leave should be subject to a quota system and that quotas should be set for levels of female representation on company boards. The state should also increase the salaries in female-dominated jobs in the public sector so that they can achieve the same level of compensation in comparable male-dominated jobs in the private sector. Proponents of this approach claim that the individual's choices are far too limited by prevailing discriminatory structures in society and that these structures must be changed or done away with, for the benefit of gender equality. If the establishment of gender equality is left in the hands of market forces, tradition, and the individual's free will, then these changes will take too long, and there is no certainty that the desired result will be achieved.

Equal opportunities or equal results?

The dividing line described in the previous section can also be discerned as the difference between gender equality understood as the provision of as *equal opportunities* and gender equality in terms of *equal results*. The first approach is called *formal equality* and the later, *substantive equality*. Formal equality emphasises the point that everyone should be provided with the same opportunities, and no one should be subject to discrimination. This approach presupposes that people possess the same potential to exploit these opportunities to the same degree. If a person wishes to take advantage of an opportunity, it is up to that individual. This principle is based on the liberal approach to the individual's rights, with minimal involvement from the state, claim Wottle and Blomberg (2011: 103). The definitions of gender equality that were cited at the beginning of this chapter emphasise the notion of 'equal opportunities' and are thus expressions of formal equality. But the definitions also contained references to equal access to resources or equal distribution of power and influence. These are expressions of substantive equality, which emphasises *equal rights* (instead of *equal opportunities*) and refer to equal or 'fair' *results*. Advocates of this approach to gender equality recommend the implementation of active measures to achieve this, including positive discrimination and the setting of representational quotas.

There is a substantial difference between these approaches to gender equality (Lerwall, 2001). Formal gender equality is expressed in the form of prohibitions, whilst material gender equality demands that positive action be taken. Consequently, the first approach tends to preserve the prevailing order, whilst the second approach is one that invokes change to this order. Both approaches appear in the legislation on gender equality and both are present in the gender equality debate, but it is less usual to note that effort is made to distinguish between the two. Two parties might be fervent supporters of gender equality but may hold quite different views on which approach should be adopted so as to achieve gender equality. If one fails to distinguish between formal and substantive gender equality, then it becomes easy for the one party to accuse the other of *not* supporting gender equality. It is important to make this distinction, so as to ensure that the debate on gender equality remains clear to everyone involved.

Fairness or a resource?

As indicated in the previous section, gender equality invokes the idea that fairness should prevail between men and women. The notion of 'fairness' is present in both approaches: fair opportunities and fair results. In many areas, including education, political representation, and opportunities for gainful employment, gender equality vastly improved during the 1900s. But one area has shown itself to be less amenable to change; namely, the proportion of women who occupy high positions in the world of business. The 'fairness' argument has not established itself in the business world.

Because of the above, an argument that invokes the notion of 'resource' has been deployed. Two variants of this approach can be discerned: it is either the case that (i) women constitute an unexploited resource, merely in terms of their numbers, or (ii) women constitute an unexploited resource in terms of the 'unique female qualities' which they bring to the organisation. Of course, it is a waste of resources to ignore half a population's competence – especially if it is the case that this half is very highly qualified. Note that women's educational attainment has surpassed, or is about to surpass, male educational attainment in most industrialised countries (Pekkarinen, 2012).

In Sweden, 60%–65% of all university degrees that have been awarded since 1985 have been awarded to women (SCB, 2014). Whilst it is true that the choice of educational programme remains informed by the graduate's sex, it is only in the areas of technology and science where the majority of graduates are male. This does not mean that there is a lack of women in these areas. According to the SCB (2014), 31% of all the degrees that were awarded in the fields of technology and manufacturing were awarded to women. For some time now, degrees in economics have been conferred equally between men and women. It should thus be profitable to recruit women.

The problem with this type of argument, however, is that it can be used to support an opposite approach; something which is often done to argue against the introduction of quotas, for example, quotas for women on the boards of listed companies. In case it is *not* profitable to recruit more women the resource argument becomes invalid. Investigations into this issue have shown results in either direction. One example, which supports the argument that women are a resource, is a study that found that the setting of a gender quota in the Social Democratic party resulted in somewhat 'average' men being replaced by more competent women (Besley et al., 2013). However, unsurprisingly, studies of changes in business profitability show positive and negative results in conjunction with setting gender quotas, in equal proportion. It is hardly worth arguing for a direct and simple causal relationship between gender and profitability because far too many other factors play a role in an organisation's profitability. What remains then is the argument based on 'fairness', which, in the final analysis, is an argument that is based on moral grounds.

I wish to now suggest to business leaders who do not think that this issue deserves to be a high priority the notion of 'fairness as a resource'. Motivational theory informs us that a person who feels that he or she has been unfairly treated by an organisation will lose motivation and thus perform poorly (Ahl, 2004: 51–52, 2006). Research has shown that experiences of fairness (or unfairness) also influence the employees' and the bosses' health (Eib, 2015; Eib et al., 2015). Systematically putting people of a certain gender at a disadvantage is a waste of resources. Consequently, there is no reason at all why one should avoid engaging in gender equality work.

What remains to be done?

Legislation against gender discrimination can be a necessary point of departure for the HR specialist to have reason to, and the mandate for, engaging in gender equality work. But support from the law only is not a sufficient cause for this work to be successful. Individuals who work on implementing gender equality within an organisation must first possess knowledge about gender and sex, and about the different ways gender equality can be argued for, as summarised in the present chapter. These individuals must scrutinise their own position on this issue, by asking themselves the following questions: *What is my position on the debate on gender equality? Can I consider that gender can be expressed in a variety of different ways, or do I hold onto fixed notions about what is 'natural' for men and woman?* This may well be a difficult process to undergo, especially since attitudes and predispositions about gender constitute the fundamental building blocks of one's own identity. Both men and women are disposed to recreate safe and well-known patterns and structures; something which can actually put us at a disadvantage in this debate.

Once the HR specialist has become thoroughly acquainted with the issues at stake, then the managers of the organisation need to go through the same process. If this is not done, then it is difficult to get everyone in the organisation to work together on these issues. Preconceptions of what is 'masculine' and what is 'feminine' and what the purpose of gender equality is can, in some case, pose as obstacles to the gender equality work that is to be done. Those individuals who strongly believe that it is best and the most secure if the boss is male find it more difficult to accept women's advancement.

The person who is responsible for gender equality within an organisation must first obtain knowledge and reflect over this knowledge. This person then needs pedagogic tools to provide the managers and other employees opportunity to support the establishment of gender equality. Without this knowledge and awareness of the issues at hand, there is a serious danger that, just as was claimed by the editorial in the *Östgötakorrespondenten*, plans to establish gender equality are reduced to mere 'paper tigers'. However, by working together with knowledge about gender, sex, and equality, our work on gender equality can be a very powerful agent of change and subsequent improvement. An organisation that is seen to be fair by all of its employees will also be a healthy and productive organisation.

Suggested reading

Textbooks and research articles

Acker, Joan (1990). Hierarchies, jobs, bodies: A theory of gendered organizations. *Gender & Society*, 4(2), pp. 139–158.

Alvesson, Mats & Billing, Yvonne D. (2009). *Understanding gender and organizations*: London: Sage.

Kanter, Rosabeth M. (1977). *Men and women of the corporation*. New York: Basic Books.

Kvande, Elin (2007). *Doing gender in flexible organizations*. Bergen: Fagbokforlaget.

Practical resources

Equal Guide on Gender Mainstreaming (2004) http://ec.europa.eu/employment_social/equal/data/document/gendermain_en.pdf.

Includegender.org, a resource portal for gender equality which offers information and news about gender equality as well as practical examples and concrete tools for gender equality work: www.includegender.org/facts/gender-equality/.

References

Ahl, Helene (2004). *Motivation och vuxnas lärande: En kunskapsöversikt och problematisering*. Stockholm: Myndigheten för skolutveckling.

Ahl, Helene (2006). Motivation in adult education: A problem-solver or a euphemism for direction and control? *International Journal of Lifelong Education, 25*(4), pp. 385–405.

Arbetsdomstolen (2001). Arbetsdomstolens domar. *AD 2001*, nr 13. Hämtat från www.notisum.se/rnp/domar/ad/AD001013.htm [2015-02-18].

Arbetsdomstolen (2005). *AD 2005*, nr 87. Hämtat från. https://lagen.nu/dom/ad/2005:87 [2015-03-09].

de Beauvoir, Simone (1953). *The second sex*. London: Jonathan Cape.

Besley, Timothy, Folke, Olle, Persson, Torsten & Rickne, Johanna (2013). *Gender quotas and the crisis of the mediocre man: Theory and evidence from Sweden*. Stockholm: Research Institute of Industrial Economics.

Council of Europe (2016). Gender Equality Glossary. https://rm.coe.int/16805e55eb. Retrieved 2018-02-02.

Corren.se (2015-02-13). Fluffig plan i guldig ram. [Vague plans in golden frames] Retrieved 2015-02-16.

Doyle, James A. & Paludi, Michele A. (1998). *Sex and gender: The human experience.* (4 Suppl.) San Francisco: McGraw-Hill.

EC Fact Sheet (2016). http://ec.europa.eu/justice/gender-equality/files/gender_balance_decision_making/1607_factsheet_final_wob_data_en.pdf. Retrieved 2018-02-02.

Eib, Constanze (2015). *Processes of organizational justice: Insights into the perception and enactment of justice.* Stockholm: Stockholm University, Department of Psychology.

Eib, Constanze, Bernhard-Oettel, Claudia, Näswall, Katharina & Sverke, Magnus (2015). The interaction between organizational justice and job characteristics: Associations with work attitudes and employee health cross-sectionally and over time. *Economic and Industrial Democracy, 36*(3), pp. 549–582.

EIGE (2018). What is gender mainstreaming? http://eige.europa.eu/gender-mainstreaming/what-is-gender-mainstreaming. Retrieved 2018-02-02.

Eurostat (2017). Gender pay gap statistics. http://ec.europa.eu/eurostat/statistics-explained/index.php/Gender_pay_gap_statistics. Retrieved 2018-02-02.

Försäkringskassans nyhetsbrev (2015). Föräldraskap och sjukskrivning. www.forsakringskassan.se/wps/wcm/connect/b98dd1f6-4350-4ed4-b6a6-abb25b54e220/socialforsakringsrapport-2015-03.pdf?MOD=AJPERES. Retrieved 2018-07-20.

Hirdman, Yvonne (1990). *The gender system: Theoretical reflections on the social subordination of women.* Stockholm: Maktutredningen.

Hirdman, Yvonne (1992). *Den socialistiska hemmafrun och andra kvinnohistorier.* [The socialist housewife and other women stories] Stockholm: Carlssons.

Hirdman, Yvonne (1998). State policy and gender contracts. In Eileen P. Drew, Ruth Emerek, & Evelyn Mahon (eds.), *Women, work and the family in Europe* (pp. 36–46). London: Routledge.

Ibarra, Herminia (1992). Homophily and differential returns: Sex differences in network structure and access in an advertising firm. *Administrative Science Quarterly, 37*(3), pp. 422–447.

Kanter, Rosabeth M. (1977). *Men and women of the corporation.* New York: Basic Books.

Lerwall, Lotta (2001). *Könsdiskriminering.* [Gender discrimination] Uppsala: Iustus.

Pekkarinen, Tuomas. (2012). Gender differences in education. *Nordic Economic Policy Review, 1,* pp. 165–195.

SCB (2014). *Women and men in Sweden: Facts and figures 2014.* Örebro: Statistics Sweden.

SCB (2016). *Women and men in Sweden: Facts and figures 2016.* Örebro: Statistics Sweden.

SFS (2016:828). *Diskrimineringslag.* [The law against discrimination] Stockholm: Socialdepartementet.

UNdata (2012). *Gender inequality index.* Retrieved from http://data.un.org 2014-02-19.

UNESCO (2003). UNESCO's gender mainstreaming implementation framework. www.unesco.org/fileadmin/MULTIMEDIA/HQ/BSP/GENDER/PDF/1.%20Baseline%20Definitions%20of%20key%20gender-related%20concepts.pdf. Retrieved 2018-02-02.

UN Women (2011). Gender equality glossary. https://trainingcentre.unwomen.org/mod/glossary/view.php?id=36&mode=letter&hook=G&sortkey=&sortorder=aschttps:/. Retrieved 2018-02-02

WHO (2011). Gender, equity and human rights. Glossary of terms and tools. www.who.int/gender-equity-rights/knowledge/glossary/en/. Retrieved 2018-02-02

Wottle, Martin & Blomberg, Eva (2011), Feminism och jämställdhet i en nyliberal kontext 1990–2010. *Tidskrift för genusvetenskap, 2011*(2–3), pp. 97–115.

8

HETERONORMS, LGBTQ, AND QUEER AT THE WORKPLACE

Frida Ohlsson Sandahl

The previous chapter dealt with equality between women and men and about the importance of questioning female and male norms in an attempt to achieve inclusiveness and equal treatment at the workplace. But this is not enough. There are many more norms which create discriminatory structures and behaviours which should be challenged. Heteronorms include different norms for gender, romantic relationships, sexuality, and family. Judith Butler (1990) has called this 'the heterosexual matrix'. Norms which assume that everyone is heterosexual permeate all of society, including places of work, and this has consequences for those who do not comply with these norms. Many employees hide their sexuality or gender identity at work. By examining the norms which prevail at the workplace, it is possible to reinforce that which is good and change those norms which cause some people unhappiness.

Traditionally, work on inclusiveness has focussed on increasing tolerance, with emphasis on how 'the other' lives. The problem with 'tolerance' is that it risks reinforcing differences between groups. A better alternative is to investigate and closely inspect prevailing norms. By raising one's consciousness about norms and organisational cultures, one is provided with good opportunities to reinforce that which is considered to be good and change that which excludes employees and clients.

Norms are social rules which govern the particular ways how people should behave. Most people can 'read' norms and they know approximately what is expected of them at a workplace, even though norms can be sometimes very subtle. Newly employed people are often extra sensitive to reading the workplace culture.

Individuals who are seen as norm bearers – they satisfy what is considered to be the norm – often enjoy certain privileges; for example, they are free from being questioned and thus reach positions of power more easily. But what happens to the person who breaks workplace norms? Fear of being the target of discrimination or the experience of being bullied causes poor mental health. This, in turn, leads to poor work performance. By working together in an inclusive manner, employing a perspective that is critical of prevailing norms, is a sustainable way of working with the psychosocial environment and deploying human resources. Such 'norm-critical' work is queer theory put into practice.

The present chapter provides an introduction to heteronorms, LGBTQ, and queer theory and provides a number of practical tips on how the workplace can be made more inclusive. I begin by explaining what queer theory is. Then I will introduce and explain a number of concepts which are used in the context of gender identity and sexual orientation.

Queer theory as a point of departure

Queer is an English word which means 'odd' or 'strange'. Previously, it was used as a name of abuse for people who broke norms governing gender and sexuality, but it has since acquired new meaning from activists and by academics. One activist group which renegotiated this term was Queer Nation, based in New York. In the early 1990s, their slogan was "We're here, we're queer, get used to it" (Rosenberg, 2006: 14).

Queer theory has emerged via postmodern feminism and in conjunction with work done with supporting LGBTQ individual's rights. The previously called 'Homo Movement' discovered that, quite frequently, 'normal' equality activists and supporters did not reveal their own experiences and conditions. During the 1960s and 1970s, lesbians and feminist activists had different goals and relied on different theories. The movement thus developed in different directions, and by the 1980s the division between the two approaches was quite evident. This caused the use of static labels and a belief that there was a common solution for everyone to become problematic. Queer theory, on the other hand, questions definitions and static divisions as previously made in terms of woman::man and homo::hetero. Queer theory interrogates that which is considered to be 'normal' and 'usual', so as to reveal what takes place in the relationship between 'norms' and 'deviance from norms'. Michel Foucault (1979) argued that people must set free from labels because definitions limit people.

One theory which has enjoyed some success in both Queer Theory and Feminist Theory is Judith Butler's (1990) theory of gender performativity, which argues that people are copies of earlier copies of culturally created categories. By repeating behaviours that are 'approved' by society, in terms of the role ascribed by someone else, categories and that which is considered to be 'normal' are affirmed. If someone transgresses the bounds of what is considered to be acceptable, then the person can be punished. One can consider a violation of a norm as a game with identities and the individual's factual possibility to be the person the individual wishes to be. Butler claims that Queer Theory is a deconstructive strategy and an approach, which is the opposite of the earlier Homo Movement's 'identity politics'. *Deconstruction* entails a pulling apart; in this case, norms about gender and sexuality are pulled apart and something new or quite different is reconstructed. Butler criticises feminism's focus on 'women' and 'men', because such labels confirm the limiting, two-gender norm.

One point of criticism that has been directed at Queer Theory is that, if an individual can always choose a way to express a certain identity, then the individual is thus responsible if the environment becomes hostile to the individual. Another point of criticism is that it is not always possible to choose certain expressions, including one's body, physical ability, age, and skin colour. The point of departure for a queer perspective is one that questions norms and categories. For example, if the word *woman* is to be used, then a definition must first be provided. Organisations thus need to discuss what different words mean and what definitions of certain words emerge in the daily work done in the organisation.

Queer Theory is an academic point of departure; in practice, it is an approach that is norm-critical. Which norms should be subject to Queer Theory interrogation? A common language and a shared array of concepts facilitates our identification of norms, thus I will discuss a number of the different concepts that are used in this theory.

Explaining cis, HBTQ, trans, and queer

Cis

The cis-norm is one of the strongest and yet one of the most invisible norms. *Cis* is Latin for 'on this side of' (cf. *trans* 'across'). Cis is based on the notion that there are only two gender alternatives: male or female. A cis person has every perspective on gender 'on the same side'; including one's *mental* gender (the gender that a person identifies with), one's *legal* gender (the gender that appears on one's birth certificate), one's *biological sex* (the body that one is born with – note that there are more than two variations of this), and one's *social* gender (the gender that one is seen as possessing by one's social environment). A cis-man and a cis-woman are thus people whose gender identity is congruent with his or her biological, legal, and social gender.

A cis-person very seldom needs to defend his or her gender identity, since it is more or less taken as given. In the cis-norm, everyone is expected to be cis-people until it is shown to be otherwise, for example, until a person comes out as a transgender people. A transgender person is consequently a person who does not have all four gender perspectives 'on the same side'. It is important to remember that neither cis nor trans have anything to do with sexual orientation, and it should be noted that the person himself or herself always has the right to make his or her own gender identification.

Signe Bremer (2013), in her chapter in the anthology *Genusyrsel and normupppror*, argues that the two-gender norm controls how people are treated. She claims that the norm demands that we all fit into the two-gender principle because "to be recognised as *real* people, we are expected to agree with this principle" (2013: 107).

Related to the two-gender norm is the twosome togetherness norm, where everyone is expected to want to enter into a couple relationship, 'the nuclear family norm', and have a family, with children. Elvin-Nowak and Thomsson (2012: 152, author's translation) write that

> two adults of the same or different gender are usually perceived as a couple, not as a family. To be a family, children are needed. […] To be a real family, there has to be the correct number of adults (2), and the correct number of genders (2).

Gender identity, trans, and queer

As mentioned above, gender identity is the gender that a person self-identifies with. It also coincides with the person's mental gender. Everyone has one or more gender identities. Because of the influence of hetero norms, gender identity can be of great importance to how included a person may feel. Everyone is limited by cis norms in that there are expectations that stem from a person's gender identity and gender expression. These expectations are a function of a *gender hierarchy*.

There exists a multitude of gender identities. Note that these are terms that people use as part of their identity, and consequently, gender is a complex issue. To provide some examples of the variety and complexity of gender identity, consider the following list of gender identities: *agender, androgyn, bigender, binary, cis-woman, cis-man, cis-person, crossdresser, demiboy, demifemme, demigender, demigirl, demiguy, female to male, girlboy, FtM, FtX, genderbender, genderfluid, genderqueer, genderfree, gender neutral, gender neutral person, non-binary, intergender, intersexual, woman, man, MtX, non-binary gender, nongender, person, boygirl, queer, edited, trans★, transandrogyn, transfeminin, transboy, transwoman, transsexual, transman, transmasculine, trigender, questioning,* and *two spirit*.

Trans is a Latin prefix meaning 'over' or 'across'. *Transgender* is a term which includes all identities that in some way violate the cis norm. There is a widespread hate for and negative attitudes against trans and trans people; so-called 'transphobia'. Many employers and businesses have divided their employees and operations (restrooms, and so on) according to two genders only. Thus, every business should consider how it can become more inclusive. It is important that organisations and the work they do in establishing equality within the organisation is based on more gender identities than just two. Note too that *gender identity* or *expression* is one of the seven principles that informs the Swedish Discrimination Act (SFS, 2008: 567).

LGBTQ

The term *LGBTQ* stands for *Lesbian, Gay, Bisexual, Trans,* and *Queer*. Notwithstanding the common misconception that LGBTQ solely refers to a person's sexual orientation, note that both sexual orientation (indicated by the *LGB*) and gender identity (indicated by the *TQ*) are included in the term. The term includes a great variety of identities, but what unifies them all is that LGBTQ people can be excluded by hetero-norms.

In Swedish LGBTQ is often translated to HBTQ. Other terms, such as QTBH (*H* for *Homosexual*) and THBQ are also sometimes used, depending on which perspective is adopted. A gender hierarchy can be identified even here, so many people choose to use LBHTQ to highlight lesbians and to distinguish them from homosexual men. The terms change constantly, so our focus should not lie with the terms in themselves, but, rather, on the hetero-norms which exclude certain people and how the workplace can be changed so as to include a diversity of gender identities and sexualities.

The term *queer* in LGBTQ stands for several different identities, including people who identify themselves as queer; a person who is fluid in their gender identity and sexuality can identify as *queer*. *Queer* can also be a way to avoid, refuse, or be silent about one's identity. There is thus a freedom to choose one's identity and sexuality, free from any predetermined categories. Furthermore, *queer* can represent a norm-critical perspective, as mentioned above.

To invoke a category of people as LGBTQ is sometimes necessary, for example, when investigating any health differences between LGBTQ-identified people and cis- and hetero people. Young LGBTQ people suffer from poorer health than young cis-people and young heterosexual people. The reason for this is that they are subject to discrimination, harassment, threats of violence, and actual physical violence. Transgender people suffer from poorer mental health than homosexuals, and this is more common in young transgender people than older transgender people. Stress and fear are results of young LGBTQ-identified people's fear of discrimination at the workplace. Their mental health is impacted upon by their fear of mistreatment (Ungdomsstyrelsen, 2010: 35).

The workplace can be more inclusive if people are made aware of hetero-norms. Hetero-norms cooperate with discrimination, violence, and phobias. These norms can constitute an obstacle for a person who may otherwise wish to come out as a LGBTQ person. A person who identifies as LGBTQ may refuse to be open with others, possibly resulting in the person becoming invisible and being the subject of meanness or violence. A person who lives a hetero-normative life is privileged by not having to expend energy in avoiding breaking prevailing norms.

Sexual orientation: hetero-, homo-, and bisexuality

One's sexual orientation is how one identifies when it comes to whom one is romantically or sexually attracted to and is always self-identified. Everyone has one or more sexual orientations. However, one criticism of the term *sexual orientation* lies in the fact that it suggests that everyone is orientated at least in one direction, whilst it is the case that there are people who have several sexual identities which do not always coincide with the person's sexual practices. In the Discrimination Act (SFS, 2008: 567), three sexual orientations are mentioned: heterosexual, homosexual, and bisexual. We note that it is forbidden to discriminate against a person on the grounds of the person's sexual orientation.

The word *homo* is from the Greek word meaning 'the same'. Homosexuality entails that a person feels sexually attracted to, falls in love with, and/or wishes to enter into a relationship with someone who has the same gender identity as the first person. The meaning of the word can vary, from person to person.

Bi- is a Latin prefix, denoting 'two'. Bisexuality entails that a person feels sexual attraction, is in love with, and/or wishes to have a relationship with another person irrespective of that person's gender. The meaning of this word may vary, from person to person. Many prefer to use the term *pansexual* instead (*pan* meaning 'all' or 'every') because it does not reproduce (and thereby reinforce) the two-gender norm.

Hetero-norms assume that heterosexuality is the most common sexuality. Everyone is expected to be hetero unless something indicates that this is not the case. According to hetero-norms, there are only two genders. The point of departure is that men and women are different (as described in Chapter 7, an *essential* viewpoint is taken with respect to gender), and that they are in constant pursuit after the perfect equivalent person from the other category. One is assumed to be a 'whole person' only once one has found one's partner. This is called *gender complementarity*. A person who lives by heterosexual norms does not need to 'come out of the closet' and show their sexuality or gender identity. It is seen as something self-evident and nothing that people who know the person need reflect over. A person who lives a hetero-normative life can talk about their sexuality or gender identity without remark from someone else, whilst a person who violates hetero-norms and does the same thing can be seen as someone who is 'always talking about sex'.

Queer gender equality work

The whole gender equality discourse is based on the idea that there are two genders, which results in people who do not identify as a woman or as a man being left invisible. Gender norms, gender identities, and sexuality are all brought together in the heterosexual matrix. Queer perspectives and two-gender normative gender equality work may, at first, be opposites of each other. If gender equality work is not to torpedo the opportunities and rights of transgender people, then everyone must be included in this work, irrespective of their gender. Gender equality work which is informed by queer feminism incorporates both feminist and queer perspectives. Adopting these perspectives allows the analysis to include more genders and more sexual orientations.

Our point of departure should be one where everyone starts from being in their own 'closet'. This may include one's membership with a congregation, one's family situation, or one's disabilities. The employer should strive to establish an inclusive organisational culture which has the goal of allowing every employee feel safe and able to be open about their identity. If they want to be open about this or not is, however, a decision that they must make themselves. 50% of all employees hide their sexual orientation at work (Jansson & Jacobson, 2007).

A person who is forced to hide part of their life will avoid situations where there is a risk of being uncovered. Social encounters, for example, in the staff break room, can increase the risk, which may cause the person to be silent in such situations.

The most important thing that an organisation who wishes to achieve gender equality can do is to examine its own norms from a queer perspective. Each context has its own norm system and its own organisational culture. How easy it is to be open with one's identity is different at different workplaces. Changes in organisational culture should focus on broadening norms instead of getting everyone to 'come out of the closet'. What values characterise the employer and which norms do you endorse? The responsibility for this is especially heavy for bosses and managers. The values that the boss is seen to endorse have great influence on the organisation. Consequently, employers should pay special attention to working with the norms and values that are endorsed by the organisation's leadership. The HR specialist should ensure that as many employees as possible, in not all of them, feel responsibility for their work environment, the prevailing norms, and the organisational culture.

Achieving inclusiveness

In the work to be done to achieve inclusiveness, it is important that the employer ensure that every employee, client, and visitor feels welcome. The organisation should prepare for this *before* someone feels excluded otherwise a great deal of pressure will be placed on the person who is tasked to solve such problems. If individuals are made to feel unwelcome, then this can lead to lost customers and fewer potential employees.

The responsibility for gender equality planning and salary scales is often the HR specialist's, but the ultimate responsibility for gender equality and the organisation's inclusiveness can never be placed on a single individual or role. The organisational culture is represented by everyone, but the responsibility is to be found with the management and all of the bosses.

Below, I provide a number of practical tips on how an organisation can free up the use of language, engage in open communication, and provide space for a more gender-equal workplace:

- Ensure that every boss and manager is informed about what norms are and the Discrimination Act and any other relevant legislation.
- Ask open questions about how people live their lives, so as to avoid situations where people feel compelled to 'come out'.
- Impose a zero-tolerance policy on homo-, bi-, or transphobic jokes.
- Use words such as *different genders* or *every gender identity*, instead of *men and women*, so as to make the language used in the organisation more inclusive.

- Sometimes, it may be the case that the employer needs statistical data about gender distribution in the organisation, for example, with respect to salary scales. If legal gender is used, mention this. If it is possible, allow for other genders to be included. Ask what a person's gender identity is instead of limiting the person to a choice of either legal genders.
- Revise the organisation's internal and external communication documents. If images are included in these documents, what is represented by these images?
- Ensure that there are gender-neutral restrooms and changing rooms available, and that the signage used by the organisation is inclusive. If a restroom has a baby-changing station, consider the image that indicates this. Surprisingly often, the image used on such signs is wearing a skirt. Use Braille, symbols, and different languages.
- Transgender people are often expected to educate their environment about trans questions. Do not ask enquiring questions about gender or the trans process. Open questions are always a good rule of thumb, to avoid forcing a person to 'come out'. To show respect and to be inclusive is always the right thing to do.

Often, events that follow hetero-norms are celebrated. For example, a colleague may have had a child or got married. Organisations should consider what and who should be celebrated. Try and include different types of events, so that the celebration will contribute to profiling diversity and different people's life situations. Take note of whose responsibility it is to organise such social events.

Gender equality work must also be part of the changes made in the psychosocial work environment. The Discrimination Act includes several supporting actions which are compulsory to implement. In the third section of the law, 'Active measures' (SFS, 2008: 567), it is stipulated that employees and employers must cooperate with each other concerning the active arrangements that are needed to allow for participation from everyone at the workplace. The discrimination ombudsman argues that gender equality arrangements can, to good effect, be linked to the systematic work environment arrangements that take place within organisations as a matter of course. The best way to perform successful worker's rights advocacy is to include such work in the existing work that is done by the organisation, thereby ensuring gender equality integration.

Implementing inclusiveness is difficult, important, and fun. To succeed with the norm-critical work, one must put one's ego to the side. Everyone needs to consider how they are privileged and understand what opportunities are available to oneself to help or hinder others in their environment. Most people mean well, but sometimes misunderstandings may arise if one bases one's actions on one's own and the workplace's norms. Key to success in this endeavour is when bosses and HR specialists, and all the other employees, admit to their mistakes when mistakes are made.

There exists a great deal of good methods and informative materials on gender equality. You might even want to ask other companies! You do not have to invent the wheel over again. However, there is a constant demand for people who have competency in supporting different group's rights and equality. This chapter is hopefully one of many steps on this journey.

Recommended reading

Butler, Judith (1990), *Gender trouble: Feminism and the subversion of identity*. London & New York: Routledge.
Connell, Robert. W. (2005), *Masculinities*. Berkeley: University of California Press
Foucault, Michel (1979), *The history of sexuality*, Volume 1. Harmondsworth: Penguin.
Kugelberg, Jorun, Westerlund, Ulrika, Nielsen, Mika (2009). *Break the Norm! Methods for studying norms in general and the heteronorm in particular*. Stockholm: RFSL

References

Bremer, Signe (2013), Patienten: Vårdar du patienten eller normen? Om sjukvårdens möte med transpersoner. [The patient: Do you care for the patient or the norm? Transpersons and how they are dealt with healthcare providers] In Maria Ejd (ed.), *Genusyrsel och normuppror [Gender confusion and norm outrage]* (pp. 107–116). Stockholm: Vårdförbundet.
Butler, Judith (1990), *Gender trouble: Feminism and the subversion of identity*. London & New York: Routledge.
Elvin-Nowak, Ylva & Thomsson, Helene (2012), *Att göra kön: Om vårt våldsamma behov av att vara kvinnor och män*. [Doing gender: Our violent need to be women and men] Stockholm: Bonniers.
Foucault, Michel (1979), *The history of sexuality, Volume 1*. Harmondsworth: Penguin.
Jansson, Anna-Carin & Jacobson, Maria (2007), *Fritt fram för en god arbetsmiljö: Homo, bi & hetero*. [Moving forward to a good work environment: Homo, bi, and hetero] Stockholm: RFSL.
Rosenberg, Tiina (2006), *L-ordet: Vart tog alla lesbiska vägen?* [The L-word: Where did all the lesbians go?] Stockholm: Normal.
SFS (2008: 567), Diskrimineringslag. [The law against discrimination] Stockholm: Socialdepartementet.
Ungdomsstyrelsen (2010), *Hon hen han.* [She *hen*(he/she) him] Stockholm: Myndigheten för ungdoms- och civilsamhällesfrågor.

9

GENERATIONAL DIFFERENCES AT THE WORKPLACE

Ann-Kristin Boström

For the majority of the 1900s, for most people in Western societies, life was divided into three quite distinct stages. First was childhood and the developmental years, up until approximately 20 years of age. Then came one's working life (or higher studies and then work), up until a pensionable age of approximately 65 years old. The final stage was life as a pensioner, outside the labour market. The financing of the first and third stages was built on contributions made to society during the second stage.

This pattern is now undergoing some changes. What one might do at a particular age is no longer equally predictable. We note that many young people study for much longer than before, and we observe that many young people experience difficulties in entering the labour market. When they eventually do obtain work, they remain there for several decades, experiencing high levels of stress as they forge a career, whilst establishing their families and bringing up their children. For many, however, the more peaceful, later years at work, where one might rely on one's hard-won experience, fail to materialise because of changes in the work-life, rapid technological developments, and even age discrimination. Consequently, it is not uncommon that people suffer from involuntary unemployment after the age of 50. Age discrimination and certain preconceptions about becoming a pensioner can result in people of a pensionable age being denied the opportunity to contribute to society in different ways, even though they still wish to do so and are capable of doing so. Certain images about age and old people can also create friction and problems in cooperation across different generations at the workplace (Myers & Sadaghiani, 2010).

Against this background, we will examine the importance of how young people and older people can work together in a good way. Positive relationships between people are important for workplace cooperation, and they provide people with the safety that is needed if they are to have the courage to discuss and solve problems and to be innovative. To be able to create positive relationships, one needs to have a fundamental understanding of the differences that may exist between different generations; differences that can be related to the different conditions individuals grew up under. In this context, access to technology and IT plays an important role, but the different historical and cultural backgrounds of the different generations also influence relationships at work, and thus, the work environment.

Can we imagine a more flexible work-life where age does not play such a large role? Can we facilitate cooperation between bosses and employees at work by informing ourselves about the differences between generations and what one can do to bridge the gap between generations? Can we facilitate the learning of different generations about each other? These questions are explored in the discussion below, using the results of two investigations from Singapore and the United States, respectively. But first, we will consider learning between different generations.

Learning that transcends the generation gap: intergenerational learning

Are different generations actually different? Yes, there are differences, and they depend on where and when one was born, which, in turn, provides us with different life experiences. People have always learnt from each other. Children learn from their parents, who, in turn, were taught by their parents. Attitudes, values, skills, and knowledge have always been passed down from one generation to another.

Research on *intergenerational learning* began in the 1970s in the United States (Boström, 2014). From an international research perspective, intergenerational learning, or learning across generations, is an area that is undergoing constant development. Many researchers have now contributed to this area. Note that Klercq's (1996) publication *Talking about generations* addresses the need to perform deep investigations into the relationships between different generations. Hashimoto's (1996) *The gift of generations* is a comparative study of relationships between generations in Japan and in the United States. Newman et al. (1997) and their study, *Intergenerational programmes*, provide a description and explanation of the social developments in the United States since the 1970s. *Generations in touch* (Thang, 2001) examines the interaction between children and the elderly in Japan, whilst Kaplan et al. (2002) emphasise the importance of the transfer of habits and attitudes from one generation to the next in their work, *Linking lifetimes*.

Coombs and Ahmed (1974) claim that learning is a lifelong process which starts at childhood and continues throughout one's adulthood. They divide this learning into different types:

- *formal learning* – learning which is hierarchal and chronologically structured in an educational system, takes place within the bounds of an institution, and results in some form of qualification;

- *nonformal learning* – organised educational activities, but outside the formal system, which give selected parts of an education to specific groups in society (for example, a study circle);
- *informal learning*– the lifelong process where every individual acquires knowledge, skills, attitudes, and experiences from everyday lessons and impressions from the environment.

Informal learning takes place, as suggested by its name, in informal contexts; at home, in the playground, with friends, and so on. A large part of informal lifelong learning also takes place at the workplace (Hager, 2001; Tuijnman & Boström, 2002). In the apprentice system, which was previously quite common, the primary purpose of an apprenticeship was that the apprentice should learn a craft or set of skills from a master craftsman. Even so, attitudes, morals, and other values were transferred when people lived and worked together. Certain technological developments, urbanisation, and other demographic changes have resulted in changed conditions for informal learning, not least at the workplace. During the last 100 years (and even more so in the last 30 years, since the introduction of the PC), communication between people has changed, and continues to change. In the following section, we examine the consequences of these changed conditions.

Urbanisation and industrialisation

During the first half of the 1900s, many people moved from the countryside into large cities, often leaving behind the older generations. During the 1920s, 55% of the Swedish population lived on the countryside. In 2000, that proportion was 22% (SCB, 2014). When people moved into the cities, in response to the industrial revolution, both parents in the family began to do work outside the home and their children went to school. The previous relationships between grandparents, parents, and their children were thus disrupted. Previously, several generations of the same family would live together; now, the different generations are separated from each other by preschool, school, work, and old-age homes. We are now confronted with what I call *chimneystack generations* – generations that have grown up in the Western industrial nations and have lived in different places, but have very little time for cross-generational interaction. When people lived together on the farm, they worked together. Now most children have their own bedroom, and they can even virtually isolate themselves from others, even though they are sitting in the same room.

Demographic changes

Changes in demographics influence the conditions for cross-generational learning. More people are living for longer, and there have been periodic dips in the birth rate. Today, there are 90,000 Swedes who are over the age of 90, compared with the 2,500 of the same age in 1900 (SCB, 2014). Of those who grew up in

Sweden at the beginning of the 1900s, 60% of them lived in households where at least five people lived together, and 20% of households consisted of eight or more people. Living alone at that time was very rare; only 6% of households consisted of one person. In 2012, 38% of Swedish households consisted of one person.

We thus have a workforce in Sweden whose average age is higher than ever before, and a large part of the population lives alone. These facts constitute changed conditions for opportunities for informal learning, when compared with earlier times.

Technical changes

Technology continues to develop, faster than ever. In particular, developments in IT have radically influenced the conditions for communication. Previously, people had to meet and talk with each other, face-to-face, but now communication can take place via telephone, computers, or PC tablets. Previously, one was forced to deal with relationships with the people around you, for better or worse, whilst now, a great deal can be done *virtually*. We also note that these virtual relationships are becoming more important. As a result of this, opportunities for intergenerational learning are reduced. Another point to note is that the generations which have been brought up with IT often have a different attitude to virtual communication, when compared with people who were raised before the introduction of the PC and the Internet. At the workplace, however, different generations work together and need to learn how to cooperate with each other. Myers and Sadaghiani (2010) report that younger employees often work in groups and think that technology is important. Older employees can learn from them but also provide their younger colleagues with advice, based on their experience, when decisions that affect the business are to be made. The younger generations also appreciate having a balance between work and time off. Myers and Sadaghiani (2010) observed that, after being influenced by the younger employees, the older employees also began to think about the balance between work and time off.

The discussion above is summarised in Table 9.1.

In what follows, I present the results of two investigations into intergenerational learning at the workplace. Note that there are several different ways of defining a generation – the distinctions are drawn in different ways. In the investigations referred to below, the same distinctions are drawn, thereby allowing the results of the studies to be comparable. In the statistical data which is available

TABLE 9.1 The differences in upbringing between different societies

Farming society	*Industrial society*
Three generations together	Chimneystack generations
Work together	One's own bedroom
Face-to-face communication	IT communication

for the Swedish context (cited above), comparisons have, instead, been made between *cohorts*: individuals who were born in the same year (see the report, *Generationergenomlivet*, SCB, 2014).

Research from Singapore

In Singapore (TAFEP, 2010), a very thorough investigation into the effects of how different generations view each other has been conducted. The point of departure for this investigation is the observation that *relationships are important to people*. People build up social capital which creates trust and security and forms the basis for cooperation. Every generation is seen to be an important resource, but if different generations are to learn from each other, then good relationships between the generations are needed too.

In the Singapore investigation, 3,541 people from 30 different organisations provided answers to the researchers' questions. These participants were divided into five different generations, or age groups as follows:

- Generation Y (born after 1980),
- Generation X (born between 1965 and 1980),
- Late baby boomers (born between 1955 and 1964),
- Early baby boomers (born 1946–1954),
- Traditionalists (born before 1946).

Of course, there is a danger that one might exaggerate and generalise over stereotypical perceptions that different generations may have about each other. We should be aware of this when we highlight these differences. Such differences do exist, but with mutual respect and understanding, different generations can learn from each other; in fact they must. Even if the differences between the generations are not exactly the same as in Sweden, the investigation revealed that (i) differences do exist, (ii) what types of differences exist, and (iii) what we can learn from these differences.

The first question that was asked was: Which age group(s) do you have the most difficulty in cooperating with? See Table 9.2.

TABLE 9.2 The distribution of responses to the question: *Which age group(s) do you have the most difficulty in cooperating with?* (TAFEP, 2010: 14)

Respondent	I have difficulties in cooperating with...				
	Generation Y (%)	Generation X (%)	Late baby boomer (%)	Early baby boomer (%)	Traditionalist (%)
Generation Y	6	22	62	51	100
Generation X	17	6	11	22	0
Late baby boomer	37	31	8	3	0
Early baby boomer	34	35	12	9	0
Traditionalist	6	6	7	15	0

It is clear that the young people, Generation Y, had difficulties in cooperating with Traditionalists, and also with Late baby boomers and Early baby boomers, to a somewhat lesser degree. An obvious follow-up question would be to ask: *Why is this the case?* To answer this question, the researchers investigated how the different generations generalised over the problem that they experienced in cooperating with those generations which they found to be particularly 'difficult'. In Table 9.3, the results of this line of enquiry are shown.

The investigation that was conducted in Singapore also addressed a number of intergenerational problems but also provided a number of potential solutions to

TABLE 9.3 What the different generations say about each other (TAFEP, 2010: 14–15)

Respondents	Said about Generation Y
Generation X	They lack knowledge, have attitude problems, are arrogant, not mature, are self-centred
Early baby boomers	They are not flexible, do things in their own way, are 'job bouncers',[1] have bad moods, are immature, get tired easily
Late baby boomers	Have difficulty in concentrating for longer periods, are overbearing, impatient, selfish, focused on short-term goals, do not show interest, are too active, just want to be promoted, do not show respect for older colleagues
Traditionalists	Cannot cooperate with older people, have attitude problems, are 'job bouncers'

Respondents	Said about Generation X
Generation Y	Their brains are preprogrammed, only want to work their way, think that they are cleverer than everyone else
Early baby boomers	They are self-centred and selfish, only care about their own needs, do not accept criticism, are speculative
Late baby boomers	They are over ambitious, believe that they know everything, believe that older colleagues are old-fashioned, too demanding, are insensitive to other's needs, think that they have power

Respondents	Said about Early baby boomers
Generation Y	They are not open to new ideas, believe that they know everything and act in such a way, react according to old habits and cannot adopt other's perspectives, are not willing to learn, are stubborn to change their values or opinions, are unwilling to take risks
Generation X	They do not listen, are not flexible, do not respect younger colleagues, believe that they have the most experience and make decisions based on this belief, resist change, do things their own way, have a fixed perspective of their environment

Respondents	Said about Traditionalists
Generation Y	They are not open to accept new ideas, are slow to understand, are conservative and inflexible, have a fixed view on everything
Generation X	They are not flexible, resistant to change, are not open to criticism, do not understand the younger generations, are not open to learn new things, work slowly

these problems. In Table 9.4, we note how each of the generations ranked (from 1 to 10; 10 being last and 1 being first) ten different ways by which the problems that were identified could be solved and relationships between the generations could be improved.

After the investigation, it became apparent that many employees thought that it was important that opportunities for the different generations to work together be created. The creation of a recruitment panel consisting of several generations and the establishment of rules to govern the cooperation across generations were considered to be two unimportant suggestions, however. A number of distinct

TABLE 9.4 The ranking provided by different generations of suggestions on how relationships between the generations could be improved (TAFEP, 2010: 17)

	Generation Y	Generation X	Late baby boomers	Early baby boomers	Traditionalists
Create opportunities for employees who are of different generations to work together.	No. 2	No. 2	No. 1	No. 3	No. 4
Educate the employees so that the employees will understand each other and show respect for each other.	No. 6	No. 3	No. 2	No. 2	No. 1
Do not make assumptions about a person based on a person's age.	No. 1	No. 1	No. 3	No. 5	No. 6
Start a mentoring programme for the employees, so that the employees can receive guidance from someone who has more experience.	No. 4	No. 4	No. 5	No. 4	No. 2
Inform all employees that it is important for the workplace that several generations can work together.	No. 7	No. 6	No. 4	No. 1	No. 3
Discuss differences of all types.	No. 3	No. 5	No. 6	No. 6	No. 5
Only employ people who can cooperate with colleagues of different generations.	No. 9	No. 8	No. 7	No. 7	No. 7
Do not make expectations about a person's work performance merely based on that person's age.	No. 5	No. 7	No. 8	No. 10	No. 8
Establish rules that govern cooperation across the generations.	No. 10	No. 9	No. 9	No. 8	No. 9
Allow a recruitment panel consisting of several generations to participate during recruitment interviews.	No. 8	No. 10	No. 10	No. 9	No. 10

differences could be observed in the ranking of suggestions across the different generations. For example, Traditionalists thought that if employees could be educated, then they will understand each other and show respect for each other, whilst Generation Y did not rank this suggestion very high at all.

In another part of the study, the different generations were asked about their opinions of work meetings. The Early and Late baby boomers both preferred face-to-face meetings, whilst Generation X preferred e-mail communication and considered holding a meeting as a last resort. For Generation Y, the 'Internet generation', SMS, and e-mail were the obvious means of communication – meetings were considered to be completely unnecessary.

Research from the United States

In the United States, a number of changes, similar to those described in the Swedish context, have taken place in the workforce. If we compare the workforce in the United States 20 year ago with today's workforce, we note a large difference in the average age of the workforce. In 2012, the average age of the workforce was 41.5 years of age, but 20 years previously, the average age was 36.6 years of age. This is, in part, because the Baby boomers, who were born between 1946 and 1964, constitute the largest generation in the history of the United States. Members of this generation have also begun to consider prolonging their active working life after the pensionable age. Labour market economists predict that the number of young people on the labour market will remain constant – or may even decrease somewhat – whilst the number of older workers is expected to increase. In other words, there will be a large number of 'difficult' Traditionalists that Generation Y will have to deal with.

These changes in age demographics impact on the availability of a competent workforce. The potential selection of young employees is reduced, proportionately, and the need to acknowledge and maintain the competencies held by the older generations is going to increase. In the United States, the media have warned employers that the Baby boomer's retreat from the labour market will be the largest *brain drain* in the country's history (Sloan Center on Aging & Work, 2010). If many experienced employees leave the labour market at the same time, then operational knowledge, knowledge about important customers, and knowledge about how one solves common problems in the organisation will disappear. This can be devastating for certain organisations.

The Sloan Center of Aging & Work (2010) has investigated what motivates employees of different generations. They wished to map the levels of commitment present in today's multigenerational workplace, including what was considered important (to employees) and how one could influence employee's level of commitment at work. The same division into different generations was used in this study as was used in the study from Singapore.

The investigation revealed that older employees (Baby boomers and Traditionalists) generally had higher levels of commitment than younger employees.

The researchers also found that 'one size does *not* fit all' in this context. Different generations were motivated by different things. Consequently, employers will need to note that the factors which influence employee motivation are different for each generation of employee.

Generation Y appreciated flexible work schedules and work locations, since this allowed them to complete their work and look after their family responsibilities. Generation Y also valued professional development opportunities, whilst older employees were less interested in such things. Generation X appreciated being placed in supervisory roles. With respect to the Late baby boomers, good physical health was a factor that was associated with their level of commitment, whilst the provision of supervisory support was a factor which correlated with high levels of commitment in Early baby boomers and Traditionalists.

The consequences of generational differences and demographic changes

An aging workforce needs adapting

Employers often define the ideal employee as someone who is in the prime of his or her life, is career-orientated, independent, and determined to do his or her best for his or her organisation or career, in a nonemotional and rational manner (Sloan Center on Aging & Work, 2010).

This approach can be a problem because features which are associated with the ideal employee can create damaging stereotypes at the workplace, dictating how the employees *should be*. Difficulties may arise when the employee does not fit into the expected pattern of behaviour. When older employees wish to increase their level of participation at the workplace after the traditional pensionable age of 65 years (or they may wish to change careers and take up a different profession), this may come as a surprise to the employer. These new ideas and work patterns on the labour market represent a break with the typical concept of the ideal worker from the 1900s. Employers who assume that every employee in the organisation wants to strive towards a higher position by continually accepting more and more responsibility, status, and salary might be surprised by older employees who do not want to go on pension but are no longer interested in moving up in the organisation. Such an employer might think that the employee is uninterested in the job or lacks commitment, which is probably far from the truth.

The term *encore* has been used by Freedman (2007), amongst others, to refer to a new career that is taken up later in life. In the United States, there are many examples where people who have had a stressful and demanding job change over to a job which they think gives back to them and often makes some form of contribution to society. Employers who wish to attract potential employees to their organisations, irrespective of their age or career level, will need to broaden their conceptualisation of the ideal employee and will have to identify the steps they must take to (i) attract young, middle-aged, and older employees to their organisation; (ii) keep such employees committed to their work; and (iii) cultivate the desire in the employees to remain with the organisation. These employers will have to learn to understand what reinforces employee motivation at different ages, so that the organisation can develop policies and programmes which increase the commitment levels of the employees whilst taking their age into consideration.

Different generations need to be managed in different ways

The increasing number of differences between generations leads to an increasing need to adapt on the employer's side. Employers are recommended to examine closely the different needs and wishes expressed by the different generations. They should ask: *What do different generations think about certain work methods? Which work methods are most suitable for a certain generation? How can they assist the employees who are of different generations in understanding, appreciating, and supporting each other?*

These goals can be achieved by creating work teams consisting of different age groups. One can minimise the danger of conflict by highlighting the importance of every employee being open to each other's new ideas. Furthermore, one can use different means of communication so that no employee feels excluded. Different training courses, mentorships, or web-based courses can be offered. Employees should be encouraged to help each other; older employees can, for example, act as mentors to their younger colleagues.

Each of the generations that were included in the Singapore study realised that the most effective way to prevent opposition was to work together. Common to both investigations was the observation that the employer must be prepared to provide flexible solutions according to the needs of each generation and to provide support to every employee so that they can develop and contribute in the best possible way to the organisation.

Plan for the provision of competence

Employers in a number of industrial areas, especially those who employ a large proportion of older workers, need to be aware of the fact that the number of available new employees who are of a younger generation is must less than the Baby boomers who are at the end stages of their working lives. In certain areas, this will entail that the oversupply of workers that one has had for a long time will come to an end. Some of the employers who were questioned in the US study claimed that, without achieving a significantly higher level of productivity, they will not be able to fill all of the vacant work positions.

The changes in the population's age demographics will also have an effect on the market for the organisations' goods and services. If a large proportion of a population is old, patterns of demand are influenced. Some of the organisations included in the US study had changed their marketing strategies so that they could better attract customers from the Baby boomers. Organisations will need to understand the influence that current age-demographics will have on their businesses, not only so they can plan for the continued provision of competence in their organisations but also so that they can ensure that their organisations will continue to operate.

Recommended reading

Freedman, Marc (2007), *Encore: Finding work that matters in the second half of life*. New York, NY: Public Affairs.
Myers, Karen & Sadaghiani, Kamyab (2010), Millennials in the workplace: A communication perspective on millennial's organizational relationships and performance. *Journal of Business and Psychology, 25*(2), pp. 225–238.

Note

1 A 'job bouncer' being a person who voluntarily changes permanent, full-time jobs, multiple times each year.

References

Boström, Ann-Kristin (2014), Reflections on intergenerational policy in Europe: The past twenty years and looking into the future. *Journal of Intergenerational Relationships, 12*(4), pp. 357–367.
Coombs, Philip A. & Ahmed, Manzoor (1974), *Attacking rural poverty: How nonformal education can help*. Baltimore, MD: John Hopkins University Press.
Freedman, Marc (2007), *Encore, finding work that matters in the second half of life*. New York, NY: Public Affairs.
Hager, Paul (2001), Lifelong learning and the contribution of informal learning. In David Aspin, Judith Chapman, Michael Hatton & Yukiko Sawano (eds.), *International handbook of lifelong learning, Part 1*. London: Kluwer Academic.
Hashimoto, Akiko (1996), *The gift of generations: Japanese and American perspectives on ageing and the social contract*. New York, NY: Cambridge University Press of America.
Kaplan, Matthew, Henkin, Nancy & Kusano, Atsuko (2002), *Linking lifetimes: A global view of intergenerational exchange*. Boston, MA: University Press of America.
Klercq, Jumbo (1996), *Van generation gesproken: Leerprocessen in onzemeergeneratiesamenleving*. [Talking about generations: Learning processes in our multi-generational society] Driebergen, Netherlands: VTA Group.
Myers, Karen & Sadaghiani, Kamyab (2010), Millennials in the workplace: A communication perspective on millennial's organizational relationships and performance. *Journal of Business and Psychology, 25*(2), pp. 225–238.
Newman, Sally, Ward, Christopher R., Smith, Thomas B., Wilson, Janet & McCrea, James (1997), *Intergenerational programs: Past, present and future*. New York, NY: Taylor and Francis.
SCB (2014), Demografisk rapport (2014:2), *Generationergenomlivet: En demografiskbeskrivningavfödda under 1900-talet*. [Generations throughout life: A demographc description of those born during the 1990s] Örebro: Statistiskacentralbyrån.

Sloan Center on Aging & Work (2010), *Engaging the 21th century multi-generational workforce.* Boston, MA: Boston College.

TAFEP (Tripartite alliance for fair employment practices) (2010), *Harnessing the potential of Singapore's multi-generational workforce.* Singapore: Tripartite Alliance for Fair Employment Practices.

Thang, LengLeng (2001), *Generations in touch.* London: Cornell University Press.

Tuijnman, Albert & Boström, Ann-Kristin (2002), Changing notions of lifelong education and lifelong learning. *International Review of Education, 48*(1), pp. 93–110.

10

PROFESSIONAL DEVELOPMENT FOR OLDER COLLEAGUES

Cecilia Bjursell

The population in Sweden is living for longer and is healthier than before. As a consequence of this, the proportion of older people in the population is on the increase. In 2015, almost one in five people were over the age of 65. In 2060, it is calculated that one in four people will be over 65 years of age (SCB, 2016). Similar demographic changes are underway in many other countries. In the European Union, the ageing population is one of the most pressing social issues. The changing composition of the population will influence how companies will work on professional development within their organisations. A large number of older people have considered working for longer, past the pensionable age, but as the situation looks like now, there are a number of issues that must be solved if such a change is to be implemented with good results. There is a fear that those individuals who are ill or 'worn out' might land in a more difficult situation if they are forced to work past the pensionable age, or that those individuals who wish to continue to work will not be allowed to because of legislation or age discrimination (Bjursell et al., 2014).

This highlights a central issue about an extended working-life; namely, the importance of professional development of older workers, so that they can be better utilised within the organisation. In the Swedish *Pensionsåldersutredningen* (SOU, 2013: 25 'Retirement Age Investigation'), it is stated that an important part of an extended working-life is to provide opportunities for older workers to maintain and develop their professional competencies. This entails that a review of the relevant structures and systems with respect to professional development must take place, both in society and in organisations. Organisations should be aware of the issue of age so as to satisfy its employees' needs during different stages of their life. To offer professional development during a person's whole working life is a strategic issue for the HR department to address, and this issue demands insight into how professional development for older employees can be encouraged and structured appropriately. In the present chapter, I will demonstrate how this can take place and offer up arguments as to why older employees should be included as a relevant dimension of the strategic arrangements for professional development, from the perspective of the organisation.

Why invest in older employees' professional development?

When the issue of age is discussed in organisations, the points touched upon often include age discrimination, pension systems, or an unwillingness to invest in professional development for someone who is in the latter half of their working life or is close to retirement. In conjunction with the increasing interest from the government to raise the retirement age, it has become clear that we need changes in our current systems, attitudes, and way in which work is organised. The conditions to which older employees are subject need to change with respect to opportunities for study support and access to career advice (SOU, 2013: 25). Furthermore, adult education and labour market education systems need to be revised so as to better satisfy the needs of older employees. There are several arguments that propose that we take the issue of older employees' learning and training seriously. The workforce, irrespective of age, is faced with more and more unpredictable changes, and it is probably going to be more common that one's retirement will take place in the form of a 'phasing out from the labour market'. Thus, the adaptation and 'employability' of the current workforce will become just as important as the recruitment and introduction of new employees within an organisation (Field & Canning, 2014).

From the organisation's perspective, there are several advantages in caring for one's older employees. Older employees are often loyal to the organisation, reliable, service- and customer-orientated, possess institutional knowledge, follow a work ethic, have life experience, and are productive (Wells-Lepley et al., 2013). This cohort is generally physically and cognitively better equipped that previous generations (Swedish Government, 2014), and the provision of professional development and other learning opportunities will allow the individual's skills to be retained, if not increase such skills (Mehrotra, 2003). In Table 10.1, a number of arguments for arranging the further education, training, and professional development of older employees are summarised.

Arguments against arranging educational opportunities for the older employees are based on an assumption that such arrangements give a lower return on investment, since the older employees (as a group) have a shorter time left in the organisation (when compared with the younger employees (as a group). In today's employment market, it is, however, quite usual for an employee, irrespective of age, to change employers several times during the course of their career. In the context of 'older employees', clarification should be provided about which age group one is actually referring to. In fact, two groups are included; those who are actually pensioners but are considered to be a potential source of labour, and those who are in the latter half of their work-life. In the following section, the concept of 'age' is dealt with.

TABLE 10.1 Arguments in favour of arranging professional development opportunities for older employees

---

Organisations are faced with an increasingly diverse workforce in terms of age.

Older employees, as a group, are physically and cognitively better equipped that previous generations, and many wish to continue working.

Continual learning can contribute to maintaining or reinforcing and individual's health, knowledge, and preparedness to learn.

Demands for new knowledge and skills are constantly being made, which creates a situation where the workforce should be continually 'upgraded'.

Older employees are often stable individuals, who are loyal and productive.

The older members in an organisation constitute an important source and distribution point of knowledge within the organisation.

Who is 'older'?

The definition of who is 'older' or an 'older employee' is dependent on the context. In a primary school context, pupils who are in high school are older, whilst in later life individuals can be divided into 'old' after the age of 65, and 'elderly' after the age of 80. Studies into the learning that older people engage in usually examine learning that takes place after retirement. With respect to the context of one's work-life, the age of 65 is a pivotal age in Sweden because this age is associated with the time when one comes to the end of one's working life. 'Older' in the context of work-life is defined in relation to this time point. The Retirement age investigation (SOU, 2013: 25) has suggested increasing the retirement age, and there are now changes being made in this area which may well influence viewpoints on age in the work-life. Opportunities for education and learning are prerequisites for such changes.

A number of studies of older workers use different definitions of who is to be considered as 'older'. One study of Irish directors defined 'older' as including a wide range of ages; from 28 to 75 years old. This is somewhat unexpected when one thinks of another more common categorisation which states that older employees are 40 plus years old (McCarthy et al., 2014). The results of the Irish study could be partially explained by the fact that the Irish directors who were asked about older workers used their own ages as reference points. This is not surprising, but should be a factor which is taken into consideration before any relevant organisational decisions are made. With respect to access to professional development it is best to provide a broad definition of those who might be included in the group: 'older employees'. An important reason for this is that if the definition of 'older employee' include employees who are in the middle of their work-life, then it is possible to work proactively with arrangements to raise competencies and skills for the employees (Ilmarinen, 2001).

One alternative to solely focusing on the chronological age of the employee is to speak of 'life stages', as well as a 'third' and 'fourth age'. Another variation on this theme is to speak of different 'generational cohorts', instead of specific ages.

In today's work-life, up to five generations might work together, which may entail a great number of challenges for the HR department (Roodin & Mendelson, 2013).[1] To make proper use of the different strengths that the different generations may possess in an organisation, organisations should consider the following questions:

- How can unique, and sometimes competing, strengths in each generation be dealt with?
- Which strategies will increase each generation's productivity?
- Which strengths do older and younger employees contribute to the workplace?
- Can mentorship, coaching, or knowledge transfer contribute to intergenerational learning in your organisation?

Other ways of defining 'age', in addition to chronological age, include functional age, psychological age, organisational age, and a life-cycle perspective on age (Kooij et al., 2008; Sterns & Miklos, 1995). I will not explore further these various ways of categorising people in terms of 'age', but the point has been made that this can be done by using various points of reference. From an organisational perspective, one should consider carefully what consequences different definitions may have to arrangements that are made with people's age in mind. It is also necessary to adapt the older employees' professional development to the individual's and the organisation's unique characteristics. The benefit to be had from speaking of 'different age groups' is that it makes clear to the HR department that they can work in parallel with adapted strategies for the different generations.

Older employees' learning at work

There are only a few studies on professional development for older employees (Liu et al., 2011). The reason for this is because we are faced with a historically unique situation with the current age demographics. With respect to remaining at work, the physical work environment and psychological factors, such as preconceptions and attitudes towards older employees, are two areas that must be taken into consideration. The opportunities for learning that are offered to the individual employee are also important factors which may determine whether someone will remain in the work-life. Professional development, the work environment, and the employees' health are central areas in HR work, so it should be noted that when older employees engage in learning, this can have a positive effect on these areas. It can thus be a good idea to spend some time thinking about their needs.

It is now generally accepted that learning and professional development has moved on from being a matter related to the individual to something of importance for the organisation's development and even survival (Aronsson et al., 1996).

The individual's educational level is the one factor which, to the greatest extent, influences participation in continued studies, and this factor gains even more influence as the person ages (Bjursell et al., 2017; Skaalvik et al. in Andersson & Tøsse, 2013). The higher the educational level the individual has achieved, the more probable that the individual will engage in continued education. One reason for this is that education develops the ability to search for and sort through existing information about what is available in terms of professional development, hence these increased levels of participation (Mehrotra, 2003). Professional development which is provided so as to reinforce and develop an individual's knowledge and skills enables adaptation to and participation in the changes that take place in work-life. Professional development can provide specific knowledge and skills which are needed in the short term, but in the long term, professional development can provide opportunities where the individual's cognitive abilities are kept in good shape, in general.

The connection between health and learning, i.e., the opportunity to contribute to the individual's well-being is another benefit provided by professional development. Participation in learning activities promotes good health by providing social and cognitive stimulation. It has been claimed that the ability to learn is present even in old age (Andersson & Tøsse, 2013). Learning via cognitively demanding training and development stimulates cognitive functioning, which can be maintained throughout the years, and may even increase with such stimulus (Mehrotra, 2003).[2] Social fellowship has certain positive effects on brain function. However, certain changes in cognitive ability may occur over time. Research has shown that it can be easier for younger people to memorise data, whilst older people perform better in practical learning situations where they can become productive rapidly (Ilmarinen, 1999). It should be noted again that rough categorisations that are based purely on age can only lead to gross simplifications; in concrete situations, one must take several variables into consideration.

Retirement – preparing for take-off

The perspective that professional development is a natural part of one's career should also include a strategy for the decommissioning, or winding down, of a professional position. In today's work-life, at the time of retirement, it is usual for an individual to go 'from a hundred miles an hour to a standstill'. For the individual, such a perspective allows for an alternative to (i) either the person works or (ii) he or she does not. A more progressive approach to retirement would benefit both the individual and the organisation. Perhaps he or she can work part-time, take on a different role in the organisation, start his or her own business, or begin a new career in a completely new area.

In such a scenario, a lifelong system of study and career guidance can play an important role in the planning of professional development arrangements and career decisions for older employees who are in search of a place in the work-life which suits them (Cummins, 2014). Such a system can provide opportunities for the employee to ask questions about suitable jobs and learning activities, to consider the prerequisites that govern alternative work positions, and perhaps decide to continue with the current job or to discuss whether a reduction in work load or a transfer to another job are viable alternatives for the individual. This demands a broader perspective on professional development because such decisions may entail a new phase in the person's life, where the person can contribute to the work-life under changed conditions.

For the organisation, a transitional, or decommissioning, phase in the employee's career can offer the organisation additional flexibility in cases where the employee works only part-time. If this type of flexibility is to work optimally, then it should be informed by the individual's life conditions, so that the person can combine his or her work-life with other changes which may occur later in life (Björklund Carlstedt et al., 2017; Bjursell et al., 2014). Another benefit for the organisation with this type of 'softer' transition from work-life to retirement is that it can provide the organisation with the opportunity to collect and safeguard knowledge and skills that are possessed by the employee. For example, the employee might work in a mentor's role during the transition phase, thereby contributing to learning in the organisation. The knowledge and experience possessed by older employees are, when they are dealt with properly and 'upgraded', an asset to the organisation's professional development arrangements, in general.

Professional development via the study circle approach

An increased emphasis on professional development for older employees, together with the danger of the loss of organisational knowledge when these older employees leave the organisation, should be cause enough for the organisation to develop learning methods that are attractive to the employee. In one study of how pensioners viewed employment and learning, it was discovered that the study circle approach was the most common way of participating in education activities. In Figure 10.1, it is shown that in Bjursell et al.'s (2014) study, 102 respondents out of a total of 232 had taken part in a study circle. Educational formats numbers two and three in the figure, 'book circle' and 'senior university', were also organised in terms of the study circle approach.

The study circle approach is most closely connected to the 'folkbildning' tradition (liberal or popular adult education that does not lead to a degree). In 2012, 36% of the participants in study circles in Sweden were older than 65 years of age (Andersson et al., 2014). The study circle approach is based on the idea that each individual is involved in his or her own learning via active and equal participation (Andersson & Tøsse, 2013). The study circle approach has a long tradition within the folkbildning movement and is viewed as a democratic and emancipatory arena for adult education (Bjerkaker, 2014). There are different types of study circles, some which resemble a school classroom context, for example, for learning a foreign language (Nordzell, 2011). Notwithstanding this, the emancipatory

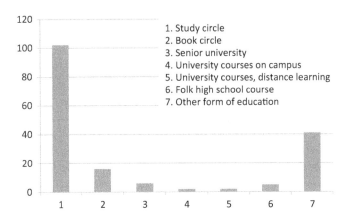

FIGURE 10.1   The number of individuals who participated in various forms of educational activities (Bjursell et al., 2014).

ambition inherent in this movement is not about 'obtaining knowledge'*per se*, but it is about challenging dominant assumptions about knowledge (Nordvall, 2002). Irrespective of the purpose of organising oneself and others into a study circle, the participants' self-education, so as to increase their knowledge in a particular area, is the main focus of such an arrangement.

Given the popularity of the study circle approach with older people, it may be of interest for us to consider whether this approach has anything to add to an organisation's professional development arrangements. Since the point of departure of a study circle is based on free and voluntary participation, at first glance, it may seem to be tricky to use the study circle approach in an organisation, where the ideal is often such that everyone is expected to 'pull their weight' in the same direction. However, there are several examples of approaches to organisational development which resemble a study circle, including; *research circles*, which have become more usual in educational institutes; *quality assurance circles*, which have emerged from the context of Japanese production industries and is now found all over the world; and *communities of practice*.

A *research circle* can resemble a study circle where one or more research competency is included (Holmstrand & Härnsten, 2003). A research circle can have different functions during the research process; from supporting the start of the research project, the analysis of the research problem, the collection of data, to the development of popular science (Abrahamsson, 2007). The group as a whole is responsible for the production of knowledge, thus the relationship between the participants is expected to be one of between equals (Holmström, 2009). An important part of this is the mix of scientifically based knowledge and experiential knowledge. A usual purpose of a research circle is professional development for teachers and lectures at school and university. Four types of research circle can be identified, based on their purpose as follows: (i) to engage in studies based on a specific theme; (ii) to be based on a subject, which is then related to didactics;

(iii) to investigate a particular issue; or (iv) to address a particular target group (Persson, 2008). Researching one's own professional practices, so as to contribute to or develop an organisation's operations, is an exciting approach which has the potential to be used outside the education sector.

Quality assurance circles were originally used in the Japanese car manufacturing industry as part of their quality assurance work, but are now also used to engage with other development areas (Dahlgaard-Park, 2011; Tang & Buler, 1997). A group of colleagues with similar tasks meet with each other under the leadership of a boss or manager with the purpose of solving any problems in one's own sphere of responsibility. Such operational improvements (i.e., solutions to any existing or anticipated problems) are then shared with the company management, who may or may not approve what is suggested by the quality circle. However, it is desirable that the employees themselves implement the new solution or operational improvement (if it is approved), since it is believed that this will promote the employees' motivation. Quality assurance circles were most popular during the 1980s, but they still can be found in different forms today. Tand and Bultler (1997) identify seven areas which are necessary for the proper functioning of a quality circle: (i) management support, (ii) the participant's commitment, (iii) good problem-solving abilities, (iv) a low staff turnover amongst the participants (i.e., employee continuity), (v) knowledge of the nature of the task, (vi) support from other people in the organisation, and (vii) access to information and adequate time to perform the task on hand. Quality assurance circles are primarily focussed on operational development, and not an individual's professional development. However, such arrangements remain a source of continual learning.

A *community of practice* constitutes a more theoretical model for collective, experiential learning (Wenger, 1998). Communities of practice focus on informal learning that may take place in a work team or a network. Depending on the timeframe and the researcher, different definitions have been provided for this term; including 'learning between an expert and novice', 'personal development', or 'a tool for management to develop the organisation' (Li et al., 2009). Despite the fact that the theory highlights the informal, experiential, and social aspects of learning, it does occur that communities of practice are used as a management tool to promote knowledge development in an organisation. One area where 'communities of practice' has become a popular tool is in the healthcare industry. A *profession* can form the basis for a community of practice which is involved in solving shared problems (Heery & Noon, 2008). In a community of practice, informal learning that is directed by the persons' interests can take place. Variations of this model include groups who have gathered their attention around a product or theme, so as to develop their knowledge and keep up to date in areas which undergo continual change.

The above discussion demonstrates that there is a whole repertoire of different approaches to professional development that are similar to the study circle. An approach based on the study circle in the context of work-life could function as a bridge between practical experience and theoretical learning (Lahn, 2003). An important contribution made by the study circle approach is the emphasis placed on the participants' commitment to, and responsibility for, organising the study circle and maintaining order in the group. This, in combination with solving problems in a particular context, can stimulate development and allow for the transfer of knowledge and experience from older employees to the organisation.

The study circle approach to professional development for older employees

The study circle approach can be of value to an organisation's professional development arrangements. Many older employees prefer the free form of learning, which is based on previous knowledge and experiences and emphasis on one's own responsibility. The following questions may provide some guidance to an organisation which may wish to decide to introduce a study circle approach in the organisation's professional development arrangements:

*   Which previous experience do the employees have of professional development? If all previous professional development activities have been passive in nature, then the employees need to be introduced to ways of working with more self-reliant and independent approaches to learning.
*   Who is ultimately responsible for the organisation and execution of the professional development arrangements? Study circles are stimulating because of the active participation and the shared responsibility of the participants, but questions remain concerning the support, time, and other resources that will be provided by the organisation.
*   Is the study circle approach fit-for-purpose for the particular area, subject, or problem that is to be the focus of investigation? The study circle approach is suitable if the framework is broad in scope with respect to the content of what is to be learnt, its implementation, and the timeframe in which the implementation is to take place. Research, development, and subject knowledge are three areas which are suited to the study circle approach to learning. If, for example, a message from the organisation's management is to be communicated to everyone in the organisation, then a study circle approach to this task would not be the most suitable approach.

Older employees as individuals and professionals

Lifelong education and learning is one way to maintain and increase an individual's knowledge, abilities, and skills. We have now discussed the study circle approach and described it as a suitable educational form which can be used to maintain and build upon the knowledge and experience that individuals have gained earlier in their work-life. This is a popular approach for older employees, but from a planning perspective, other factors must also be taken into consideration. First, there exist similar arrangements that can be used for organisational development, including research circles, quality assurance circles, and communities of practice. In addition to these, there are several other ways to engage with professional development, both within and without the organisation. An important question to ask is: *When is it suitable to use the study circle approach?*

An overarching principle to consider when one is to choose a particular approach to professional development is to note that an employee is, first and foremost, an *individual*, with a unique combination of characteristics, expectations, and abilities. It is said that we become more different from each other the older we get (Lahn, 2003). Older employees thus form a heterogeneous group, but they do have one thing in common: their participation in educational activities decreases rapidly with age (Field & Canning, 2014). Golding (2015) reports on the unwillingness of older, poorly educated men to participate in formal educational courses, but also shows that the same men are happy to participate as a group in informal learning contexts. Previous experiences and educational habits influence how an individual engages with future educational programmes or courses. Fenwick (2012) investigated older accounting consultants and discovered that a continual process of learning formed the basis of these professional's identity as specialists. The accounting consultants took individual responsibility to keep up to date in their field and employed different strategies to develop the degree of expertise which is demanded by the profession. What was missing from their professional development arrangements was a critical examination of the underlying structures and a lack of generalisations concerning knowledge. The most important point raised by Fenwick's study is how it highlights the fact that we need to understand the learning process of older people in relation to an individual, professional, and organisational context.

Golding (2015) and Fenwick (2012) both argue that learning must be organised based on the individual's conditions and commitment if such learning is to be successful. When education and learning are working well, this can induce health-promoting effects in addition to increasing the individual's knowledge and skills. From the organisation's perspective, such learning may influence the individual to remain in employment, thereby highlighting the importance of professional development throughout the employee's whole career. This entails that the HR department should adopt a life-cycle perspective so as to increase the effectiveness of its professional development arrangements with respect to the subject area that is to be dealt with, the individual's characteristics, and age (Lahn, 2003). The HR department has an important role to play in showing how the knowledge that is possessed by older employees can be used to good effect to support the professional development of older employees (Field & Canning, 2014). This is most applicable for individuals who are unused to studying and need organisational support for this. The advantages, and success, with the study circle approach is found in the fact that it places emphasis on the participant's own responsibility to engage in learning and the social dimension of learning as a group. This is something which the HR department can build upon as it formulates its strategies for the professional development of older employees.

Recommended reading

Field, John, Burke, Ronald J. & Cooper, Cary L. (eds.) (2013), *The Sage handbook of aging, work and society*. London: Sage.
Parry, Emma & McCarthy, Jean (eds.) (2017), *The Palgrave handbook of age diversity and work*. London: Palgrave Macmillan.
Thomas, Robyn, Hardy, Cynthia, Cutcher, Leanne & Ainsworth, Susan (2014), What's age got to do with it? On the critical analysis of age and organizations. *Organization Studies*, *35*(11), pp. 1569–1584.

Notes

1 The reader is also referred to Chapter 9 for a deeper discussion of intergenerational learning.
2 Physical exercise is also important to maintaining one's cognitive abilities, but the one does not exclude the other.

References

Abrahamsson, Kenneth (2007), *Från arbetarhögskola till forskningscirkel: Svenska bildningsvägar i utbildningsexpansionens samhälle*. [From a worker's college to a research circle: Swedish educational pathways in a society where education is expanding.] Halmstad: Premiss.
Andersson, Eva, Bernerstedt, Mats, Forsmark, Jan, Rydenstam, Klas & Åberg, Pelle (2014), *Cirkeldeltagare efter 65: Livskvalitet och aktivt medborgarskap*. [Study circle participation after the age of 65: Quality of life and active citizenship]. Stockholm: Folkbildningsrådet.
Andersson, Eva & Tøsse, Sivart (2013), Tid för studier efter sextiofem. [Time for studies after 65]. In Andreas Fejes (ed.), *Lärandets mångfald: Om vuxenpedagogik och folkbildning.* [The diversity of learning: About adult learner pedagogy and liberal adult education] (pp. 89–106). Lund: Studentlitteratur.
Aronsson, Gunnar, Hallsten, Lennart, Kilbom, Åsa, Torgén, Margareta & Westerholm, Peter (1996), Äldres arbetsliv – slutsatser och nya frågor. [The work-life of older adults –conclusions and new questions] In Gunnar Aronsson & Åsa Kilbom (eds.), *Arbete efter 45: Historiska, psykologiska och fysiologiska perspektiv på äldre i arbetslivet.* [Work after 45: Historical, psychological, and physiological perspectives on older adults in work-life] (pp. 261–278). Solna: Arbetslivsinstitutet.
Bjerkaker, Sturla (2014), Changing communities: The study circle – for learning and democracy. *Procedia – Social and Behavioral Sciences*, *142*, pp. 260–267.
Björklund Carlstedt, Anita, Brushammar, Gunilla, Bjursell, Cecilia, Nystedt, Paul & Nilsson, Gunilla (2017), A scoping review of the incentives for a prolonged work-life after pensionable age and the importance of "bridge employment". *Work: A Journal of Prevention, Assessment and Rehabilitation.* 60(2), pp. 175–189.
Bjursell, Cecilia, Bergeling, Ingegerd, Bengtsson Sandberg, Karin, Hultman, Svante & Ebbesson, Sven (2014), *Ett aktivt åldrande: Pensionärers syn på arbete och lärande.* [An active aging: Pensioners' views on work and learning]. Encell rapport 1:2014. Visby: Nomen/Books on demand.
Bjursell, Cecilia, Nystedt, Paul, Björklund, Anita & Sternäng, Ola (2017), Education level explains participation in work and education later in life. *Educational Gerontology*, *43*(10), pp. 511–521.
Cummins, Phyllis A. (2014), Effective strategies for educating older workers at community colleges. *Educational Gerontology*, *40*(5), pp. 338–352.

Dahlgaard-Park, Su Mi (2011), The quality movement: Where are you going? *Total Quality Management & Business Excellence*, *22*(5), pp. 493–516.

Fenwick, Tara (2012), Older professional workers and continuous learning in new capitalism. *Human Relations*, *65*(8), pp. 1001–1020.

Field, John & Canning, Roy (2014), Lifelong learning and employers: Reskilling older workers. In Sarah Harper & Kate Hamblin (eds.), *International handbook on ageing and public policy* (pp. 463–473). Cheltenham: Edgar Elgar.

Golding, Barry (ed.) (2015), *The men's shed movement: The company of men*. Champaign: Common Ground Publishing.

Heery, Edmund & Noon, Mike (2008), *A dictionary of human resource management*. (2nd edition) Oxford: Oxford University Press.

Holmstrand, Lars & Härnsten, Gunilla (2003), *Förutsättningar för forskningscirklar i skolan: En kritisk granskning*. [Conditions for research circles at school: A critical review]. Stockholm: Myndigheten för skolutveckling.

Holmström, Ola (2009), *Perspektiv på karta och terräng: Utvärdering av forskningscirklar*. [Perspectives on maps and terrain: An evaluation of research circles]. Malmö stad: Avdelning barn och ungdom, FoU-utbildning, Resurscentrum för mångfaldens skola.

Ilmarinen, Juhani (1999), *Ageing workers in the European Union: Status and promotion of work ability, employability and employment*. Helsinki: Finnish Institute of Occupational Health and Ministry of Social Affairs and Health.

Ilmarinen, Juhani (2001), Aging workers. *Occupational & Environmental Medicine*, *58*(8), pp. 546–552.

Kooij, Dorien, de Lange, Annet, Jansen, Paul & Dikkers, Josje (2008), 'Older workers' motivation to continue to work: Five meanings of age. *Journal of Managerial Psychology*, *23*(4), pp. 364–394.

Lahn, Leif (2003), Competence and learning in late career. *European Educational Research Journal*, *2*(1), pp. 126–140.

Li, Linda C., Grimshaw, Jeremy M., Nielsen, Camilla, Judd, Maria, Coyte, Peter C. & Graham, Ian D. (2009), Evolution of Wenger's concept of community of practice. *Implementation Science*, *4*(1), 11.

Liu, Su-Fen, Courtenay, Bradley C. & Valentine, Thomas (2011), Managing older worker training: A literature review and conceptual framework. *Educational Gerontology*, *37*(12), pp. 1040–1062.

McCarthy, Jean, Heraty, Noreen, Cross, Christine & Cleveland, Jeanette N. (2014), Who is considered an 'older worker'? Extending our conceptualisation of 'older' from an organisational decision maker perspective. *Human Resource Management Journal*, *24*(4), pp. 374–393.

Mehrotra, Chandra M. (2003), In defense of offering educational programs for older adults. *Educational Gerontology*, *29*(8), pp. 645–655.

Nordvall, Henrik (2002), Folkbildning som mothegemonisk praktik? [Liberal education as a diverse practice]. *Utbildning och demokrati*, *11*(2), pp. 15–32.

Nordzell, Anita (2011), *Samtal i studiecirkel: Hur går det till när cirkeldeltagare gör cirkel?* [Dialogue in a study circle: How do study circle participants create study circles?]. Stockholm: Stockholms universitets förlag.

Persson, Sven (2008), *Forskningscirklar – en vägledning*. [Research circles – a guide]. Malmö stad: avdelning barn och ungdom, FoU-utbildning, Resurscentrum för mångfaldens skola.

Roodin, Paul & Mendelson, Maeona (2013), Multiple generations at work: Current and future trends. *Journal of Intergenerational Relationships*, *11*(3), pp. 213–222.

SCB (2016), *Hur stor är Sveriges folkmängd 2060?* [How large will Sweden's population be in 2060?]. Retrieved from www.sverigeisiffror.scb.se [2016-03-15].

SOU (2013:25), *Åtgärder för ett längre arbetsliv*. [Actions for an extended work-life]. Official Reports of the Swedish Government. Stockholm: Socialdepartementet.

Sterns, Harvey L. & Miklos, Suzanne M. (1995), The aging worker in a changing environment: Organizational and individual issues. *Journal of Vocational Behavior*, 47(3), pp. 248–268.

Swedish Government (2014), Ett förlängt arbetsliv: Forskning om arbetstagarnas och arbetsmarknadens förutsättningar. Rapporter från riksdagen 2013/14:RFR8. [An extended work-life: Research into employees and labour market conditions. Reports from the Swedish Government].

Tang, Thomas & Butler, Edie (1997), Attributions of quality circles' problem-solving failure: Differences among management, supporting staff, and quality circle members. *Public Personnel Management*, 26(2), pp. 203–225.

Wells-Lepley, Meredith, Swanberg, Jennifer, Williams, Lisa, Nakai, Yoshie & Grosch, James W. (2013), The voices of Kentucky employers: Benefits, challenges, and promising practices for an aging workforce. *Journal of Intergenerational Relationships*, 11(3), pp. 255–271.

Wenger, Etienne (1998), *Communities of practice: Learning, meaning, and identity*. Cambridge: Cambridge University Press.

11

UNDERSTANDING WHY AN IMMIGRANT NEUROSURGEON IS DRIVING YOUR TAXI

On highly qualified foreign labour looking for work in your country

Roland S. Persson and Vezir Aktas

When casually discussing everyday life with the local 'pizzaiolo', one of the authors of this chapter asked what background he had and what lead him to launch his restaurant. The fact that about half of his menu featured not only a considerable variety of unusual pizzas but also a variety of Middle Eastern fast food prompted my question. 'I moved here from Iraq,' he said cordially, 'and I am an electrical engineer by trade'. I was stunned by his answer and wondered what made him choose making pizzas and serving kebabs (sometimes in combination!) over a continued career in engineering. He looked at me in frustration and replied:

> I told Swedish immigration authorities when arriving here from war-torn Iraq what profession I had and how eager I was to continue doing the same here. Their response was to send me to labour market–adapted training arguing that this was suitable as an introduction to the Swedish working context. It made perfect sense at first and I accepted the kind offer. On the very first day of training, however, I was shown by an instructor how to connect a cord to a plug that goes into the wall socket. This was electrical engineering according to the immigration authority. I have never felt so insulted in all of my life! I left angrily never to return. I decided to start my own business – any business – and I chose to do food! Everyone has to eat. Swedes love pizza. I needed a job!

My Iraqi acquaintance is by no means unique. Sweden abounds with pizzerias. They exist even in the most remote and sparsely populated communities and villages. Most of these pizzerias, if not all, have something in common; the proprietors do not stem from Italy as one would expect considering the Neapolitan origins of pizza (Helstosky, 2008). Swedish pizza-makers tend to hail from Lebanon, Syria, Iraq, and Turkey – often because there are few other options open to them in gaining access to the labour market, no matter how highly qualified they may be when they arrive to Sweden as immigrants (Hultman, 2013).

The dilemma of not effectively aligning these immigrants' qualifications and experience with suitable jobs in their new country is ubiquitous. It is an international problem interchangeably referred to as *discrimination* (Carlsson & Rooth, 2007; Dustmann & Preston, 2007), *brain abuse, brain waste* (Bauder, 2003; Brandi, 2001), or even as *ethnic penalty* in the sense that immigrant labour is, in various ways, disadvantaged by the market for not being similar enough in terms of culture and appearance to gain the same acceptance and trust that cultural natives enjoy (Carmichael & Woods, 2000; Heath & Cheung, 2006; Koopmans, 2017).

The national economy and the effects of immigration are exceedingly complex issues. Contrary to general belief, however, research has clearly shown that immigration has an overall positive effect on the receiving country's economy. It is useful to note that some of the countries which have historically received the greatest numbers of immigrants are currently also among the world's wealthiest (Bodvarsson & van den Berg, 2013). It is difficult to argue for any negative impact of immigration with reference to Australia, Canada, New Zealand, and the United States! Silicon Valley in California, for example, the arguably most important centre for IT innovation and development in the world, is not likely to have become a place of such iconic significance without the influx of skilled Asian immigrants. These account for at least one third of the Silicon Valley workforce (Saxenian, 2002). Immigration, in general, is beneficial to the recipient country. Immigrant *skilled* labour, no matter where such labour comes from, is likely to be even more beneficial to the host country, if not a *necessity* for the country's continued economic development (Borjas, 1995; Boubtane, Dumont & Rault, 2016; International Organization for Migration, 2018).

Understanding the difficulties that skilled immigrant labour endures when trying to find a suitable job will allow us to suggest useful practices for organisations and businesses which they can more effectively employ and integrate such labour at the workplace. This is especially important since most countries suffer from a shortage of suitably skilled labour. The reason for the current alarming shortage of skilled labour in many countries too is that highly qualified individuals often leave their country of origin for greener pastures as they move to other, more attractive, countries (Boeri et al., 2012; Cohen & Zaidi, 2002; Gordon, 2009). Alternatively, there is simply not a sufficient number of individuals who are being trained to satisfy national needs for certain skills and areas of expertise (Frey & Osborne, 2017; Özden & Schiff, 2006).

Much experience, expertise, and the creative benefits of different cultural perspectives risk being lost because of lengthy integration processes (for bureaucratic reasons) and because of certain difficulties posed by social-cultural dynamics. While employers cannot easily influence legislative frameworks by which immigration is organised politically, they most certainly can influence the social dynamics within their own organisation and thereby benefit from foreign skilled labour who might apply for work in their company. The objective of this chapter, therefore, is to propose how individual companies and organisations can implement human resource practices which are based on a better understanding of social-cultural dynamics, for the benefit of the company or organisation, as well as for the benefit of their immigrant employees.

The ordeals of an immigrant employee

The short supply of skilled labour is indeed a current problem worldwide (Frey & Osborne, 2017; Michaels, Handfield-Jones & Axelrod, 2001; World Economic Forum, 2016). It is easy to understand why many policymakers and employers have almost desperately turned their attention to finding skilled labour from overseas since their own resources are no longer sufficient. Terms such as *brain drain, brain gain, brain waste,* and so on have emerged to describe the growing migration of much-needed human capital between countries and continents. Owing to conflict and war, however, such human capital is also increasingly becoming part of the millions of refugees across the world who are seeking a new home in other countries. It would seem that the individuals with the means to escape are also often people with professional experience and university qualifications. The number of highly qualified immigrants is consistently rising. In 2014, they accounted for 31 million migrants in the OECD countries, yet their unemployment rate is surprisingly 50% higher than that of the natives of these countries (OECD, 2014). In the European Union, 25% of all migrants arrive with completed university training (OECD/EU, 2015). Where skilled labour is in short supply, this addition to a national workforce would, in all likelihood, solve quite a few pressing problems. Their arrival to another country and their subsequent entry into the labour market, however, is rarely an easy process. Highly skilled job applicants are forced to face many an obstacle which they cannot themselves influence. Instead, they often become innocent victims of bureaucratic inertia and social-cultural dynamics.

Fettered by an ethnocentric bureaucracy

Highly skilled immigrants will usually have to pass formal 'equivalency' evaluations of their previous training before being allowed to apply for certain jobs, notwithstanding the fact that they may have already successfully worked in these professional positions for a long period of time at home. No matter how highly qualified and experienced these immigrants might be, their education is as a rule ethnocentrically viewed as *less* valid in comparison to equivalent training offered in the recipient country. This bias is particularly true in high-income countries (Bauder, 2003; Bonfanti & Xenogiani, 2014; Ferrer & Riddell, 2008; Huddleston, Niessen & Tjaden, 2013; Nieto, Matano & Ramos, 2015; Nordin, 2011). While waiting for such 'equivalency' validation, or in the end failing to obtain it, these immigrants, if they are to survive, have no choice but to seek and accept work for which they are often grossly overqualified. A Somali neurosurgeon is likely to be driving your taxi or an Iraqi electrical engineer will be making you lunch in a Scandinavian pizzeria (Quintini, 2011). Studies have shown that these immigrants' professional situation occasionally improves over time. As they develop their language skills further and become more integrated into society, they also tend to land better jobs. However, these are not necessarily the same highly qualified jobs as they once held (Huddleston, Niessen & Tjaden, 2013; Latif, 2015). Astonishingly, for some, their professional prospects have not improved at all, not even after a decade. National bureaucracy is usually to blame (Szulkin et al., 2013).

Dealing with suspicion and xenophobia

Any migrant will face a degree of acculturation stress; this includes encountering different values, traditions, and behaviours foreign to what they are used to. Such stress will be more severe and be more difficult to resolve the greater the cultural differences are between their native country and their new country (Gupta, Hanges & Dorfman, 2002). If the skilled immigrant also has refugee status, then stress reactions are likely to be much more complex. In addition to coping with new cultural patterns, they are also waiting for decisions to be taken by authorities whether they will be allowed to stay in the host country or not. This is their greatest source of stress, by far (Hallas et al., 2007; Laban et al., 2004).

Encountering natives of the new host culture will be the first social challenge. Foreigners are not always immediately accepted by the residents of the host country. Attitudes towards immigration vary depending on age, level of education and income, political orientation, the current condition of the national economy, the number of immigrants already in the country, and to some degree also on personal dispositions (Ervasti, 2004; Paas & Halapaluu, 2012). Although the attitudes which immigrants encounter have a complex origin, the younger generation with a university education generally tend to be more accepting of immigration and foreigners, whereas members of the older generation often tend to resist change and be less tolerant (Chandler & Tsai, 2001; Hainmueller & Hiscox, 2007; McLaren, 2001; Winkler, 2015).

Dealing with discrimination

The degree of discrimination that immigrants have to deal with varies from country to country, but it is known that it is more common that women and labour from low-income and developing countries are discriminated against (OECD/EU, 2015). Interestingly, being treated unfairly in the new country is a problem that arises irrespective of the immigrant's competence, training, and experience (Arai, Bursell & Nekby, 2008; Bertrand & Mullainathan, 2004; Lamba, 2003; Rydgren, 2004). For example, job applicants who have a foreign name are less likely to be offered an interview (Carlsson & Roth, 2007). Foreign labour will have to make much more of an effort in finding a job. To finally receive a positive reply from a potential employer, they will have had to submit three to five times as many applications as any native candidate (Zegers de Beijl, 2000).

To resolve this situation, some immigrants give in and decide to marry a native. Surprisingly, this increases their chance of employment by 11%. The reasons for this increase are unknown, but gaining access to a social network that might otherwise be inaccessible to them has been suggested as one explanation for this increase (Chi, 2015; Furtado & Theodoropoulos, 2009).

Not getting access to suitable work and discovering that they are being discriminated against adversely affects many immigrant job applicant's health. Highly qualified immigrant labour is particularly prone to suffering from mental health problems, such as stress-related illness and depression because of their continued struggle with trying to find suitable work (Ahlsten, Davin & Lindholm-Billing, 2013; Dean & Wilson, 2009).

Why are employers (and quite a few other individuals) xenophobic?

It is a fact that nationality, or group membership, most often take precedence when there is a choice to be made between (i) an expert with great experience and skills but of foreign extraction and (ii) a lesser skilled and experienced candidate but of the same country and culture as the recruiting company (Jureidini, 2003). Why is it that an employer is prepared to settle for a candidate who is less suitable and less competent in such a situation?

Xenophobia, or the fear of strangers, is fundamental to human behaviour, and is apparent already during childhood. It sets a limit on the outward reach of identification and imitation. Konner (2007) explains that such behaviour is motivated by children staying close to their primary caregivers, thereby strengthening the bond between family members. As the child grows older, this automatic fear turns into suspicion and prejudice against everyone who the child cannot identify with or relate to. Put into more technical terms: 'xenophobia is an important component of the human behavioural repertoire. It is a phylogenetic adaptation [...]' (Eibl-Eibesfeldt, 1989: 174). In other words, being afraid or suspicious of individuals who we do not know, cannot recognise, behave differently, look differently, and speak a language that we cannot comprehend triggers a mechanism we are all born with (CeaD'Ancona, 2016; Hjerm & Nagayoshi, 2011; Raijman, Semyonov & Schmidt, 2003). Importantly, however, this human universal function is subject to modification by learning. Once strangers become more familiar and we learn to recognise them and relate to them in various ways, then fear and suspicion are likely to subside and eventually disappear altogether.

Continued fear and suspicion into adulthood is often more an indication of a lack of experience and knowledge of foreign cultures and behaviours than it is of an intentional ideological stance. We rarely make a conscious and intentional effort to be discriminatory or prejudiced! More qualified applicants for a certain job position may well be discarded because the employer is faced with someone culturally unknown. Unfortunately, this reaction wrongly translates into 'not as competent, suitable, or trustworthy as someone from my own country'. Or as expressed in a somewhat crude but effective idiom: 'Better the devil you know than the devil you don't.' The solution to the problem, at least in part, is to obtain information and experience of cultures other than your own!

Practical advice to human resources personnel

Immigration and integration are both dependent on government policies. There are, however, some aspects of labour market integration which HR departments may influence to the benefit of the organisation, the business, as well as the immigrant skilled work force in general as follows:

- Avoid underestimating employees from different cultures and the experience that they already have in their chosen profession. Diversity of knowledge, experience, and points of view constitute a fertile ground for innovation and creativity (Davison & Ekelund, 2004; Schmidt & Rosenberg, 2014; Snell et al., 1998). Its opposite – homogeneity, dogmatism, and no or little experience of other cultures and ways of thinking – is likely to have the opposite effect. Such an attitude prevents new ideas and fresh approaches from emerging (Forte, 2008; Horwath, 2012; Lamprecht & Ricci, 2009).
- It would be wise to become familiar with the notion of 'ethnocentrism' and what it means in theory and practice. To be informed about various ethnicities in a multicultural and diverse society is, beyond doubt, the most effective way of avoiding misunderstanding and discriminatory behaviour. Being unfamiliar with cultural diversity automatically *distorts* the perception of someone's suitability, even when this person holds tremendous formal credentials and experience. The immigrant skilled labour that was discarded might well have been someone who could turn a business or an organisation into a considerable success.
- Note that a vast majority of immigrants are eager to normalise their everyday life. Like every native to any society, immigrants want an everyday life by acquiring a job, a place to live, and obtain a normal existence. This means that it is also likely that because of their social status as a resident in a new country, they are *strongly* motivated to integrate and do a given job extremely well, perhaps even much better than expected by the employer. Never underestimate the motivating force of wanting to 'fit in' (Baumeister, 2012; Hällgren, 2005; Neuberg, Smith & Asher, 2003). Seeking social approval and acceptance will make most immigrant labour both willing and able to 'walk the extra mile', even if this is not required.
- Never ignore the fact that cultural differences strongly affect expectations on who should do what and how. This includes how employees relate to leadership and team work, and how they understand seniority and gender roles, since these may differ between cultures. Avoid allowing these different understandings to be a cause for conflict. Problems can be easily averted if both native and immigrant employees are offered opportunities to learn

about each others' cultural differences, and how these differences might relate to the organisation and its own culture (see, for example, Meyer, 2014).

- At the outset, it might be wise to allow immigrant employees to work with
younger well-educated colleagues for the simple reason that they tend to
be more welcoming of cultural diversity than the older generation, and are
often more able to use diversity to everyone's advantage.

Recommended reading

Browaeys, M. J., & Price, R. (2008). *Understanding cross-cultural management*. Harlow, UK:
Prentice-Hall/Financial Times.
Jandt, F. E. (2016). *An introduction to intercultural communication: Identities in a global commu-
nity*. London: Sage.
Meyer, E. (2014). *The culture map. Decoding how people think, lead, and get things done across
cultures*. New York: Public Affairs.
Shukla, N. (2014). *The good immigrant*. London: Unbound.
Tan Chen, V. (2015). *Cut loose. Jobless and hopeless in an unfair economy*. Oakland, CA:
University of California Press.

References

Ahlsten, M., Davin, K., & Lindholm-Billing, K. (2013). *A new beginning; Flyktingintegra-
tion i Sverige: Det handlar om tid!* [A new beginning; Refugee integration in Sweden:
It is all about time!] Stockholm: United Nations High Commissioner for Refugees,
Regional branch for Northern Europe.
Arai, M., Bursell, M., & Nekby, L. (2008). *Between meritocracy and ethnic discrimination: The
gender difference* (Discussion paper no. 3467) Bonn, Germany: Institute for the Study
of Labor, http://ftp.iza.org/dp3467.pdf (Accessed 4 January 2018).
Bauder, H. (2003). 'Brain abuse'. Or the devaluation of immigrant labour in Canada.
Antipode, 35(4), 699–717.
Baumeister, R. F. (2012). The theory of belonging. In P. A. M. Van Lange, A. W.
Kruglanski, & E. T. Higgins (Eds.), *Handbook of theories of social psychology: Volume two*
(121–140). London: Sage Publications.
Bertrand, M., & Mullainathan, S. (2004). Are Emily and Greg more employable than
Lakisha and Jamal? A field experiment on labor market discrimination. *American Eco-
nomic Review*, 94, 991–1013.
Bodvarsson, Ö. B., & Van den Berg, H. (2013). *The economics of immigration: Theory and
policy* (2nd edition). New York: Springer.
Boeri, T., Brücker, H., Docquier, F., & Rapoport, H. (Eds.). (2012). *Brain drain and brain
gain. The global competition to attract high-skilled migrants*. Oxford, UK: Oxford Univer-
sity Press.
Bonfanti, S., & Xenogiani, T. (2014). Migrants' skills: Use, mismatch and labour market
outcomes – A first exploration of the international survey of adult skills (PIAAC), in
Matching economic migration with labour market needs (249–312), Paris: OECD Publishing.
Borjas, G. J. (1995). The economic benefits from immigration. *Journal of Economic
Perspectives*, 9(2), 3–22.
Boubtane, E., Dumont, J. C., & Rault, C. (2016). Immigration and economic growth in
the OECD countries 1986–2006. *Oxford Economic Papers*, 68(2), 340–360. doi:10.1093/
oep/gpw001.

Brandi, M. C. (2001). Skilled immigrants in Rome. *International Migration*, 39(4), 101–131.

Carlsson, M., & Rooth, D. O. (2007). Evidence of ethnic discrimination in the Swedish labor market using experimental data. *Labor Economics*, 14, 716–729.

Carmichael, F., & Woods, R. (2000). Ethnic penalities in unemployment and occupational attainment. *International Review of Applied Economics*, 14(1), 71–98.

Cea D'Ancona, A. (2016). Immigration as a threat: Explaining the changing pattern of xenophobia in Spain, *International Migration & Integration*, 17, 569–591.

Chandler, C. R., & Tsai, Y.-m. (2001). Social factors influencing immigration attitudes: An analysis of data from the General Social Survey. *The Social Science Journal*, 38(2), 177–188. http://dx.doi.org/10.1016/S0362-3319(01)00106-9.

Chi, M. (2015). Does intermarriage promote economic assimilation among immigrants in the United States? *International Journal of Manpower*, 36(7), 1034–1057.

Cohen, M. S., & Zaidi, M. A. (2002). *Global skill shortages*. Cheltenham, UK: Edward Elgar.

Davison, S. C., & Ekelund, B. Z. (2004). Effective team processes for global teams. In H. W. Maznevski, M. L. Mendenhall, & J. M. E. McNett (Eds.), *The blackwell handbook of global management* (pp. 227–249). Oxford, UK: Blackwell.

Dean, A. J., & Wilson, K. (2009). 'Education? It is irrelevant to my job now. It makes me very depressed…': Exploring the health impacts of under/unemployment among highly skilled recent immigrants in Canada. *Ethnicity & Health*, 14(2), 185–204.

Dustmann, C., & Preston, I. P. (2007). Racial and economic factors in attitudes to immigration. *The Berkley Electronic Press Journal of Economic Analysis & Policy*, 7(1), 1–39.

Eibl-Eibesfeldt, I. (1989). *Human ethology*. New York: Aldine de Gruyter.

Ervasti, H. (2004). Attitudes towards foreign-born settlers: Finland in a comparative perspective. *Yearbook of Population Research in Finland*, 40, 25–44.

Ferrer, A., & Riddell, W. C. (2008). Education, credentials and immigrant earnings. *Canadian Journal of Economics*, 41(1), 186–216. doi:10.1111/j.1365–2966.2008.00460.x.

Forte, S. (2008). *Dare to be different! A complete guide for those who want to make it to the top*. Oxford, UK: Management Books 2000.

Frey, C. B., & Osborne, M. A. (2017). The future of employment: How susceptible are jobs to computerisation? *Technological Forecasting and Social Change*, 114, 254–280.

Furtado, D., & Theodoropoulos, N. (2009). 'I'll marry you if you get me a job: Marital assimilation and immigrant employment rates. *International Journal of Manpower*, 30(1/2). 116–126.

Gordon, E. (2009). The global talent crisis. *The Futurist*, 43(5), 34–39.

Gupta, V., Hanges, P. J., & Dorfman, P. (2002). Cultural clusters: Methodology and findings. *Journal of World Business*, 37, 11–15.

Hainmueller, J., & Hiscox, M. J. (2007). Educated preferences: Explaining attitudes toward immigration in Europe. *International Organization*, 61(2), 399–442.

Hallas, P., Hansen, A. R., Staehr, M. A., Munk-Andersen, E., & Jorgensen, H. L. (2007). Length of stay in asylum centres and mental health in asylum seekers: A retrospective study. *BMC Public Health*, 7, 288–294, doi:10.1186/1471–2458-7-288.

Hällgren, C. (2005). 'Working harder to be the same': Everyday racism among young men and women in Sweden. *Race Ethnicity and Education*, 8(3), 319–342.

Heath, A., & Cheung, S. Y. (2006). *Ethnic penalties in the labour market: Employers and discrimination* (Research report no. 341). London: Department for Work and Pensions, available at http://webarchive.nationalarchives.gov.uk (Accessed 28 December 2017).

Helstosky, C. (2008). *Pizza: A global history*. London: Reaktion Books.

Hjerm, M., & Nagayoshi, K. (2011). The composition of the minority population as a threat: Can real economic and cultural threats explain xenophobia? *International Sociology*, 26(6), 815–843.

Horwath, R. (2012). To realize your potential, 'dare to be different'. *On-line: CNN International Edition*. http://edition.cnn.com/2012/02/24/opinion/horwath-strategy-different/index.html (Accessed 4 January 2018).

Huddleston, T., Niessen, J., & Tjaden, J.D. (2013). *Using EU indicators of immigrant integration. Final Report for Directorate-General for Home Affairs*. Brussels: European Commission.

Hultman, H. (2013). *Liv och arbete i pizzabranschen* [The life and business of Swedish piz-zaioli] (Doctoral dissertation in sociology). Lund, Sweden: Arkiv Förlag.

International Organization for Migration (2018). *World Migration Report 2018*, Geneva, CH:IOM,www.iom.int/ (Accessed 22 March 2018).

Jureidini, R. (2003). *Migrant workers and xenophobia in the Middle East* (Identities, conflict and cohesion programme paper no. 2). Geneva, CH: United Nations Research Institute for Social Development.

Konner, M. (2007). Evolutionary foundations of cultural psychology. In S. Kitayama & D. Cohen (Eds.), *Handbook of cultural psychology* (77–108). New York: Guilford Press.

Koopmans, R. (2017). *Assimilation oder Multikulturalismus? Bedingungen gelungener Integration* [Assimilation or multiculturalism? Conditions for successful integration]. Münster, Germany: LIT Verlag.

Lamba, N. K. (2003). The employment experiences of Canadian refugees: Measuring the impact of human and social capital on quality of Employment. *Canadian Review of Sociology/Revue Canadienne de Sociologie*, 40(1), 45–64. doi:10.1111/j.1755-618x.2003.tb00235.x.

Laban, C. J., Gernaat, B. P. E. H., Komproe, I, H., Schreuders, B. A., & De Jong, T. V. M. J. (2004). Impact of long asylum procedure on the prevalence of psychiatric disorders in Iraqi asylum seekers in the Netherlands. *The Journal of Nervous and Mental Disease*, 192(12), 843–851.

Lamprecht, J. L., & Ricci, R. (2009). *Dare to be different! Reflections of certain business practices*. Milwaukee, WI: ASQ Quality Press.

Latif, E. (2015). The relationship between immigration and unemployment: Panel data evidence from Canada. *Economic Modelling*, 50, 162–167.

McLaren, L. M. (2001). Immigration and the new politics of inclusion and exclusion in the European Union: The effect of elites and the EU on individual-level opinions regarding European and non-European immigrants. *European Journal of Political Research*, 39(1), 81–108.

Meyer, E. (2014). *The culture map. Decoding how people think, lead, and get things done across cultures*. New York: Public Affairs.

Michaels, E., Handfield-Jones, H., & Axelrod, B. (2001). *The war for talent*. Boston, MA: Harvard Business School Press.

Neuberg, S. L., Smith, D. M., & Asher, T. (2003). Why people stigmatize: Toward a biocultural framework. In F. H. Heatherton, R. E. Kleck, M. R. Hebl, & J. G. Hull (Eds.), *The social psychology of stigma* (pp. 31–61). New York: The Guildford Press.

Nieto, S., Matano, A., & Ramos, R. (2015). Educational mismatches in the EU: Immigrants vs. natives. *International Journal of Manpower*, 36(4), 540–561.

Nordin, M. (2011). Immigrants return to schooling in Sweden. *International Migration*, 49(4), 144–166.

Organization for Economic Co-Operation and Development (2014). *International migration outlook 2014: Special focus – mobilising migrants' skills for economic success*. Paris: OECD Publishing.

Organization for Economic Co-Operation and Development & European Union (2015). *Indicators of immigrant integration 2015: Settling in*. Paris: OECD Publishing.

Özden, Ç., & Schiff, M. (Eds.). (2006). *International migration, remittances & the brain drain*. Washington, DC: The World Bank/Palgrave MacMillan.

Paas, T., & Halapuu, V. (2012). Attitudes towards immigrants and the integration of ethnically diverse societies. *Eastern Journal of European Studies*, 3(2), 161–176.

Quintini, G. (2011). *Over-qualified or under-skilled: A review of existing literature* (OECD Social, Employment and Migration Working Papers, No. 121). Paris: OECD Publishing, http://dx.doi.org/10.1787/5kg58j9d7b6d-en.

Raijman, R., Semyonov, M., & Schmidt, P. (2003). Do foreigners deserve rights? Determinants of public views towards foreigners in Germany and Israel. *European Sociological Review*, 19(4), 379–392.

Rydgren, J. (2004). Mechanisms of exclusion: Ethnic discrimination in the Swedish labour market. *Journal of Ethnic and Migration Studies*, 30(4), 697–716.

Saxenian, A. L. (2002). Silicon Valley's new immigrant high-growth entrepreneurs. *Economic Development Quarterly*, 16(1), 20–31.

Schmidt, E, & Rosenberg, J. (2014). *How Google works*. London: John Murray.

Snell, S. A., Snow, C. C., Davison, S. C., & Hambrick, D. C. (1998). Designing and supporting transnational teams: The human resource agenda. *Human Resource Management*, 37(2), 147–158.

Szulkin, R., Nekby, L., Bygren, M., Lindblom, C., Russell-Jonsson, K., Bengtsson, R. & Normark, E. (2013). *På jakt efter framgångsrik arbetslivsintegrering* (In search of successful labour market integration. Research report 2013:1). Stockholm: Institute for Future Studies.

Winkler, H. (2015). *Why do elderly people oppose immigration when they're most likely to benefit?* Washington, DC: Brookings.

World Economic Forum (2016). *The future of jobs. Employment, skills and workforce strategy for the fourth industrial revolution*. Geneva, CH: World Economic Forum.

Zegers de Beijl, R. (2000). *Documenting discrimination against Migrant workers in the Labour market: A comparative study of four European countries*. Geneva, CH: International Labour Office.

12

FUNCTIONAL WORKPLACES FOR PEOPLE WITH DISABILITIES

Joel Hedegaard and Martin Hugo

A disability, contrary to what many people believe, is *not* an attribute possessed by the individual. A *disability* is defined as an interaction between the person with a disability and the obstacles, in terms of attitudes and environmental obstacles, which the person is confronted with. If one can change attitudes or make certain adaptations to the environment, then 'disabilities' can be limited. This implies that employers, sometimes by quite simple means, can readily make use of the resources (in terms of knowledge and skills) that individuals who are disabled possess.

There are many different disabilities; each demanding its own adaptations. In this chapter, we use the results of a study into the inclusion of young adults associated with high-functioning autism (previously known as *Asperger's Syndrome*) to demonstrate how employers, HR managers, and HR departments can ensure that inclusion at the workplace actually takes place and to ensure that diversity is found within the workplace. Different groups of people may need different adaptations; the study that we report on is used to illustrate how this can be achieved for one particular group.

Note that many countries also legislate for the employer's responsibility for preventing discrimination against people with disabilities; for example, by passing laws that determine how the work environment should be adapted and the nature of the work that can be done by people with disabilities. Below, we report on a number of international conventions on the right to social inclusion and participation. We then focus on the Swedish law governing inclusion and participation, as an example of a national application of such a convention. We describe how many people in Sweden suffer from social exclusion because of a disability and we discuss some of the challenges that these people are faced with because of their disability. We then move on to a discussion of a group of young adults which we have studied in the past and what current research has to say about the needs that people with high-performing autism have. This is followed by an introduction to an educational project which we investigated and the results of this investigation. This chapter ends with a list of recommended readings on this topic.

The right to social inclusion and participation

In the UN convention on human rights for people with disabilities (United Nations, 2008), the right to work on equal grounds is established. Furthermore, the State is mandated to make arrangements so as to ensure that people with disabilities are able to find employment opportunities, receive employment, remain in employment, and be able to return to such employment, as need arises. Work, or meaningful occupation, is one of the most important factors in one's participation in society. Having the opportunity to provide for oneself can improve one's financial situation and allow for the possibility for one to engage in more active leisure time. The UN convention also defines *disability* as an interaction between people with a disability and the obstacles that are contingent on other people's attitudes and the environment which counteract against the disabled person's full participation in society, at least on equal grounds. In the introductory paragraph of the first chapter of the convention, the following is stated:

> The purpose of the present Convention is to promote, protect and en- sure the full and equal enjoyment of all human rights and fundamental freedoms by all persons with disabilities, and to promote respect for their inherent dignity.
>
> *(United Nations, 2008: 4)*

In addition to the United Nations, the European Union has also highlighted the need for social inclusion and has emphasised the point that the labour market should take responsibility for creating a suitable physical and psychosocial work environment which does not contribute to the exclusion of people with disabilities (European Commission, 2010). Thus, we note that it is the conditions that are set for the individual which are subject to change (subject to being 'normalised'), and *not* the individual who has to change. This is what the 'principle of normalisation' is based upon (Nirje, 2003). In response to these stated rights, certain concepts such as 'social entrepreneurship', 'corporate social responsibility' (CSR), 'social economy', and 'social enterprise' have become more and more popular, and they have been deployed by the UN, the EU, and by national and regional authorities. What these concepts have in common is that they unify (i) the individual's need for work with the labour market's need for goods and services and (ii) society's need for rehabilitation services and new work opportunities. These efforts are usually financed by public funds with the caveat that any profit that is made be reinvested in similar enterprises. A vast majority of these social work placements are in the public sector. However, more and more private companies have shown interest in this issue, motivated by marketing opportunities which might enhance their branding (European Commission, 2014; Nordiska Ministerrådet, 2015).

The reality of exclusion – a Swedish example

Despite existing laws, directives, and policies, there remains a great deal more to be done to ensure entry into the labour market for those people who are currently far from being offered employment. In Sweden, this includes young adults who are not engaged in further studies (Arbetsförmedlingen, 2013), people with a foreign background (LO, 2015), and people with disabilities (The National Board of Health and Welfare, 2012; Arbetsförmedlingen, 2015). These three groups find it the most difficult to enter the labour market. There exists a large number of people who are ready and willing to work, but they are not given the opportunity to do so. It is a great challenge to the individual to dismantle the condition of social exclusion and to then enter the regular labour market. This is caused, in part, for example, in Sweden, because there has been a tradition of creating *special employment* for groups of people who have certain needs, instead of adapting the conditions of *normal employment* in the regular labour market (Nygren et al., 2013). The unemployment rate is higher for people who suffer from some sort of disability than the rest of the population. Numbers from Statistics Sweden show that, in 2014, the unemployment figure for people between 16 and 64 years of age was 8%, whilst 10% of people with disabilities were unemployed. Amongst people with disabilities which have reduced their ability to work, the rate of unemployment was 13% (Statistics Sweden, 2015). Note, however, that the phrase *people with disabilities* refers to a very heterogeneous group of people, and great variation can be found with respect to unemployment figures within this group. It is no easy task to obtain statistics for specific groups of people who are on the autistic spectrum, but those individuals who face the most challenges in obtaining gainful employment are those who have psychological disabilities (Lindqvist, 2012).

The progressively deregulated labour market in Sweden has contributed to the establishment of striving for efficiency in the workplace, including an increase in work production, increased demands on competencies, and more streamlined organisational structures. These are contributing factors to the reduction of opportunities for vulnerable and marginalised individuals as they try to enter the labour market (Ahrne et al., 2013). A similar situation exists for people associated with high-functioning autism. Many of these individuals face difficulties in obtaining employment and retaining their position (Larsson Abbad, 2007; Hendricks, 2010; Krieger et al., 2012; Roy et al., 2015). In 2006, it was estimated that only 10%–15% of people with high-functioning autism were gainfully employed (Andersson, 2006). Even those individuals who possess desirable educational qualifications and competencies find it a significant challenge to present themselves as 'employable' (Andersson, 2008). According to Statistics Sweden (2015), people who are disabled are four times more likely to experience discrimination on the labour market than the rest of the population.

Many different arrangements must be deployed to remedy this negative situation, including short- and long-term reforms and a thorough overview of all the forms of subsidised employment schemes which are intended to ease the entrance of these individuals into the labour market. Furthermore, efforts should be made to improve the business climate and workplace culture so as to reduce prejudice and discrimination (Jansson, 2010). Nowadays, there is a specific strategy behind the introduction of legislation for disabled people in Sweden where it is stipulated that the employment rate for people with disabilities must be raised and that the matching of disabled job-seekers with suitable employment opportunities should be made more efficient (Ministry of Health and Social Affairs, 2011). In addition to the above, employers need to offer a variety of adaptations in the workplace, so that the employment of disabled employees is sustainable and, potentially, for the long term. These needs, however, stand in contrast to the striving for efficiency which permeates today's work-life (Ahrne et al., 2013); something which causes employees to view their place of work as merely interchangeable, in their efforts to develop professionally (Ellinger & Ellinger, 2014) or move forward in their career (see Chapter 4 for further discussion of this point).

High-functioning autism

People associated with high-functioning autism often experience difficulties in reading social codes and behaviour. However, many of these individuals possess the ability to concentrate on an assignment for a long period of time and to pay close attention to a number of details. Certain computer programming companies have concluded that these abilities may provide them with a competitive advantage and thus only employ people with high-functioning autism. However, such companies are more the exception than the rule; more often than not, the unique skills that these individuals possess are not taken advantage of. A large majority of young people who have been diagnosed with high-functioning autism have had problematic school careers because their unique needs were not met (Simmeborn Fleisher, 2012). This group of people often find themselves excluded from others in their environment; a condition which becomes more and more apparent the older these people get. This exclusion is often the cause of unemployment and a lack of psychological well-being (Attwood, 2000; Jackson, 2011).

In addition to the stigma of the social exclusion that is suffered by the individual, a significant financial cost is paid by the public purse as a result of this exclusion. The cost over the lifetime of each young person who suffers from social exclusion is estimated to be between 11 and 14 million SEK (one British pound (GBP) is in time of writing the equivalent of about 12 Swedish crowns (SEK)) (Nilsson & Wadeskog, 2012).

Social exclusion can be very difficult to break away from. Psychological research (Bandura, 1982; Cron et al., 2005) has shown that people most often enter into activities which they believe in (and have experience of) their own success. Individuals who have previously experienced failure develop a psychological resistance to engaging in activities where there is a perceived risk that they might fail again. In terms of Antonovsky's (1991) 'KASAM' concept, individuals need to feel that their work-life is meaningful if new failures are to be avoided. This entails, for example, that the workplace is one which can satisfy these individuals' needs and is adaptable, so that they can feel safe and be allowed to succeed in their work.

People associated with high-functioning autism quite frequently need special support systems. These support systems may include aspects of the person's work routine, communication and social interaction, and aspects of the person's work performance, all of which need to be understood from the high-functioning autistic person's perspective, so that they can feel secure in their employment (Hendricks, 2010; Krieger et al., 2012).

Specific research-based models have been developed with the purpose of highlighting the most important work-related support systems for disabled people. *Individual placement and support* (IPS) (Bond et al., 1997) has attracted a great deal of attention in this area because it has been shown to be a successful approach to improving the conditions for people associated with high-functioning autism (Mueser et al., 2011; Giarelli & Fisher, 2013; Nygren et al., 2013; Bond et al., 2014; Marshall et al., 2014). IPS also supports *integrated rehabilitation*. The goal of this approach is to find a 'normal' job on the open labour market, without having to train the candidate or evaluate the candidate's ability to work in advance. A special 'programme trust scale' is used in the IPS framework, consisting of 8 principles (Bond et al., 2014) as follows:

The goal is to obtain employment on the open labour market.
Participation in the IPS model is based on the client's desire to work.
Work rehabilitation is integrated with the neuropsychiatric treatment that the client receives.
The client's willingness to work and his or her interests are the starting point for the programme.
Economic advice about financial self-maintenance is provided early on.
The search for work takes place at an early stage.
There is a systematic search for and creation of relationships with new employers.
The support that is provided is not time-limited.

We researched an educational programme in IT for young adults associated with high-functioning autism as an example of a venture which was intended to break the state of isolation and exclusion that these young adults suffer from. Many of the ideas behind the IT programme are based on the foundational principles of *supported education* (Waghorn et al., 2004), which can be seen as the educational institute's answer to the labour market's IPS approach. The goal of the IT programme was to prepare the students for work in the regular labour market. Note that the student's work-related success would be dependent on how socially responsible potential employers and businesses are.

How the IT programme was arranged and its purpose

The IT programme at Eksjö is special in that it is aimed at young adults associated with high-functioning autism. The educational programme is also aimed at breaking down the student's state of social exclusion, by preparing the student for work in the regular labour market. The programme has 15 placements. The students who participate in the programme have, for some period of time, found themselves to be in a state of social exclusion, related to them being unemployed, and they have experienced a feeling of meaninglessness since they feel that they cannot contribute to society. Many of the students report on bouts of long-term depression and attempted suicide related to being depressed. A majority of the students have previous negative experiences of academic failure and that the 'ordinary' school system was not adapted to meet their needs (Hedegaard & Hugo, 2017; Hugo & Hedegaard, 2017).

The programme is for candidates who have an expressed interest in IT, are motivated to study, and have a desire to work in the field of IT. Campus i12, in Eksjö municipality, is the owner of the project and is responsible for providing the IT programme. Campus i12 offers IT students associated with high-functioning autism their own entrance, specially adapted rooms, small study groups, fixed workstations, individual study plans, a small team of teachers, and access to a work therapist and a psychologist. Campus i12 has a close, cooperative working relationship with the national Labour Office, Social Security, and the county's psychiatric care provider. Teaching takes place between 12:00 and 16:00, Monday to Friday. The content of the IT programme consists of *computer-aided design* (CAD), *computer programming*, and *computer systems*. The content of the programme has been chosen in response to the large demand for people with competencies in these areas in the labour market. Another important part of the programme includes a workplace-based internship which provides the students with the opportunity to train at a real workplace and to also demonstrate their competencies to others.

Breaking down feelings of isolation and the experience of participation in a meaningful social context

The research project that we report on here was conducted during the autumn of 2014. The method of data collection included participatory observations, naturally arising conversations, research interviews with students, and a focus-group interview with the staff. The students reported that their studies on the IT programme had allowed them to break away from their previous state of isolation, which consisted of long periods of idleness and loneliness. Their studies in the IT programme increased their sense of participation, adaptability, and meaningfulness, with a belief in a brighter future as a result. Four graduates from the programme have obtained gainful employment. With respect to the teaching format and the other adaptations that were made in conjunction with the teaching, the students highlighted the importance that (i) they were able to work at their own fixed workstation, (ii) they could work at their own pace, (iii) they were free to decide on the time they spent on their studies, (iv) they received individual help from teachers (who made themselves available for consultation), and (v) they had the opportunity to focus on one course at a time, as they progressed through the programme. The aspect of learning that was most apparent in the students' narratives included, besides the actual content of the courses that they took, was the social learning that took place. Step by step, they reported that they had begun to function better socially in their interactions with other people, and by doing so had developed the ability to ask for help, to speak in front of a group of people, and to develop a better structure to their everyday lives.

What can employers learn from the IT programme?

As mentioned previously in this chapter, disabled people's ability to work is defined in terms of the employer's ability to adapt the workplace, including a conscious effort to improve the workplace climate, so that more and more people with disabilities can find work in the labour market and thus contribute with their skills and competencies. In addition to certain formal requirements (the correct education, desired experience, and so on), certain intrapersonal aspects are of importance to a person's employability, including aspects of self-awareness and self-confidence. The students, who had previously lived in a state of long-term isolation and social exclusion, in addition to receiving their education, also need to be present in an environment where they can slowly build up their self-confidence, as well as their other competencies. Without being provided with this supportive environment, these students run the risk of failing once again, either by failing to be hired or failing to maintain their employment status, and may well return to a life of exclusion and isolation.

The IT programme is a good example of a venture which has broken down the state of exclusion and isolation in the participating students and has also provided these students with useful competencies and skills in the IT field. What then can an employer learn from the IT programme so as to make it possible for them to employ someone with high-functioning autism? First, we should state that the adaptations that were made within the framework of the IT programme were successful since the students felt that they were understood and were provided with the opportunity to succeed with their studies. It is usually the case that individuals associated with high-functioning autism are described as 'gifted' and are thought of as having the potential to develop a special degree of competence in the area(s) that they are interested in (Volkmar et al., 2014). Consequently, employers who are capable of making the necessary adaptations at the workplace can create the conditions where individuals with high-functioning autism are provided the opportunity to perform at a high level, within their area of competence. In the IT programme, we found that the most important adaptations which an employer should be aware of (so as to create conditions conducive to sustainable positions of employment) were (i) a suitably adapted work environment, (ii) structure and clarity, and (iii) a teacher, work leader, or mentor who understands the individual. These observations are developed further in the section below.

The importance that the employer adapts the work environment

During our interviews, it became apparent how important it was that the work environment was adapted to the students' needs. Several students reported that they experienced difficulties in concentrating if there were disturbances in their environment. The fact that they had their own dedicated workstations was also rated as important. One of the students put it thus:

> You have your own workstation...I am really grateful for that...instead of being in an open computer room, you know...you can do your computer lab work as if you were in a large computer room...I find it very difficult to concentrate when there are loads of people around.

At the IT programme, all of the students either have their own room to work in or they can create a private space around them by using movable screens. Similar opportunities should be afforded them by future employers; for example, if they have to sit in an open plan office space, then they should be provided with movable screens so that they can choose when they wish to interact with their environment. Many of the students work in a very focussed manner on the assignments that are given to them, to the point where they are sure that they are on the right track. Many of the students want to be left in peace whilst they work, but they do not necessarily wish to be alone. Two different students reported the following:

> I mostly work on my own. I know that they [the other students] usually go out for coffee and the like...I'm not a person who is interested in that kind of thing. I am very much the individual. I come here for the sake of my work...then I focus on my work. I am not a very social person. I do socialise, but I don't like crowds. That's how I usually am.
>
> *(S1)*

> I am one of *them*, of course...I hate people, they are the worst thing I know. [...] I prefer to keep to myself and I never take a break or such. I just work at my computer and that's where I am. If someone talks to me, then of course I will

talk back to them…but I would never start a conversation […] I think that it is really great to be able to sit here and program, and it's even better when there is no other damn person left here […] then it's so damn quiet everywhere…just me… Then I feel a peace within my body that is quite unbelievable.

(S2)

Work assignment structure and clarity

It is crucial that high-functioning autistic employees are given work assignments that are structured and clear to the employee. Problems often arise when such employees have several different work assignments to complete at the same time. It is desirable that the work manager assigns just one work task at a time, so that the employee can focus on its completion. This approach contributed to the success of the students on the IT programme, since the students often completed one assignment at a time within one academic course. Students did not commence with a new course until they had completed the previous course. Many of the students reported, for example, that one of the problems that they had encountered in the elementary school system was that they had to study many different subjects in parallel. Many of these students achieved considerably better study results at the high school level, where they had a mentor who was able to adapt the syllabus so that particular subjects could be studied one at a time.

A work leader/mentor who understands the individual

During the interviews with the students, they reported on how important their relationships with their teachers were. For many of the students, the teacher was one of the most important sources of motivation. The teachers' didactic subject competence was not the primary factor in this context, but, rather, the teachers' ability to see, acknowledge, and meet with the individual student, thereby providing a sense of security and enabling the student to build up his or her self-confidence (something which was often lacking prior to enrolling in the programme). One student described her teacher in the following words:

He gets you, you know, to feel at peace here. He gets you to feel calm. And he makes you feel welcome […] and it is thanks to him and that he is himself and he is so calm as possible and, you know…he gets you to feel calm. You know, when you are around him, then you get calming energy and so you become calm too…and this is the biggest support that he has given to me.

(S3)

This type of work leader, or mentor, is also needed at the workplace. These are people who take on additional responsibility for this type of employee and continually ensure that a peaceful atmosphere is present at the workplace. This does not necessarily entail a great deal of extra work on the work leader's part, since most of these employees merely wish to be left in peace to do their work for most of the day; but they also do not necessarily wish to be alone whilst they do their work. A mentor who is available and approachable, who is available when needed, and who is sensitive to, and takes note of, what the employee is able to do is crucial to the success of such employees at the workplace.

We claim that the adaptations mentioned above will facilitate the employment opportunities for many of our fellow human beings who are associated with high-functioning autism. Note, however, that this group of people is not completely homogenous; different individuals have different needs. Further to this, we need to develop our understanding that other, more general, support systems, at work and outside of work, can also impact on people in different ways. Thus we should always be ready to modify these support systems. The correct adaptations and support from a work leader or mentor can result in a 'normalisation' of the conditions that the individual finds himself or herself in, and thus provide opportunity for the individual to succeed. It is very important that the individual experiences being part of a social context when he or she feels that he or she is appreciated by others in his or her environment. The students in the IT programme felt appreciated and their levels of self confidence increased, but, notwithstanding this, they still expressed some concern about their future performance in the 'real world' of work-life. One of the programme's teachers made the following remarks during the focus group interview:

> The issue of self confidence...what he is building up is, of course, self confidence...but it is a self confidence in the context of the educational situation...It is not the case that self confidence automatically extends itself into the work situation.
>
> *(T1)*

Future employers are faced with the challenge of implementing the adaptations that were made in the IT programme, including the accommodating and accepting culture that permeates the programme. Such a culture can also be created in the workplace by future potential employers. These are our suggestions of how employers and HR departments can implement adaptations which can lead to conditions that promote inclusion and diversity at the workplace.

Concluding remarks concerning fixed or dynamic competencies

The central point raised in this chapter is that adaptations in the context of academic studies or at the workplace are prerequisites for the proper functioning of people associated with high-performing autism. Whether it is the adaptations and the support that these individuals need that scares potential employers away from hiring these individuals is difficult to access, but it is quite clear that the teachers at the IT programme note that it is difficult to induce employers to take on these students, even as apprentices. One (somewhat pointed) question that arises is whether it is not the case that in most, if not all, instances where someone is employed that a certain degree of adaptation and support is demanded by the newly employed person, irrespective of the status of that person? Most of us have been forgiven for instances of lower than expected levels of performance when we excuse ourselves by saying that we are new to the job and we do not yet know all the rules and work routines. A gradual increase in demands is made on our performance the longer we are employed in a certain job. In other words, we claim here that it is not fully trained individuals who are employed at a new job, but rather, each individual is naturally given the time and space to develop, *as he or she becomes more experienced in doing the particular job.*

One of the main results of our research project was the observation that the students underwent a process of social learning which found expression in an increased capacity to feel empathy, better performance in social contexts with other people, and an increase in self-confidence to the point where the students dared to speak in front of a group of people. These are quite wide-ranging personal developments from a learning process which took place in a relatively short period of time. When we consider the lack of abilities that are sometimes ascribed to people associated with high-functioning autism (in terms of a lack of social skills, poor communication skills, and a purported lack of imagination), and the fact that the diagnosis for this condition is often described as 'static' (Helles et al., 2016), it was very surprising to note how much the students had learnt and developed in these areas (social skills, communication, and creative imagination) during their attendance at the IT programme (Hedegaard & Hugo, 2017; Hugo & Hedegaard, 2017). Given this, it is quite reasonable for us to expect that they could develop and learn in a similar fashion at a workplace which also features an understanding and accepting work climate and work environment.

The results of this study also indicate that people associated with high-functioning autism can become productive colleagues, contingent on certain adaptations at the workplace being made. In conjunction with their offer of employment, employers are also provided with the opportunity of making an important social contribution. Thus, the needs of other groups of people, who suffer from different disabilities, can be positively responded to, for the sake of these individuals and for the improvement of the organisation and society as a whole.

Suggestions for further reading

Literature on 'inclusion'

Jaeger, Paul T. & Bowman, Cynthia Ann (2005), *Understanding disability: Inclusion, access, diversity, and civil rights.* Westport: Praeger Publishers.
Rimmerman, Arie (2013), *Social inclusion of people with disabilities: National and international perspectives.* New York: Cambridge University Press.
Tasso Eira de Aquino, Carlos &[Robert W. Robertson, Robert W. (Eds.) (2018), *Diversity and inclusion in the global workplace: Aligning initiatives with strategic business goals.* Cham: Springer International Publishing.

Literature on 'high-functioning autism' and/or 'Asperger's Syndrome'

Attwood, Tony (2008), *The complete guide to Asperger's Syndrome*. London and Philadelphia: Jessica Kingsley Publishers.

Fast, Yvona (Eds.) (2004), *Employment for individuals with Asperger Syndrome or non-verbal learning disability: Stories and strategies*. London and Philadelphia: Jessica Kingsley Publishers.

McPartland, James C., Ami Klin, Ami & Volkmar, Fred R. (Eds.) (2014), *Asperger Syndrome: Assessing and treating high-functioning autism spectrum disorders*. New York: The Guilford Press.

Tincani, Matt & Bondy, Andy (Eds.) (2016), *Autism spectrum disorders in adolescents and adults: Evidence-based and promising interventions*. New York: The Guilford Press.

Interest organisations

Autism Society (US)
The National Autistic Society (UK)

References

Ahrne, Göran, Roman, Christine & Franzén, Mats (2013), *Det sociala landskapet: En sociologisk beskrivning av Sverige från 1950-talet till början av 2000-talet.* [The social landscape: A sociological description of Sweden from the 1950s to the beginning of the 21st century] Göteborg: Korpen.

Andersson, Torbjörn (2006), *Asperger syndrome och liknande autismtillstånd hos vuxna: En grundbok.* [Asperger syndrome and similar autistic conditions in adults: A journal] Göteborg: Andet utbildning och förlag.

Andersson, Torbjörn (2008), *Asperger, ADHD och arbete.* [Asperger, ADHD, and work] Göteborg: Andet utbildning och förlag.

Antonovsky, Aaron (1991), *Hälsans mysterium.* [Unraveling the mystery of health: How people manage stress and stay well] Translated by Magnus Elfstadius. Stockholm: Natur och kultur.

Arbetsförmedlingen (2013), *Ungdomar på och utanför arbetsmarknaden: Fokus på unga som varken arbetar eller studerar.* [Young adults inside and outside the labour market: Focus on young adults who neither work nor study] Stockholm.

Arbetsförmedlingen (2015), *Arbetsförmedlingens återrapportering 2015: En strategi för genomförandet av funktionshinderpolitiken 2011–2016.* [The Swedish labour exchange's yearly report 2015: A strategy for the implementation of the disabled person's policy 2011–2016]. Arbetsförmedlingen: Stockholm.

Attwood, Tony (2000), *Om Aspergers syndrom: Vägledning för pedagoger, psykologer och föräldrar.* [Asperger's syndrome: Guidlines for pedagogs, psychologists, and parents] Stockholm: Natur & Kultur.

Bandura, Albert (1982), Self-efficacy mechanism in human agenda. *American Psychologist,* 37(2), pp. 122–147.

Bond, Gary R., Becker, Deborah R., Drake, Robert E. & Vogler, Kathleen M. (1997), A fidelity scale for the individual placement and support model of supported employment. *Rehabilitation Counseling Bulletin, 40*(4), pp. 265–284.

Bond, Gary R., Drake, Robert E. & Campbell, Kikuko (2014), Effectiveness of individual placement and support supported employment for young adults. *Early Intervention in Psychiatry, 10*(4), pp. 300–307.

Cron, William L., Slocum, John W., VandeWalle, Don & Qingbo, Fu (2005), The role of goal orientation on negative emotions and goal setting when initial performance falls short of one's performance goal. *Human Performance, 18*(1), pp. 55–80.

Ellinger, Alexander E. & Ellinger, Andrea D. (2014), Leveraging human resource development expertise to improve supply chain managers' skills and competencies. *European Journal of Training and Development, 38*(1), pp. 118–135.

European Commission (2010), *Communication form the European Commission to the European Parliament, the council, the European Economic and Social Committee and the Committee of the Regions. European disability strategy 2010–2020: A renewed commitment to a Barrier-Free Europe.* Brussels: European Commission.

European Commission (2014), *Corporate social responsibility national public policies in the European union. Compendium 2014.* Brussels: European Commission.

Giarelli, Ellen & Fisher, Kathleen (2013), Transition to community by adolescents with Asperger syndrome: Staying afloat in a sea change. *Disability and Health Journal, 6*(3), pp. 227–235.

Hedegaard, Joel & Hugo, Martin (2017), Social dimensions of learning - The experience of young adult students with Asperger syndrome at a supported IT education. *Scandinavian Journal of Disability Research, 19*(3), pp. 256–268.

Helles, Adam, Wallinius, Märta I, Gillberg, Carina, Gillberg, Christopher & Billstedt, Eva (2016), Asperger syndrome in childhood – personality dimensions in adult life: Temperament, character and outcome trajectories. *British Journal of Psychiatry, 2*(3), pp. 210–216.

Hendricks, Dawn (2010), Employment and adults with autism spectrum disorder: Challenges and strategies for success. *Journal of Vocational Rehabilitation, 32*(2), pp. 125–134.

Hugo, Martin & Hedegaard, Joel (2017), Education as habilitation: Empirical examples from an adjusted education in Sweden for students with high-functioning autism. *Andragogic Perspectives, 23*(3), 71–87.

Jackson, Luke (2011), *Miffon, nördar och Aspergers syndrom.* [Freaks, nerds, and Asperger's syndrome] Lund: Studentlitteratur.

Jansson, Li (2010), *Handikappolitiken – en björntjänst i all välmening: Hur fel focus i sysselsättningspolitiken minskar tillgängligheten till arbetsmarknaden.* [Disabled politics – a misguided disserve: How the wrong focus in labour policies reduces access to the labour market] Stockholm: Svenskt Näringsliv.

Krieger, Beate, Kinébanian, Astrid, Prodinger, Birgit & Heigl, Franziska (2012), Becoming a member of the work force: Perceptions of adults with Asperger syndrome. *Work, 43*(2), pp. 141–157.

Larsson Abbad, Gunvor (2007), *"Aspergern, det är jag": En intervjustudie om att leva med Asperger syndrom.* ["Asperger's. Who I am." An interview study into living with Asperger's syndrome] Linköping: Linköpings universitet, Institutionen för beteendevetenskap och lärande.

Lindqvist, Rafael (2012), *Funktionshindrade i välfärdssamhället.* [The disabled in a welfare society] Malmö: Gleerups.

LO (2015), *Etablering i skuggan av hög arbetslöshet, skillnadsskapande och migrationseffekter.* [Settling in in the shadow of high unemployment, social differences, and the consequences of immigration] Stockholm: Landsorganisationen i Sverige.

Marshall, Tina, Goldberg, Richard W., Braude, Lisa, Dougherty, Richard H., Daniels, Allen, Ghose, Sushmita Shoma & Delphin-Rittmon, Miriam E. (2014), Supported employment: Assessing the evidence. *Psychiatric Services*, *65*(1), pp. 16–23.

Ministry of Health and Social Affairs (2011), *En strategi för genomförande av funktionshinder-spolitiken 2011–2016.* [A strategy for the implementation of the disabled person's policy 2011–2016] Stockholm.

Mueser, Kim T., Campbell, Kikuko & Drake, Robert E. (2011), The effectiveness of supported employment in people with dual disorders. *Journal of Dual Diagnosis*, *7*(1–2), pp. 90–102.

Nilsson, Ingvar & Wadeskog, Anders (2012), *Utanförskapets ekonomiska sociotoper: Socioekonomisk analys på stadsdelsnivå inom ramen för Healthy Cities.* [The sociotopes of economic social isolation: A socio-economic analysis of a city borough within the framework for Healthy Cities] Karlshäll: SEE AB.

Nirje, Bengt (2003), *Normaliseringsprincipen.* [The normalisation principle] Lund: Studentlitteratur.

Nordiskaministerrådet (2015), *Sosialt entreprenørskap og sosial innovasjon: Kartlegging av inn-satser for sosialt entreprenørskap og sosial innovasjon i Norden.* [Social entrepreneurship and social innovation: A report on social entrepreneurship and social innovation schemes in Scandinavia] Köpenhamn.

Nygren, Ulla, Markström, Urban, Bernspång, Birgitta, Svensson, Bengt, Hansson, Lars & Sandlund, Mikael (2013), Predictors of vocational outcomes using individual place-ment and support for people with mental illness. *Work*, *45*(1), pp. 31–39.

Roy, Mandy, Prox-Vagedes, Vanessa, Ohlmeier, Martin D. & Dillo, Wolfgang (2015), Beyond childhood: Psychiatric comorbidities and social background of adults with Asperger syndrome. *Psychiatria Danubina*, *27*(1), pp. 50–59.

Simmeborn Fleischer, Ann (2012), Support to students with Asperger syndrome in higher education: The perspectives of three relatives and three coordinators. *International Journal of Rehabilitation Research*, *35*(1), pp. 54–61.

Statistics Sweden (2015), *Situationen på arbetsmarknaden för personer med funktionsnedsättning 2014.* [The situation on the labour market for disabled people 2014] Örebro: Statis-tiska Centralbyrån.

The National Board of Health and Welfare (2012), *Sysselsättning för personer med psykisk funktionsnedsättning: Utvärdering av statsbidrag under åren 2009–2011.* [Employment rates for people with psychological disabilities: An evaluation of government funding between 2009–2011] Stockholm.

United Nations (2008). *Convention on the rights of persons with disabilities and optional protocol.* New York: United Nations.

Waghorn, Geoffrey, Still, Megan, Chant, David & Whiteford, Harvey (2004), Special-ised supported education for Australians with psychotic disorders. *Australian Journal of Social Issues*, *39*(4), pp. 443–458.

Volkmar, Fred R., Klin, Ami & McPartland, James C. (2014), Asperger syndrome: An overview. In James C. McPartland, Ami Klin & Fred R. Volkmar (eds.), *Asperger syndrome: Assessing and treating high-functioning autism spectrum disorders* (pp. 1–43). New York: The Guilford Press.

13

WORKING IN KNOWLEDGE-INTENSIVE ORGANISATIONS WHEN IT IS IMPOSSIBLE TO BE PHYSICALLY PRESENT

Female employees who suffer from chronic illnesses

Claudia Gillberg

This chapter examines workplace participation of people suffering from a disability caused by chronic illness who cannot be rehabilitated or are considered to be incurable. The fact that rehabilitation and medical treatment is not possible for certain illnesses can be difficult to accept and deal with. Everyone wants to get better and enjoy good health, and, in this context, it should be noted that employers have a statutory duty to offer rehabilitation and workplace adaptations to employees who need it. For example, many employers follow routines which work well for a range of disabilities, but for many people who are chronically ill, it is the demand that they be *physically present* at their place of work that causes an obstacle to their participation at work. Disabilities caused by chronic illness are often not visible to the casual observer; there being no overt signs that the person is disabled, for example, in the same way a wheelchair might signal a disability.[1]Awareness about these types of disability is consequently low compared to other disabilities; for example, disabilities associated with a person's ability to move unaided. In such cases, urgent information campaigns have led to a more inclusive existence for such people.

The question remains: *What can employers and employees do about employees who suffer from chronic illnesses?* At a university, a government office, or other places of work where there are many highly educated employees, there is often a certain amount of flexibility with respect to the *format* of the work that is to be done; with such flexibility, the emphasis is shifted from the physical presence of the employee to the intrinsic value of the work done. However, it is quite unusual for an employer to allow an employee who cannot *ever* be physically present to continue to be employed. This chapter will demonstrate that such arrangements do not need to be onerous for the employer.

In the first section of this chapter, we examine empirical material which will inform us of the danger of exclusion facing people who have a disability caused by chronic illness. This forms the foundation for various suggested actions which an employer might perform to avoid such exclusion. The chapter offers a discussion of these issues and actions which, hopefully, may lead to new forms of participation in the workplace.

Exclusion and a loss of knowledge

As discussed by Hedegaard and Hugo (Chapter 12), the exclusion of people with disabilities from the workplace is a serious problem in terms of feelings of alienation and the competencies that are left dormant and underutilised. Whilst Hedegaard and Hugo discuss how disabled people can be brought into the labour market, in this chapter, I will highlight the problems associated with the loss of knowledge and the feelings of exclusion which may arise when a person initially becomes ill or an already present illness becomes worse. To prevent a person from becoming excluded (something which is difficult to reverse), employers and their representatives should understand that this is a serious situation. The loss of knowledge which can occur because a person is off sick from work is also serious, especially since diversity in the workplace is not only determined by the employee's social and ethnic backgrounds, but also by the different knowledge and skills which each employee possesses.

To suffer from serious illness is an upsetting experience. Irrespective of age, gender, family situation, or other circumstances, most people who work in knowledge-intensive organisations wish to return to work as quickly as possible. Such employees have invested many years in their education. They often possess a strong work ethic and passion for their work, as shown by the experiences reported on below of 29 female academics from twelve different countries. The academics were interviewed between 2012 and 2017. These academics have met with each other online for a period of five years in different forums and media, which, in some cases were initially completely independent of their work or illness. It was in my conversations with these ladies, who mostly lived in Western countries, that I began to notice the shape and form of a previously unknown sense of exclusion and alienation. This form, which I could not initially grasp, prompted me to start a research project, which continues today. The method that is used for data collection is a narrative analysis of life stories (Andrews & Squires, 2013; Frithiof, 2007; Perry & Medina, 2015; Ribbens & Edwards, 2009). I also form part of these narratives since I am a female academic who suffers from a chronic illness. Consequently, the presentation of the research area and the issues therein are coloured by my understanding of them and my own embodiment of these issues (Reid & Gillberg, 2014; Wendell, 1996).

The most prominent contours of the issue under investigation, *exclusion*, were the difficulties in being heard when the women turned for help from their healthcare services, irrespective of the country they were in or their age. Most of them had waited for a long time before they sought care; thus, they went to work, even though they were ill, for weeks, months, and in some cases, years before they were compelled to seek medical care. The healthcare providers, irrespective of country, thought the women had quickly turned to the healthcare system after a short period of discomfort, and so most of them were refused treatment. In those cases where action was taken, prescriptions for antidepressant drugs or advice about massages and mindfulness were given to the women. Initially, 19 of the 29 women were incorrectly diagnosed, and of these 19, 8 eventually received diagnoses of brain tumours, neuroendocrine cancer, breast cancer, MS, and Addison's disease. The incorrect diagnoses fell predominantly into the category of psychological illness, for example, 'fatigue syndrome'.

Reference to figures and numbers in this chapter is not intended to provide a statistically significant representation of reality. However, the fact that 29 women who were unknown to each other, from 12 different countries, all shared similar stories of gradual exclusion from knowledge-intensive organisations must be taken account of. A contributory factor to their gradual exclusion was how they were treated by the healthcare system, i.e., in terms of preconceived gender stereotypes (Begum, 1996; Schenck-Gustafsson & Dahlin, 2014; Schenck-Gustafsson & Johnston-Holmström, 2011; Socialstyrelsen, 2014). One woman who was diagnosed as suffering from 'burnout' (fatigued) died in 2016. The doctors had failed to diagnose her breast cancer. I had significant contact with her during the period when the process of her obtaining sick leave became increasingly frustrating. At that time, she reported that the pain she was suffering was almost unendurable. She continued to work, part-time, and did her best to ignore the symptoms when she was told that there was nothing wrong with her. This is a problem which requires further research, but this is not within the scope of the present chapter. Notwithstanding, this problem needs to be understood by employers since it is a gender equality problem and issue of inequality for patients in the healthcare system, and employers are directly affected by the way their employees are treated, even though the patient is the one hardest hit by this type of (mis)treatment. On average, it takes five to six years before a chronic illness is correctly diagnosed. During these years, a great deal of understanding and compassion needs to be shown by the employer, even though one might not be able to accurately identify what illness the employee is suffering from.

Organising work tasks during a chronic illness – some problems

According to employees who are off sick from work for a long time, a feeling of shame is associated with a bad conscience because they have 'betrayed' their employer, colleagues, students, and other people due to being off sick. No matter how ill one might be, one may often question how bad one's condition is (Mallett & Runswick Cole, 2014; Wendell, 1996). Most people have the propensity to see themselves as healthier than they are; something that the HR specialist should keep in mind when interacting with an employee who is off sick.

The life stories which constitute the empirical material for this chapter reveal several different distinct stages, during which the sick employee goes through various changes. These stages can also be described as a balancing act, where the employee's choice is either to continue work whilst ill or risk being alienated. These stages are (i) to engage in proactive dialogue with the employer, (ii) to work as a physically nonpresent employee, and (iii) to hold fast to one's job or slip away. These stages are further commented on below.

With respect to the dialogue between the employee and employer, it is often the case that they agree with each other *about the wrong things*. Both often have good intentions about continuing the employee's participation, but despite this, things can still go wrong. The problem is that a chronically ill person's reality is fundamentally different from the reality that people with healthy bodies inhabit (Wendell, 1996). The problem with accessibility, for example, is so large for the chronically ill, that there is not enough space in this chapter to do it justice (Swain et al., 2005). For example, someone with MS or ME may need several hours to get out of bed, get dressed, and eat breakfast. The person then might be exhausted from this activity for several hours, even before the issue of doing some work presents itself. This does not mean that the work will suffer; it is just that it is cannot be done in the usual work hours that are followed by the other employees. An office meeting for someone who suffers from severe insomnia – a common symptom for many people who are chronically ill – is almost impossible to attend. Deadlines can be met by such employees, but the route they take to meet a deadline may be different to other employees.

To engage in a proactive dialogue about such issues with the employer is made more difficult by the fact that people suffering from a chronic illness may not, for a long time, consider themselves as disabled (Wendell, 1996). The fact that they are disabled is not something that most people will initially consider. The shame felt about this (as mentioned in the introduction to this chapter) is another problem to consider. No one wants to admit that they do not get out of bed until eleven o'clock and then need an hour to get dressed. Such a confession is difficult to reconcile with the integrity and dignity that everyone aspires to achieve and maintain in the public sphere. In such cases, a dialogue demands a significant amount of mutual trust and presupposes sensitivity and understanding on the employer's part (Goodley, 2014).

Being able to work as a nonphysically present employee is made difficult by other factors. The salary that is to be awarded has serious consequences for the employee. In general, many work assignments are performed within a set number of hours, irrespective of the employee's health status. Thinking, reading, planning, writing, analysing research data, formulating an application, preparing a presentation, developing or revising an educational course, or providing academic supervision are all tasks which can be done at home, and for the majority of healthy and full-time employees who work in knowledge-intensive organisations, they have performed these tasks at some time of their career without carefully recording the exact number of hours they spend doing them. The more abstract a work assignment is, the more difficult it is to be paid for it when it is performed *outside* the physical building (place of work) or fixed structures which inform a particular professional position. When a chronically ill employee expresses a desire to continue contributing to the organisation, a problem arises since such contributions can only be 'fragmentary', from the organisation's perspective. Organisations are used to situations where the employee can provide the 'whole package' of work assignments, and not only parts of an assignment. The employer is confronted with the following question: How can parts of a work assignment be properly evaluated, when all the other 'normal' employees (i.e., those who are physically present at the workplace) perform these assignments as part of an integrated portion of their permanent full-time jobs? One such example is the supervision of essays at a university, where many lecturers, irrespective of their academic discipline, spend more time on each essay than they are paid for by the university.

Employers use the notion of 'confidence work time' (as part of an honour system on the part of the employee, to complete work done at home in a timely fashion) to make things easier for their employees (i.e., allowing the employee the flexibility to do work at home, instead of coming into the workplace). But this raises the question of the value of the work when individual parts are removed from the collective whole of the work which the employee performs at a knowledge-intensive organisation. The salary which is paid out is seen as a whole sum, from which one might allocate a certain portion of for hours used on performing certain tasks, but the *exact* allocation of time (and hence a proportion of the salary) is not clear and is somewhat fuzzy. One might say that some time that was allocated for one job has been moved over to another. Such opportunities to reallocate time across different tasks do not exist for a person who, for example, can only provide online academic supervision. As soon as a student exceeds the prescribed number of hours (of supervision), the supervision must come to an end, or it continues even though the money and time allocated to this task have been used up. When tasks are performed without compensation, then hours which could have been spent on performing assignments which one can get paid for are used up; thereby creating a negative spiral which affects the disabled employee's finances negatively.

These forms of internal work arrangements are frequent and should be considered the rule, rather than the exception. But when one is chronically ill, this freedom becomes a problem because the individual work tasks that are performed outside a given (and taken for granted) whole are not given a price tag. Such part-assignments or tasks are seen merely as part of a *whole*, which is paid for as a *whole* monthly salary. Conventional work arrangements, which are taken for granted and are viewed as the 'normal' way of doing things, do not seem normal for a person who cannot complete all aspects (subtasks) of a particular work assignment. This is a problem which cannot be solved by the individual.

In such situations, the employer's creativity wanes. Instead, they invoke prevailing administrative procedures and routines, but these do not work for chronically ill employees. For example, the Swedish Social Security Office's rules for being off sick from work and the compensation that is due are incompatible with both the character of the work, which is done at knowledge-intensive organisations, and with the regulations covering work-time allocation. The Social Security Office's approach to what *per hour* (i.e., an hourly pay rate) means is quite different to what a chronically ill employee understands it to mean, since (in some cases) an hour's work might take a whole day to complete. It is understandable that the employer is not inclined to report incorrect details about work hours completed and percentages of a full-time position to the Social Security Office, but a strict adherence to the Social Security Office's rules and regulations entails that, nowadays, employers are often forced to let their employees with chronic illnesses down because their reality and their way of working fails to comply with the demands set by the Social Security Office. To get left behind in such a situation happens easily. The individual's participation in such circumstances becomes more difficult and questionable (Ståhl et al., 2011).

Measures that can be taken

During the research study, it was primarily Swedish academics who highlighted that regulation of work-time, as generous as it is, causes a type of depreciation of the work that is done, which, in their opinion, should be valued more highly. This issue is not visible in the everyday work that is done at a university, but a discussion of this issue attracts lively attention from those who suffer from chronic illnesses. The academics, researchers, lecturers, and doctoral candidates have great difficulty in reconciling their chronic illness with a paid academic position because they can only perform certain parts of the usual work assignments associated with such professional positions. It has been shown that prevailing administrative systems hinder, instead of help, the chronically ill, because chronic illness can fluctuate in terms of the sufferer's symptoms (cf. Ståhl et al., 2011).

There is always a certain amount of consternation when something which has been invisible for most people is revealed. The present discussion aims to highlight the issues that impact on the chronically ill and thereby encourage a debate of the same. It is exciting to bring people's attention to issues which have been hidden behind the façade of what is supposedly 'normal' for knowledge-intensive work contexts and how they are organised (Goodley, 2014; Wendell, 1996). We need to reflect on these issues wisely and engage in dialogue that can gradually lead to change at the workplace, which the employer can initiate, encourage, and support, by reinforcing the HR function within the organisation.

The re-evaluation of physical presence by the routine application of online tools

Regardless of the Social Security Office's ungainly collection of rules and regulations, there are concrete measures which employers can take to alleviate some of the problems faced by chronically ill employees. Regan and Delaney (2010) present a thorough discussion of the technological workplace which can function in an inclusive way, irrespective of the geographical location of the employee (cf. Chapter 12). The use and integration of programs such as Skype and Adobe Connect are examples of simple tools which can enable the chronically ill to participate at work, on their terms.

The use of online solutions on their own is not enough, however. Transformational work must also take place. Currently, an employee's physical presence at the workplace is valued higher than an employee's online participation. Work and perspectives on work are strongly connected to the physical body and its presence in a concrete, physical space (Wendell, 1996). This claim is supported by the fact that it is hardly possible to find an online job advertised by a serious employer. On the Arbetsförmedlingen's (the Swedish Employment Service) homepage, tens of thousands of jobs are advertised, but seldom are there qualified work vacancies which can be undertaken from home. Digital participation, as a substitute for a physical body at a physical place of work, is not a self-evident substitution. But at the same time, it is this type of online participation that the chronically ill need if they are to continue to contribute to their employer's organisations.

Distribution of work assignments and making resources available

If chronically ill employees are given the opportunity to perform certain work tasks normally performed by colleagues who are physically at work, then this will make certain resources available for the healthy employees to use, so that they can busy themselves with tasks that they might prefer to do instead. Such negotiations are, however, complex for a person who is not physically present within the organisation, including negotiations about arrangements that can be planned either formally or informally. The HR department can play a key role in such situations, but at many universities and government authorities the HR function has been reduced to a purely administrative role, with few exceptions being made for rehabilitation. The ability to think and act in an innovative fashion is crucial in a complex situation. Merely following fixed routines is not the way forward for a HR department when exclusionary mechanisms for the chronically ill are to be dismantled. The first constructive steps in this direction should include taking the initiative to start new discussions about long-term sick leave, perhaps via a series of workshops, lectures, and other arrangements where people's opinions can be heard.

The reappraisal of employers to create workplaces which are characterised by equality and diversity

As described in Chapter 7 by Helene Ahl, gender equality work is something that must be done at each place of work; employers are given a sociopolitical assignment to promote gender equality and to actively counteract forces that justify unfair salary structures between the different genders. The employer should thus be reappraised as a copartner in creating and maintaining as just a society as possible.

The phenomenon of long-term sick leave must be considered as a gender equality issue as well (Socialstyrelsen, 2014). Nowadays, most organisations have gender equality plans or policies, which are subject to regular revision. Such plans or policies can thus include new relevant areas, for example, issues relevant to employees who are on long-term sick leave. This is of particular relevance to chronically ill women as described in this study because autoimmune conditions are more prevalent in women (SBU, 2003; Schenck-Gustafsson & Dahlin, 2014; Schenck-Gustafsson & Johnston-Holmström, 2011). Consequently, the gender aspect of this complex problem must be of particular interest to employers.

The Swedish government's 2003 white paper on medical evaluations (SBU) states in its summary of the relevant research in the area that more specific and better quality research is needed in the area of long-term sick leave. The paper highlights several points which are of particular interest for employers and their representatives, where they were informed that they should discuss and cooperate with other actors on issues that have a direct bearing on the opportunities and obstacles facing employers as they continue to integrate chronically ill employees into their organisation's operations. SBU (2003) requested more knowledge with respect to the following issues and questions:

Why do only certain people take long-term sick leave?

Why do certain people return to work more quickly than others, after being off sick?

How can we identify those people who would benefit from early support measures so that long-term sick leave can be avoided?

What are the positive and negative consequences for the individual when being on long-term sick leave and taking early retirement are compared with each other?

How can any negative consequences caused by being on sick leave be detected and prevented?

What are the consequences of coming to work when ill, for the individual and for the employer, for colleagues and possible clients/customers?

What role do the employee's socioeconomic conditions play with respect to long-term sick leave?

What attitudes are displayed by the general public, patients, doctors, and officers at the Employment Office with respect to long-term sick leave, and what influence do these attitudes have on people who may wish to take long-term sick leave?

What forms of fruitful cooperation can different interests in the area of health insurance engage in?

What comparisons can be made with Sweden and other countries with respect to long-term sick leave?

According to the experiences of the chronically ill employees who are included in the current, ongoing study, it is only the employer who is considered the source of grounded common sense in an otherwise tumultuous and demanding state of illness. It is often felt, however, that the employer is unaware of the important role that the employer plays for the employees who suffer from a chronic illness. For example, the employer can be of great assistance when dealing with overwhelming bureaucratic demands. An investment in hiring an HR specialist with competence in this area would be a desirable step forward in assisting chronically ill employees. HR specialists have helped many employees in their interaction with the Social Security Office and other officials, and they play a role in signalling to these officials, doctors, and others that such employees are of value to the employer. Such representation may also aid an employee's smooth journey through the so-called 'care pathways'. The quicker the chronically ill employee receives proper care from the healthcare system, the better this is for them and their employer.

The female participants in this study report that there is a continual questioning of whether they are actually sick by the healthcare workers who they meet. This delays the delivery of proper care. These women also report that they are offered antidepressants long before they are properly diagnosed. Interestingly, this occurs regardless of the country they reside in (cf. Mallett & Runswick-Cole, 2014; Socialstyrelsen, 2014; Wendell, 1996). This problem is something that some employers continue to propagate (in a complicated manner) when they claim that they do not know when or whether the employee can continue working at the company. Consider the following report:

> My manager and I talked about the use of anti-depressive drugs quite a bit. She could not understand why the doctor did not conduct a proper investigation and just assumed that I was 'burnt out'. Weeks passed before I even met a doctor who seemed serious. It was then revealed that I had a neuroendcrine tumour. Really scary! Obviously I wasn't getting better, but I heard from the healthcare providers that I was not being cooperative because I refused to take the anti-depressant drugs.
>
> *(bio-chemist at a large research institute, 53 years old)*

Employers at knowledge-intensive organisations have often shown themselves to be generous, understanding, and responsive to the employee's needs, in the beginning. Some of the participants in the study have committed employers who have tried to positively influence the healthcare providers' and other officials' decisions about their employees. We also have examples where the employer has clearly stated to the relevant doctors and the Social Security Office that the employee would never stay at home if they were not seriously ill, and it is up to the healthcare system to ensure that the employee receives the best possible care:

> And so the Dean said to my social security officer and to my doctor at a status meeting that they should do a proper job since I am an appreciated and likable employee. My boss also said that she did not want me at work until I received proper treatment and was better, but she also did not want to see me disappear on what is called the 'healthcare merry-go-round' just because my symptoms seem to be diffuse. I almost laughed with relief and happiness.
>
> *(university lecturer, 44 years old)*

Such attitudes are of great value to a person who is ill and in a difficult situation. Employers have also shown the proper spirit by adapting the workplace to better accommodate the ill employee, or by maintaining contact with the employee, at least during the first year of the employee's absence. But what is most worrying is that this nearly always leads to a life outside the labour market for the chronically ill employee; even the most well-meaning employer loses interest in an employee who is off sick for a long time. There is not enough space in the present chapter to discuss why this is the case, but it remains an important point that deserves discussion. Universities and knowledge-intensive organisations, to a larger degree than occurs at present, should see themselves as opinion shapers regarding offering the chronically ill the opportunity to participate in work in ways that challenge current rules and regulations (cf. Regan & Delaney, 2010; Ståhl et al., 2011).

Rigid sick-leave reporting processes and rehabilitation processes and an overarching social security system and other regulatory guidelines are not at all equipped to deal with complex illnesses and the complicated life conditions that the chronically ill must deal with in a flexible way (Ståhl et al., 2011). The Social Security Office's rules and regulations, as is the case in all EU countries, is an expression of such a rigid system, which can lead to the exclusion of many chronically ill people who report that they can perform work, but not as much work as the rules demand they perform (SBU, 2003; Ståhl et al., 2011).

It is quite imaginable for employers to engage in the social and political debate on the issue of long-term sick leave to a greater extent, for example, in cooperation with the Social Security Office. Such engagement, which could be bolstered by an interest in learning something new about sick leave and employee inclusion, could provide the necessary space for constructive interaction at an HR department or between an employer and the Social Security Office. At present, no such initiatives exist. The focus of HR departments and the Social Security Office remains on rehabilitation and the so-called 'care chain'. The Social

Security Office's regulations, for the above reasons, have been criticised as being "not fit for purpose" (Ståhl et al., 2011).

Challenging the norm that one should be physically present at work

The dismantling of the mechanisms which cause the chronically ill and disabled people to be excluded is desirable for several reasons, including those discussed in the preceding section. The inclusion of employees, which ignores current norms about a person's physical, healthy body, demands careful consideration, new perspectives, and profound changes in people's perspectives. The norm governing one's physical presence at work is well justified; one's physical presence promotes collegiality, the exchange of knowledge and experience, and allows people to be comfortable. Being physically present acts as a social cement, bonding people together into a social continuum. It is obvious that employers wish to create so-called 'living' workplaces. No matter what one's opinion is of the matter, the fact is that the physical body plays an important symbolic function in signalling efficient or 'real' work; and stands in contrast to work which is done half-heartedly or as a compromise. But it is possible to challenge this notion of the 'physical body' and its relationship to 'work'. The preconception that an employee's mere physical presence is something positive needs to be challenged and other, innovative, ways of working should be examined.

The changes required do not necessarily need to be particularly burdensome and nor does one need to start a huge expensive project to achieve these changes. At many Swedish workplaces, work is already being done to ensure diversity and gender equality with the aim of preventing or correcting exclusionary practices. Given information and knowledge about chronic illnesses, it is quite possible for an HR department to revise existing diversity and gender equality plans. The current dominant (and seemingly taken-for-granted) discourse about the physically present body at work should be questioned and be gradually replaced by other discourses. Inclusion presupposes one's preparedness to use different tools to achieve one's goals, and the use of the correct tools requires that one engages in perceptive communication. Most employees wish to remain employed, or at least participate at work, which is of great value to the whole of society.

At knowledge-intensive organisations, especially the *content* of the work done should be highly valued, disconnected from the person – and the person's physical body – who produced the work. A new focus on 'disembodied' knowledge and competence is crucial to the inclusion of people who suffer from a chronic illness.

'Participation' and 'the right to work', as discussed by Hedegaard and Hugo in the previous chapter, are concepts that demand a radical *openness* between people if they are to apply to individual people. Diversity and participation demand a multitude of different ways of organising work, especially, as this study has shown, in the context of the elusive, physically absent body that appears to be a particular challenge to the able-bodied community. Knowledge-intense organisations, somewhat surprisingly, are no exception to the rule, although they could be at the forefront of setting new examples, as this chapter demonstrates. Now that we are surrounded by digital tools and social media, it should be easy to imagine an inclusive workplace where the physical body of the employee does not play a particularly important role in the execution of a range of work assignments.

Recommended reading

WHO (2015), Road Map for Action (2014–2019). Integrating Equity, Gender, Human Rights, and Social Determinants into the Work of WHO. Report. World Health Organisation. www.who.int/gender-equity-rights/knowledge/web-roadmap.pdf?ua=1.
Gillberg, Claudia (2016), A Troubling Truth: Chronic Illness, Participation and Learning for Change. Sheffield, UK. Centre For Welfare Reform, Series Discussion Papers. www.centreforwelfarereform.org/library/by-az/a-troubling-truth.html.

Note

1 Examples of chronic illnesses include multiple sclerosis (MS), myalgic encephalomyelitis (ME), Parkinson's disease, diabetes, Endometriosis, heart- and vascular disease, cancer, Crohn's disease.

References

Andrews, Molly & Corinne Squires (2013), *Doing narrative research*. London: Sage.
Begum, Nasa (1996), Doctor, doctor … Disabled women's experience of general practitioners. In Jenny Morris (ed.), *Encounters with strangers: Feminism and disability* (pp. 168–193). London: The Women's Press.
Frithiof, Elisabeth (2007), *Mening, makt och utbildning: Delaktighetens villkor för personer med utvecklingsstörning.* [Meaning, power, and education: Conditions for participation for people with developmental disabilities] Växjö: Växjö University Press.
Goodley, Dan (2014), *Dis/ability studies: Theorising disableism and ablism.* New York: Routledge.
Mallet, Rebecca & Katherine Runswick-Cole (2014), *Approaching disability: Critical issues and perspectives.* London: Routledge.
Perry, Mia & Carmen Liliana Medina (2015), *Methodologies of embodiment: Inscribing bodies in qualitative research.* Routledge Advances in Research Methods. London: Routledge.
Regan, Elizabeth & Chester Delaney (2010), Brave new workplace: The impact of technology on location and job structures. In Margaret Malloch, Len Cairns, Karen Evans, & Bridget N. O'Connor (eds.), *The Sage handbook of workplace learning.* (pp. 431–442). London: Sage.
Reid, Colleen & Claudia Gillberg (2014), Feminist participatory action research. In David Coghlan & Mary Brydon-Miller (eds.), *The Sage encyclopedia of action research* (pp. 344–348). London & New York: Sage.
Ribbens, Jane & Rosalind Edwards (2009), *Feminist dilemmas in qualitative research: Public knowledge and private lives.* London: Sage.

SBU (2003), *Sjukskrivning – orsaker, konsekvenser och praxis: En systematisk litteraturöversikt.* [Being off sick – causes, consequences, and common practices: A systematic literature overview]. SBU: Stockholm.

Schenck-Gustafsson, Karin & Johnston-Holmström, Nina (Eds.) (2011), *Kvinnohjärtan.* [The female heart] Lund: Studentlitteratur.

Schenck-Gustafsson, Karin & Sara Dahlin (2014), *Underlag till Jämställdhetsutredningen U2014:06. Områdesrapport utöver de jämställdhetspolitiska delmålen: Hälsa.* [Initial study for the investigation into equalityU2014:06. Subject report concerning the social equality policy sub-aim: Health.] Karolinska institutet och Karolinska universitetssjukhuset. Stockholm: Socialstyrelsen.

Socialstyrelsen (2014), *Ojämna villkor för hälsa och vård. Rapport.* [Inequalities in healthcare provision] Stockholm.

Ståhl, Christian, Ulrika Müssener, & Tommy Svensson (2011), *Sjukskrivningssystemet och dess aktörer: Efter införandet av rehabiliteringskedjan.* [The sick reporting system and the people involved: After the implementation of the rehabilitation chain] Helix Working Papers. Linköping: Linköpings universitet.

Swain, John, Sally French, & Cameron Colin (2005), *Controversial issues in a disabling society.* Maidenhead: Open University Press.

Wendell, Susan (1996), *The rejected boy: Feminist philosophical reflections on disability.* San Francisco: Jossey-Bass.

14

THOSE WHO KNOW MORE THAN YOU

Talent management in the Google era

Roland S. Persson and Vezir Aktas

Along with the increasing importance of strategic knowledge in the global economy, a new research area has opened up for study and application; namely *talent management*. The term refers to the strategic management of human resources, the recruitment and retention of such resources, as well as career planning for the human capital that is employed by an organisation to realise the organisation's goals and purpose. In most cases (but not always), this entails maximising different *business* goals (Chambers et al., 1998). The use of the term *human capital* suggests that the employees are seen as an investment made by the employer. Regardless of how one might define *talent management*, the strategies that are associated with this term are seen as something positive and necessary in the present, and future, competition for the most attractive workforce (Bethke-Langenegger et al., 2011).

Some researchers claim that, after careful calculation, most of an organisation's production can be traced back to just a small proportion of all of the organisation's employees. According to these calculations, approximately 60%–80% of employees produce under the average performance figure, whilst between 1%–5% of employees are responsible for 10%–26% of the organisation's production in total (O'Boyle & Aguinis, 2012). Those employees who are at this top level of performance are often called *talents*. But to think of a talent as someone who only produces at a high level is, however, a problem. That which makes individuals to be classified as high-level performers, creative, problem-solvers, and leaders is much more complex than what is shown by their production output. An individual may come up with a fantastic idea which may have great importance to an organisation, whilst ten other employees might produce 500 good ideas, which are all of use, but may not be as important as one revolutionary idea.

There is currently no consensus on how *talent* should be defined (Persson, 2014). The market has thus often chosen to simply ignore who these outstanding, creative, and productive individuals are and what it is that allows these individuals to do what they do. Attention has only been given to the result that is produced (Brown & Hesketh, 2004). This is a problem because it entails that one is not provided with the opportunity of finding out how these individuals function. Consequently, one cannot offer them attractive employment situations.

The present chapter primarily deals with these outstanding individuals who are capable of producing unique ideas, services, and goods. They undeniably belong to the top levels in the group of talents which companies desperately search for but do not always find because they do not really know who they are. Google call such people *smart creatives*. They are characterised by, amongst other things, their very high intellectual capacity, their creativity, their expertise in several areas, and their ability to solve problems (Schmidt & Rosenberg, 2014). The market has a lot to learn from Google in terms of how one might search for, understand, employ, and encourage these individuals. This is talent management, of course, but it is talent management that has been updated by experience that has been taken from many, relatively isolated, knowledge areas and studies of human capabilities (Persson, 2016).

American ideas and changing ideals

The fact that talent management is a relatively new area in the labour market and in academic research is not without its problems. The need for strategies which can actually optimise employees and their production increases much more quickly than what research and experience can satisfy. The difference between existing knowledge and this need has resulted in a large number of recommendations and advice which often lack support in empirical research and properly tested experience. Dries' (2013) analysis of approximately 7,000 published articles (and book chapters) which specifically dealt with *talent management* showed that only 100 of these articles had been published in traditional, peer-reviewed journals. A significant number of these articles were American in origin, which suggests that the application of the recommendations and ideas which appear in these articles is strongly bound to American culture.

Talent management is thus, primarily, an American invention. Besides being built on a certain cultural value system, American talent management is based on a legal system which is often at odds with the legal systems of other countries. In Europe, the hiring and firing of employees, workplace codetermination, and the influence of labour unions is regulated to a much higher degree than it is in the United States (Brewster et al., 2008). Consequently, it is not recommended, from a European perspective, that one uncritically looks for advice and guidance about talent management from the American literature or the American experience, or from consultants who are inspired by these American sources (Ralston et al., 1997).

One important difference between the American literature and the emergent European literature on the topic of talent management is that the American literature primarily focuses on particularly promising individuals in companies and organisations. European companies often prefer not to identify and construct a career plan for individual employees; at least not without also doing so for every employee (Diener, 2011; Fuchs, 2014). In Sweden, researchers at the Stockholm School of Economics have identified three different ideals, according to which talent management has been operationalised in a number of select Swedish companies (Bolander et al., 2014). These ideals are (i) *humanist*, (ii) *competitive*, and (iii) *entrepreneurial* in nature. The *humanist* approach states that everyone is included in different ways to further develop themselves for the organisation's best. Promising employees thus very seldom benefit from special conditions or privileges. However, in Sweden there are also approaches which are based on *competitive* conditions – and are closely related to American values and ideas – where one does not hesitate in searching for particularly promising employees within and without one's organisation. Such employees follow an individualised career path, the success of which is constantly followed-up on, evaluated, and adjusted. The third strategy can be seen as a hybrid mixture of the humanist ideal and competitive beliefs. The *entrepreneurial* strategy exposes every employee (not only specially chosen talents) to performance evaluations and assesses their continued career. "Win or disappear" is how this strategy is described by the researchers from the School of Economics.

It is hardly new that organisations wish to search for, and keep, employees who seem to possess the best abilities that will possibly benefit the organisation. The predecessor to talent management was called *strategic human resource management* (SHRM). The development towards talent management proper has echoed changes in society; the movement towards a global knowledge economy where the workforce which represents expert knowledge in different ways is expected to be flexible and mobile, in contrast to earlier expectations where such employees were permanent, and fixed in one location. Talent management is more elitist than its predecessor. Those individuals who potentially 'have talent' in an organisation are assumed to have different needs, in addition to having different backgrounds. Consequently, they are treated somewhat differently to other employees. They are expected to have greater demands on their conditions of employment and on the benefits which they contractually expect from their employer. In step with this, the employer's demands of the talents who are employed also increase, and expectations of what a newly appointed talent can do from the very beginning are also increased (Dries, 2013). The difference between the old paradigm and the new approach is summarised in Table 14.1.

The ability to predict possible potential in the future has been displaced by an immediate manifestation of what talent can do, here and now; an impatience of the market's behalf which is not particularly successful. A talent management strategy which does not build upon a properly researched understanding of how individuals operate in an organisation will lead to a situation where one spends all one's time looking for 'better' individuals, instead of

TABLE 14.1 An overview of the shift that has occurred over time with respect to typical issues dealt with by management

Then	*Now*
Strategic human resource management	Talent management
Focus on potential talent with respect to production and performance in the future	Focus on talent which can immediately perform and produce
People need companies	Companies need people
Machines, capital, and geographic location are competitive advantages	Talented individuals provide a competitive edge
Talent makes a certain difference	Talent is crucial
There are not many jobs	There are not many talented individuals
Employees are loyal and jobs are permanent and safe	The workforce is mobile and the employees' contracts are short-term contracts
Employees accept the salary and other benefits that they are offered	Employees have higher demands with respect to salary and other benefits

Adapted from Fuchs (2014) and Michaels et al. (2001).

improving upon the culture and working conditions of one's own organisation; the very conditions which perhaps pose a hindrance to current employees from doing their best (Pfeffer, 2001). Even if it has a talent management strategy in place, an organisation must continue to be interested in its other employees, their needs, and their development within the organisation (Swailes & Blackburn, 2016).

Irrespective of which ideals or research that talent management is based upon, what all models and suggestions in this area have in common is that they *structure* companies and organisations in a manner which is assumed to benefit the organisation in the global knowledge economy, and as a rule, this is from a point of departure where the *individual* employee and this person's function and value is compared to intended goals (Lewis & Heckman, 2006).

Before one can structure an organisation in accordance to the tenets of talent management, a reasonable point of departure is to first define what is actually meant by *talent*. This is more easily said than done!

What is talent?

The study of talent has a very long tradition. Even during the Middle Ages, people thought about what it was that enabled some individuals to know more than others, and to do things faster, better, and more efficiently than others. When this happened, people were worried and claimed that if this were to continue then it would inevitably lead to sickness and madness. Talents during the Middle Ages were thus encouraged – to the extent that they were noticed – to 'take things easy' (Grinder, 1985).

In the present work-life context, which is characterised by a strategic war over the recruitment and retention of the best talents, hardly anyone would entertain the idea of asking talents to take things easy and decrease their energy levels and rate of production. Quite the opposite! The more productive and frenetic one is, the better it is for the employer; a situation that many have paid for by losing their health. A total of 51% of the American population lie awake at night because of stress (APA, 2015). The cult of hyperperformance which permeates knowledge economies creates stress even when people are trying to be happy. We compete against each other to see who is the most successful. Paul Verhaeghe (2014) claims that the results of this intense competition for a great number of people are disorientation, a twisted sense of self, and despair.

Perhaps people in the Middle Ages were somewhat correct about talented people, despite the fact that their ideas and conclusions were built on classical assumptions about the importance of the theory of the four humours – blood, yellow bile, black bile, and phlegm – of which a proper balance should be maintained if a person is to enjoy good health. Of course, the talent is not the problem in itself, but rather, how the talent is (mis)used by the talented person and by employers, to the detriment of the talented person's health. The current social developments often entail a threat against stressed, talented people and the global population in general (McMichael & Beaglehole, 2000).

Despite a somewhat lengthy tradition of philosophical speculation and rigorous studies in several different academic disciplines, there remains no consensus on what *talent* represents and how we might best define it (Dai, 2010; Gallardo-Gallardo et al., 2013; Persson, 2014). To make the situation even more complicated, different interests in society use different terms, including *gifted*, *specially gifted*, *creative*, *high-performing*, *expert*, *eminence*, *genius*, and *excellence*, to name but a few. According to Brown and Hesketh (2004: 194), "a further problem is that talent has little meaning in the abstract". They continue:

> Many organizations have become impatient. They want more than someone with potential; the want people who can 'hit the ground running.' They want people who can add immediate value.

Thus we note that talent in the labour market and in the current political discourse is understood as immediate, profitable, human capital which is worth investing in (Florida, 2002), all the while the academic world continues to focus on an abstract understanding of how and why talents exist. The market needs to take heed of academic researchers, and vice versa.

The world's best Google?

Google, currently the world's most attractive and probably the most well-known employer, has a well-established reputation of being able to attract the best available talents (Dill, 2014; Schmidt & Rosenberg, 2014). Google has a great deal to say about talent and the attributes which they expect their employees should possess. There is even a special term for these desirable attributes: *Googleyness*. This term stands for a complex collection of attributes which are assumed to describe a talented person; for example, hedonistic and seeking amusement, intellectual humbleness, conscientiousness, tolerant of ambiguity, independent, and able to take calculated risks (Baer, 2015).

What is of interest is that Google, as a company, sometimes supersedes what the academic world has to say about creative people's behaviour, as they create their own conceptualisation of differentiating between individuals and how employees are expected to work and act within the organisation (Schmidt & Rosenberg, 2014). Some of these ideas are ground breaking and are well worth taking seriously, whilst others should be seen as expressions of wishful thinking and myth creating. For example, consider Google's individual, and very generous, salary scales. They argue that talent should be generously rewarded. But when the employees at Google recently found out how large the differences in salaries actually were, there was a mini revolt at the company, which caused problems for the company's management (Owen, 2015). Many employees felt that they had been treated unfairly. Google had simply not understood that there are limits to the differences in salary that can be given to employees, and when these limits are crossed then this has a negative effect on the other employees. When the differences in salary are too large, dissatisfaction and rebellion is the result, instead of employee cohesion and satisfaction (Beer & Katz, 2003; Wilkinson & Pickett, 2009).

Google's employees are called *smart creatives*. One of the attributes which characterises these individuals, according to the company, is supposedly of value to a more general talent management model, namely: *The person who is more knowledgeable and creative than you is talented*. For Google's employees, this entails that it is a particularly positive situation if the person who is applying for a job eclipses the people who are recruiting candidates for a particular job. Consequently, at Google, every employee is expected to participate in the selection of candidates for a particular position, not only the HR department. The engineers select those engineers who they would wish to work with, and designers choose the designers who they wish to work with, in their team. In this peculiar recruitment arrangement, the new people who are employed are expected to exceed the brilliance shown by current employees. Google warns against making only the HR department responsible for recruitment. If the HR department is left solely responsible for recruitment, then this often leads to a situation where the employees are *less* brilliant than what one wanted.

Of course, there is no guarantee that brilliant engineers will select engineers who are even more brilliant than themselves to work with. There is research that shows that collectives (for example, a work team) actually do not like to work with individuals who are considerably smarter than themselves (Judge et al., 2004). Google also underestimates the fact that the more extremely creative and/ or intelligent an individual is, the more difficult it is to establish a functional team which includes such an individual (Lévy, 1994; Nijstad & Paulus, 2003). In this regard, the American work culture is somewhat paradoxical. The individual's uniqueness and ability to take the initiative is highly valued, but at the same time, unreasonable demands are often placed on this unique individual, for example, that he or she must be part of a well-functioning group. It may be the case that a group of people can be both more creative and more intelligent together than what an individual might be. The task is to successfully bring a group together where everyone accepts and respects each other, and everyone complements everyone else and is attuned to each other. To put together a successful work team is a challenge under normal circumstances (Belbin, 2010). To put together a functional team of smart creatives is even more difficult because of the extreme individualism that often characterises gifted individuals (Nauta & Ronner, 2013; Persson, 2009).

The problem with creating functional work groups is not, however, the same as not being able to use these particularly insightful, high-performing, and creative individuals as a significant asset within an organisation. Zvi Sever (2011: 454) writes enthusiastically that

> Nurturing the gifted and talented students will guarantee a constant reservoir of individuals who will later lead both this research and development, and education, thus continuing to propel recruitment of the community, the State, and humanity at large toward a knowledge-based economy.

Instead of assuming that these individuals be placed in different predetermined work groups, one should take their individualism into account.

Extreme talents

Extremely creative and/or intelligent individuals are often passed over during traditional recruitment processes because of misunderstandings. These applicants might behave in a manner different to what the employer might expect during the recruitment process. Furnham (2008), for example, observed that highly creative individuals seeking work are often overlooked when hiring because they do not really fit into anticipated pattern and are often also seen as trouble makers.

Brown and Hesketh (2004), rather cynically, call this category of job applicants "the iffies". They note that these applicants often fail to be convincing during recruitment interviews. They give the impression that they lack intensity, professionalism, and enthusiasm for the very job that they are applying for. They are often very socially competent, but are seen as being far too idealistic and naïve by potential employers. A Canadian HR manager (in Kelly-Streznewski, 1999: 132) described the situation as:

> We had one very gifted young chap. He came up with two ideas which we have unashamedly stolen. But he never learned to follow normal procedure.

Couldn't fill out a PY3 form to save his life. He left us after seven months and I think it was for the best.

These 'different' individuals could probably be able to solve many of the company's problems and give them a competitive edge over their competition, but because the labour market so seldom knows how this category of job-seekers or employees operate, it is not unusual that the 'baby is thrown out with the bathwater'. These extremely talented (but often ignored) people are subject to boredom and alienation at work, whilst employers, on their part, are frustrated by the fact that these employees do not fit into a preconceived pattern and they do not like being questioned because their decisions might be illogical.

A Swedish study showed that 75% of employees with an IQ of 130 or higher were completely underutilised (as a resource) at their job, and were consequently quite unhappy at work (Person, 2009). They did the work which they were contractually obliged to perform, but not a jot more, and without any enthusiasm. Twenty-five percent of the group, however, were very happy with their job. They were seen to be unbelievably creative, productive, and efficient. They felt that their work was very satisfying, and the levels of satisfaction were high. In contrast to the larger and somewhat unhappy group of employees, the smaller and more productive group consisted of high-level managers and business owners. One spontaneously wrote to us and reported the following (as translated from Swedish):

> I have several of my own companies because, amongst other things, I want to avoid those moments of frustration that one almost inevitably is subject to when one is an employee. But it is also great fun to be able to develop one's own ideas and concepts. Of course, one is still bound to relate to one's employees, but this is offset by the fact that one still has room to manoeuvre in.
>
> *(Male business owner, pc, 2011)*

Room to manoeuvre in is key to understanding that a person's relative freedom is perhaps the most important factor which prompts these particularly talented individuals to be engaged, creative, and productive. For researchers of creativity, this is already well known (Amabile, 1996; Csikszentmihalyi, 1996; Sosniak, 2006). Excellence in all of its forms is never solely dependent on individuals; excellence is a manifestation of a system which consists of individuals *and* the surrounding environment, which must be accepting, supportive, and encouraging.

As noted earlier, Google has understood the importance of this relative freedom with respect to recruitment (Schmidt & Rosenberg, 2014). Not only does every employee have 20% time off (free time) during which they are expected to work with whatever inspires them (which is often, but not necessarily, a developmental idea that is related to Google's wide range of technologies and IT services). These employees are encouraged to take risks with their ideas and inventions. Every company accepts success, of course, but Google also accepts possible failure and unsuccessful efforts. With this security net in place, Google's engineers are especially active and productive.

It has been known for some time that 'room to manoeuvre in' and relative freedom enables creativity and innovation within organisations (Lobel, 2013). But companies and organisations have often ignored this knowledge, in the erroneous belief that the same results can be achieved by rigorous quality control and strict management instructions, something which is typical in the knowledge economy. However, the more control over the work a smart creative experiences, the less creative and less productive this person becomes. The same does not necessarily apply to nonsmart creatives. A more average employee has, as a rule, more tolerance for control, a lack of logic in the instructions received, and routine work assignments. But even these employees have their breaking point; and so the ethics of applied control makes itself felt. What constitutes 'too much control'? When do one's work conditions and one's work environment become dehumanising? (Haslam et al., 2008). Differences in tolerance levels in different groups of employees can cause conflicts. The tacit, but often incorrect, assumption is that everyone is the same in all respects, but this is hardly ever true.

Now we are in a position to formulate several suitable general guidelines which can be used to optimise the work situation for those employees who may well be more brilliant and productive that what you yourself are.

Talent management for extreme talents

Of course, this group of particularly gifted individuals is a relatively small group compared to the rest of society. Approximately 2% of the population possesses an IQ of 130 or more. It is quite possible that you have at least one such colleague at your place of work, but the question is whether you can identify this person. Their behaviour might be interpreted incorrectly because of a lack of knowledge about what characterises these individuals. A summary list of the relevant features is provided in Table 14.2 (as inspired by Lackner, 2012; Nauta & Ronner, 2008, 2013).

In the current competition over the world's best talents, researchers have begun to pay attention to this extremely gifted group of individuals (Michaels et al., 2001). They have not only discovered these individual's often isolated position in society, but they have also come to understand the underutilised resource that these people are in society and at work. However, these people need to be identified, accepted for who they are, and employed in a manner which promotes their inspiration and abilities.

If particular work tasks are adapted to suit gifted employees, instead of trying to get them to adapt to the work tasks, then it will be more probable that the relationship between employer and employee will be mutually beneficial.

TABLE 14.2 Correct and incorrect interpretations of the behaviour of gifted colleagues which colleagues and managers may make at work

Observation	Incorrect conclusion	Correct conclusion
The colleague works quickly and efficiently despite the fact that the work assignment is a new work assignment.	The area of work being done is of interest to the colleague and is thus quite suitable for the colleague.	The rapid mastery of a new area is typical of a gifted colleague, but is not proof of a particular interest in the work being done.
The colleague finishes assigned tasks quickly.	The colleague must learn to work more slowly, or else he or she might make a serious mistake.	Particularly gifted colleagues are often very meticulous in their work. They can be given additional work tasks to complete.
The colleague often assumes responsibility for several work assignments at the same time.	The colleague has difficulty in concentrating on one assignment, and is in danger of getting bogged down with too much work.	Particularly gifted colleagues can process very complex themes and can synthesise them into something that is understandable and can be applied in practice.

Note: As developed by Lackner (2012).

The following tips have been provided by researchers who have studied these specific questions (Lackner, 2012; Nauta & Ronner, 2008, 2013):

> Learn how to identify specially gifted candidates during the recruitment process. They will probably behave in a manner which is unexpected, but this is not necessarily negative. Examine your own expectations with respect to how a 'suitable' candidate should behave.
>
> Avoid assigning specially gifted employees work tasks which do not pose enough of a challenge to them. Instead, trust them to perform advanced and sufficiently demanding tasks, under relative freedom.
>
> If possible, limit the specially gifted employee's interactions with the different hierarchical functions in the organisation. It is better for them to be responsible to one manager, so as to avoid their interaction with several management levels.
>
> Avoid formal procedures, routines, and bureaucracy in favour of activities that are considered to be meaningful for the employee.
>
> Allow for productive conflicts. Misunderstandings often cause conflict, so provide space in which these can be dealt with.

Note that conflicts can be constructive, but certain cultural differences in the Western nations may cause certain employees to avoid any perceived conflict if they are dissatisfied or cannot agree with others at the workplace.

Careful consideration should also be made before an intellectually gifted person is to be promoted to a top management position. It may well be a good strategy to determine whether the person will be the manager of evenly matched colleagues (Dauten, 1999). However, the greater the difference in abstract thinking ability between the management and the other employees, the more difficult communication becomes between these two groups. Simonton (1994) observes that modern leadership – creative leadership as well as political leadership – demands a level of knowledge which is equivalent to a bachelor's degree if such leadership is to work in our modern and complex society. However, Simonton claims that the higher the employee's formal educational achievement is, past the bachelor's degree level, the more difficult it is for them to be outstanding and to make a historical impression. This researcher calculates that the person's optimal abstract thinking ability (measured in terms of the person's IQ) should be between 105 and 119. The higher the manager's IQ, the fewer sympathisers and admirers that person will have. When a person has an IQ of 156 or more, then that person will have no sympathisers or admirers at all. A workforce who is led by an incredibly intelligent manager will have great difficulties in understanding how that person thinks, and vice versa. To be the project manager working under specially adapted and time-limited conditions is one thing, but to place a intellectually gifted employee in a top management position often leads to disappointment; unless the person is *primus/prima inter pares*, 'first among equals'.

Recommended reading

Ivancevich, John M. & Duening, Thomas M. (2001), *Managing Einsteins: Leading high-tech workers in the digital age*. New York: McGraw-Hill.
Nauta, Noks & Ronner, Sieuvke (2013), *Gifted workers hitting the target*. Maastricht, NL: Shaker Media.
Robertson, Alan & Abbey, Graham (2003), *Managing talented people: Getting on with – and getting the best from – your top people*. London: Pearson Education.
Schmidt, Eric & Rosenberg, Jonathan (2014), *How google works*. London: John Murray.

References

Amabile, Teresa M. (1996), *Creativity in context*. Boulder, CO: Westview Press.
APA (2015), *Stress in America: Paying with your health*. Washington, DC: American Psychological Association.
Baer, Drake (2015), 13 qualities Google looks for in job candidates. *Business Insider*. Retrieved from www.businessinsider.com [2015-09-11].
Beer, Michael & Katz, Nancy (2003), Do incentives work? The perception of a worldwide sample of senior executives. *Human Resource Planning, 26*(3), pp. 30–44.
Belbin, R. Meredith (2010), *Team roles at work*. (2nd edition). Amsterdam, NL: Elsevier.
Bethke-Langenegger, Pamela, Mahler, Philippe & Staffelbach, Bruno (2011), Effectiveness of talent management strategies. *European Journal of International Management, 5*(5), pp. 524–539.
Bolander, Pernilla, Asplund, Kajsa & Werr, Andreas (2014), *Talent management in a collectivstic and egalitarian context: The Swedish case*. SSE/EFI Working Paper Series in Business Administration No. 2014:2.

Brewster, Chris, Dickmann, Michael & Sparrow, Paul (2008), A European perspective on HRM. In Michael Dickmann, Chris Brewster & Paul Sparrow (eds.), *International human resource management: A European perspective* (pp. 9–18). London: Routledge.

Brown, Philip & Hesketh, Anthony (2004), *The mismanagement of talent: Employability and jobs in the knowledge economy.* Oxford: Oxford University Press.

Chambers, Elizabeth G., Foulon, Mark, Handfield-Jones, Helene, Hankin, Steven M. & Michaels, Edward G. (1998), The war for talent. *The McKinsey Quarterly Online, 3,* pp. 1–8.

Csikszentmihalyi, Mihalyi (1996), *Creativity: Flow and the psychology of discovery and invention.* New York: Harper.

Dai, David Y. (2010), *The nature and nurture of giftedness: A new framework for understanding gifted education.* New York: Teachers College Press.

Dauten, Dale (1999), *The gifted boss: How to find, create and keep great employees.* New York: William Morrow.

Diener, Fredy (2011), ABB: Talente fördern für die Zukunft. [Promoting talent for the future] In Adrian Ritz & Norbert Thom (eds.), *Talent Management: Talente identifizieren, Kompetenzen entwickeln, Leistungsträger erhalten* [Identifying talent, developing competencies, and retaining top performers] (pp. 69–82). Heidelberg: Gabler.

Dill, Kathryn (2014), The world's most attractive employers 2014. *Forbes online.* Retrieved from www.forbes.com [2015-09-06].

Dries, Nicky (2013), The psychology of talent management: A review and research agenda. *Human Resource Management Review, 23,* pp. 272–285.

Florida, Richard (2002), The economic geography of talent. *Annals of the Association of American Geographers, 92*(4), pp. 743–755.

Fuchs, Maria (2014), *Engineering professionals: A comparison between U.S. and Austrian talent management systems.* A Marshall Plan Scholarship Paper. Retrieved from www.marshallplan.at [2015-08-09].

Furnham, Adrian (2008), *Personality and intelligence at work: Exploring and explaining individual differences at work.* London: Routledge.

Gallardo-Gallardo, Eva, Dries, Nicky & Gonzalez-Cruz, Tomás F. (2013), What is the meaning of talent in the world of work? *Human Resource Management Review, 23,* pp. 290–300.

Grinder, Robert E. (1985), The gifted in our midst: By their divine deeds, neuroses, and mental test scores we have known them. In Frances Degen Horowitz & Marion O'Brien (eds.), *The gifted and talented: Developments and perspectives* (pp. 5–36). Washington, DC: American Psychological Association.

Haslam, Nick, Kashima, Yoshihisa, Loughan, Stephen, Shi, Junqi & Suitner, Caterina (2008), Subhuman, inhuman, and superhuman: Contrasting humans with nonhumans in three cultures. *Social Cognition* (special issue: *Missing links in Social Cognition*), *26,* pp. 248–258.

Judge, Timothy A., Colbert, Amy E. & Ilies, Remus (2004), Intelligence and leadership: A quantitative review and test of theoretical propositions. *Journal of Applied Psychology, 89*(3), pp. 542–552.

Kelly-Streznewski, Marylou (1999), *Gifted grown-ups: The mixed blessings of extraordinary potentials.* Hoboken, NJ: Wiley.

Lackner, Maximilian (2012), *Talent-Management spezial: Hoch-Begabte, Forscher, Künstler ... erfolgreich führen.* Wiesbaden: Gabler.

Lévy, Pierre (1994), *Collective intelligence: Mankind's emerging world in cyberspace.* Cambridge, MA: Perseus Books.

Lewis, Robert E. & Heckman, Robert J. (2006), Talent management: A critical review. *Human Resource Management Review, 16,* pp. 139–154.

Lobel, Orly (2013), *Talent wants to be free: Why we should learn to love leaks, raids, and free riding*. New Haven, NJ: Yale University Press.

McMichael, Andrew J. & Beaglehole, Robert (2000), The changing global context of public health. *The Lancet, 356*, pp. 495–499.

Michaels, Ed, Handfield-Jones, Helene & Axelrod, Beth (2001), *The war for talent*. Boston, MA: Harvard Business School Press.

Nauta, Noks & Ronner, Sieuvke (2008), Hoogbegaafdheid op het werk Achtergronden en praktische aanbevelingen. [Giftedness at work: Background and practical recommendations] *Tijdschrift voor Bedrijfs- en Verzekeringsgeneeskunde, 16*(9), pp. 396–399.

Nauta, Noks & Ronner, Sieuvke (2013), *Gifted workers hitting the target*. Maastricht, NL: Shaker Media.

Nijstad, Bernard A. & Paulus, Paul B. (2003), Group creativity: Common themes and future directions. In Paul B. Paulus & Bernard A. Nijstad (eds.), *Group creativity: Innovation through collaboration* (pp. 326–339). New York: Oxford University Press.

O'Boyle, Ernest & Aguinis, Herman (2012), The best and the rest: Revisiting the norm of normality of individual performance. *Personnel Psychology, 65*(1), pp. 79–119.

Owen, Jonathan (2015), Google employees are comparing their salary details in a bid to be fairly paid. *The Independent*. Retrieved from www.independent.co.uk [2015-09-08].

Persson, Roland p. (2009), Intellectually gifted individuals' career choices and work satisfaction: A descriptive study. *Gifted and Talented International, 24*(1), pp. 11–24.

Persson, Roland p. (2014), The needs of the highly able and the needs of society: A multidisciplinary analysis of talent differentiation and its significance to gifted education and issues of societal inequality. *Roeper Review, 36*, pp. 1–17.

Persson, Roland p. (2016), Human nature: The unpredictable variable in engineering the future. In Don Ambrose & Robert J. Sternberg (eds.), *Giftedness and talent in the 21st century: Adapting to the turbulence of globalization* (pp. 65–80). Rotterdam, NL: Sense.

Pfeffer, Jeffrey (2001), Fighting the war for talent is hazardous to your organization's health. *Organizational Dynamics, 29*(4), pp. 248–259.

Ralston, David A., Holt, David H., Terpstra, Robert H. & Kai-Cheng, Yu (1997), The impact of national culture and economic ideology on managerial work values: A study of the United States, Russia, Japan, and China. *Journal of International Business Studies, 28*(1), pp. 177–207.

Schmidt, Eric & Rosenberg, Jonathan (2014), *How google works*. London: John Murray.

Sever, Zvi (2011), Nurturing gifted and talented pupils as leverage towards a knowledge-based economy. In Qing Zhou (ed.), *Applied social science: ICASS 2011. Volume one* (pp. 454–458). Newark, DE: IERI Press.

Simonton, Dean Keith (1994), *Greatness: Who makes history and why?* New York: Guilford Press.

Sosniak, Lauren A. (2006), Retrospective interviews in the study of expertise and expert performance. In K. Anders Ericsson, Neil Charness, Paul J. Feltovich & Robert R. Hoffman (eds.), *The Cambridge handbook of expertise and expert performance* (pp. 287–301). Cambridge: Cambridge University Press.

Swailes, Stephen & Blackburn, Michelle (2016), Employee reactions to talent pool membership. *Employee Relations, 38*(1), pp. 112–128.

Verhaeghe, Paul (2014), *What about me? The struggle for identity in a market-based society*. Brunswick, VIC: Scribe.

Wilkinson, Richard & Pickett, Kate (2009), *The spirit level: Why equality is better for everyone*. London: Penguin Books.

CONCLUSION

HR work – a balancing act with integrity

Ingela Bergmo-Prvulovic and Karin Kilhammar

Each chapter of this book has touched on a variety of themes which are all relevant to how HR work is performed. There are a number of common denominators found in each chapter which form a pattern which should inform the reader what future HR work might look like and what stimulating and sometimes difficult tasks that HR departments perform today. In this concluding chapter, we identify those features which we consider to be the book's central ideas. The following central notions are gaining importance in HR work: *cooperation, reciprocity, shared responsibility*, and *inclusion*. Each of these ideas entails a continual balancing act between different interests, perspectives, and needs. In this context, the ability of the HR department to communicate in a pedagogic and ethical manner is crucial. These observations have led us to formulate three concrete challenges which we believe will be particularly prominent for future HR work. The challenges are to adopt and preserve (i) a critical approach towards current trends and conditions, (ii) a relational and holistic perspective on HR work, and (iii) a positive view of people and an ethical approach to HR work.

Dealing with these challenges demands special competencies. Using Illeris' (2011, 2013) conceptualisation of 'competence' (where he identifies critical perspectives, the potential to show opposition, combinatorial abilities, empathy, creativity, imagination, flexibility, and intuition as central elements of 'competence'), we discuss why and how these elements are also central to those individuals who work in HR.

Challenges for the HR work of the future

The fact that a rapid rate of change currently permeates work-life and organisations is no longer new to people. During the last few decades, many researchers, using different approaches and perspectives, have investigated what the change to a global knowledge economy entails for organisations and for people (Ekstedt, 2009; Ekstedt & Sundin, 2006). Using the ideas discussed in the various chapters of this book as points of departure, we note that there are several areas which HR work is generally concerned with. These areas are presented as specific to HR work, are generally accepted (and thus stable), and are prominent in the literature that deals with the core areas of HR work (Björkman & Stahl, 2006; McGuire, 2014).

Ulfsdotter Eriksson (2013) describes HR work's central areas as *the employee's life-cycle*, which consists of four parts: *attract, develop, retain,* and *retire*. HR work can thus be described in terms of a so-called 'whole chain approach'. Nilsson et al. (2011) employ a similar model, including three phases of the 'competence provision process'. These three phases are (i) IN – *attract, recruit*; (ii) REMAIN – *introduce, develop, evaluate, reward, retain*; and (iii) OUT – *retire, replace*. These models that describe the core areas of HR work reveal that this work is primarily about people's lives as they relate to an organisation, and the employee's *movement to the organisation, movement into the organisation, movement within the organisation,* and *movement out from the organisation*. All of the chapters in this book touch on this life-cycle in different ways, focussing on different aspects.

However, even if it is the case that these core areas are 'stable' in the sense that they continually reappear and clearly characterise HR work, they are still influenced by trends and changes that take place within, and outside the organisation. They are also influenced by the perspectives which the organisation's leaders and employees bring with them, including trends and ideas which people fondly embrace, care about, and try to implement. They are also influenced by the people inhabiting the organisation, and their reactions and ways of managing and coping with changes they are involved in. The book's first part introduces a number of terms which clearly show how certain ideas and perspectives impact on the trends and ways of speaking about areas that are directly connected to HR work. These include *co-workership* (Chapter 1), *career* (Chapter 4), and *creativity* (Chapter 5).

Our work-life and the society that we live in is inundated with new key terms which inform our daily work-life. These different terms appear in our everyday speech, in businesses strategy documents, in national and international policy documents, and in the media. Sometimes these terms are used uncritically, and primarily to signal that the person who is using them is 'up to date' with the latest trends (cf. Illeris, 2013). So why do certain key terms have more impact than others at different times? It probably depends on which need is in focus in the public debate at each time point and on who is driving the agenda forward with the most convincing rhetoric (Abrahamson, 1996).

Today, we observe that economic interests are dominant. For example, a number of trends have emerged in association with a new interest in strategies for lifelong learning. 'Lifelong learning' was originally a humanistic concept which argued for the provision of education to adults (Rubensson, 2006). With the rise of globalisation and the emerging knowledge economy, the needs of organisations and social and economic conditions have come to the fore (Jarvis, 2009), thereby establishing new key terms. *Competence* is a term that rose to prominence in Sweden in the beginning of the 1980s. It was characterised by a perspective on work management and motivation which was developed under *human resource management* (HRM) (Illeris, 2011, 2013). Changes in work- and competitive conditions, with an increasing focus on external efficiency, the market, and one's customers contributed to the rise in prominence of *competence* as a key term. Further to this, there has been an increasing emphasis in social debates and policy documents on the individual's responsibility to drive forward, control, and develop their career, competence, flexibility, and adaptability in the face of repeated changes (see, e.g., Bengtsson, 2011; Bergmo-Prvulovic, 2012). These trends have come to characterise the way education and work-life are spoken about, thereby influencing the choice of key terms that are used and come to dominate these conversations. Many researchers who have examined the use of different key terms (as they are trending) in policy documents concerning education, work-life, and the labour market have shown that the language used in these texts is clearly influenced by economic perspectives and market logic (see, e.g., Bergmo-Prvulovic, 2012; Fejes, 2010). Using Thompson's (1967) arguments about uncertainty (to wit, that it is a fundamental problem which must be dealt with and solved in complex organisations), we come to understand these trends as just *reactions to uncertainty* in organisational contexts.

Different key terms thus become established in our everyday speech, in our organisations, and our daily lives, at different time periods. Government authorities and organisations express their declarations of intent via their policy documents (Sparrhoff, 2016). We must thus attempt to understand and become aware of the key terms which are currently *en vogue* and understand why these particular key terms are dominant when they are. Consequently, the specific core areas of HR work must also be understood in relation to the time period and context they find themselves in, and be interrogated in relation with current trends and perspectives. It is clear that the questions that the HR function has to deal with are very complex. Thus the HR specialist needs to be able to examine problems from different perspectives which are grounded in a number of different scientific disciplines, including pedagogics, psychology, sociology, business economics, and law studies (Ulfsdotter Eriksson, 2013).

This book, as a whole, presents a number of discussions on different *concepts and ideas and their influence on the core areas of HR work*. The book also uncovers a number of risks that are associated with an uncritical acceptance and an overemphasis of certain perspectives in prevailing trends and attitudes, at the potential cost of other important perspectives on the multidisciplinary area that is the domain of the HR specialist.

We are now in a position to formulate the first challenge for HR work in the future:

Challenge 1: adopt and preserve a critical attitude towards current trends and conditions

Our first challenge is partly connected to what other researchers have said in the field, and partly to the core issues which are dealt with in the various chapters of this book. To understand and deal with the present time which we live in with awareness and in a balanced way, it is important that we keep ourselves updated with current changes in society. It is quite clear that we find ourselves in the middle of a transition to a knowledge-based, globalised society. This has direct implications with respect to recruitment and ways of retaining and re-warding one's employees. When we move to a situation where new structures are being established, what we knew and understood previously is challenged. We are engaged in an ongoing transition from old to new perspectives. Add to this the fact that work-life is now characterised by a new dynamic; namely the ability of people and organisations to be mobile, locally, nationally, and even globally. Furthermore, demographic changes must be dealt with by HR depart-ments, including issues about a prolonged work-life and an increasingly ageing population.

Whilst all these changes take place simultaneously, it is not strange to note that organisations are searching for different strategies to manage the uncertainty which is present in the current work-life. We claim that it is very important that HR students and professionals adopt and develop a critical attitude towards these trends. To be able to maintain a critical perspective on how trends, concepts, and ideas can influence one's daily HR practice, the HR specialist needs to continu-ally keep up to date with current research in various disciplines, which in various ways touch upon the core areas of HR work. Nilsson et al. (2011) highlight how the gap between research and practice can be bridged is an important challenge for future HR work. However, Haake and Löfgren Martinson (2016) demon-strate that HR students at university, despite acknowledging their training in critical reflection during their time as students, fail to practice critical reflection once they are actually employed as HR specialists because they do not have time to do so. Thus our challenge for the HR specialist is to continually remain a critical, reflective practitioner.

Potential friction that is caused by change within an organisation must be dealt with by the HR department by revealing, handling, balancing and bridg-ing people's different perspectives on the same concepts and phenomenon. For example, old, traditional and 'taken-for-granted' perspectives on what a career is may be challenged by new perspectives on careers (see Chapter 4). It is quite understandable that confusion and uncertainty may emerge in the tension be-tween different perspectives of careers. Friction may also be caused by different perspectives on the value of competence; between competence that is recruited from the local national labour pool and competence that is recruited from overseas (see Chapter 11). HR departments also need to deal with and unite different perspectives that are held by different generations; between young employees and the older employees (see Chapters 9 and 10). It is important to understand that each generation's perspective on different work-related questions is a function of the context and social era they are members of. It is thus natural that the older generation will subscribe to perspectives that are characterised by work-life conditions, structures, and ways of organising and rewarding work of an earlier age.

Several chapters in this book reveal a number of risks which today's multi-faceted and complicated work-life may pose for several different groups of people. The risk of *marginalisation, exclusion,* and *discrimination* is quite clear. These problems are highlighted by Hedegaard and Hugo (Chapter 12) and by Gillberg (Chapter 13). Both chapters deal with the perspectives which characterise the competence recruitment process. Gillberg emphasises the rehabilitation process for chronically ill people that is provided by HR departments, and the danger for marginalisation which can be the result of ways of working that lack flexibility (on the part of the employee). Gillberg sheds light on the dangers of loosing valuable knowledge from the organisation's perspective, and, on the other side, the dangers of marginalisation and exclusion on the employee's part. Hedegaard and Hugo also emphasise the importance of alternative ways of thinking about how work can be organised, so that people who suffer from different disabilities can be properly included as employees and given the opportunity to contribute to the organisation with their unique competencies.

If we continue with ingrained ways of working, without reflection, or if we uncritically accept trends that supposedly inform us how problems can be quickly resolved, a clear danger emerges that HR work might fail to notice what current and potential employees can contribute to the organisation. Instead of properly thought-out long-term plans, we run the risk of focusing on superficial issues, providing rapid solutions, satisfying short-term cost-effectiveness, and uncritically communicating the demands we make on people to take responsibility for their own adaptation to the organisation's needs.

The emphasis on the individual's responsibility to keep themselves 'employable' by continually developing their competence, participating in various learning activities, and being flexible enough to quickly 'reset' is an expression of the discourse of 'individualised responsibility' (Hobbins, 2016). Metaphorically, one might say that current employees are responsible for 'shaping up', so that they can fit precisely into the organisation's jig-saw puzzle. This is in agreement with currents in society which are characterised by increased levels of individualisation and a concomitant weakening of the worker's collective. Since HR work is inherently relational, the observations above highlight the issue of responsibility: What division of responsibility is made between the employee and the employer? The question of responsibility is clearly a question of mutual character. This leads us to our second challenge for future HR work.

Challenge 2: adopt and preserve a relational and holistic perspective on HR work

A theme that is common to all of the chapters of this book refers to human beings within organisations and the relationship between human beings and organisations. This relationship is one of mutual exchange. The employees' abilities, competence, and work efforts contribute to the organisation's operations and success. Human beings who are committed to the organisation receive a platform for the development and proper utilisation of their competencies. They become part of the context where they can find expression for their abilities and their creativity. Hopefully, through the execution of their work, they may come to feel that they are doing something meaningful (Antonovsky, 1987). One trend that has been observed is the increased influence of market forces, where 'profitability' and 'economic growth' are in focus. At the same time, 'competence'is said to be crucial to an organisation's success. Note that it is *human beings* in the organisation who are bearers of this competence.

One expression of the relationship referred to above is *talent management* (see Chapter 14), where companies and other organisations actively work to recruit specific talents to the organisation so as to use their competence. *Human capital* is a term that is also used to refer to the economic aspects of the human contributions that are made to an organisation. A great deal takes place according to the organisation's conditions, where people are often just pawns in a game. The exchange comes second place, even if a win-win situation can be achieved, where the people in the organisation can benefit too. Bergmo-Prvulovic, in Chapter 4, describes two variations of the HRM approach. The first approach, called 'hard HRM' focuses on the organisation only. The second variation, called 'soft HRM', more clearly emphasises the interaction between the individual and the organisation. This is the approach which she recommends, as it relates to the concept of 'careers'. Kilhammar (Chapter 1) also highlights the necessary mutual relationship between people and the organisation, where the development of co-workership cannot take place according to conditions set by the organisation only. Employees have to be engaged and create the co-workership in the organisation, and attention should be paid to the employees' perspective too. In other words, it is all about *interplay* between humans and organisation.

To this mix we add the complex nature of human beings, which should prevent people from being treated as things or as machines. These aspects of human nature and of human needs cannot be ignored; they must be taken into consideration and confronted if both people and organisations are to succeed. In addition to certain generally accepted aspects – such as people need to be recognised and acknowledged, be allowed to use their abilities, and feel that their work is meaningful – people have special needs that should be satisfied too. These needs are discussed in the second part of this book. Different groups of people are discussed, but it is noted that within groups of people we still differentiate between individuals, based on their needs, abilities, and interests.

Basing one's actions on the individual's and the group's conditions

Throughout the book, the necessity to adapt the work and the work environment to different individual's and group's conditions has been emphasised. The reason for this being that they should have opportunity to work and, for those who have work, they should be provided with the best possible conditions to function in their job and contribute to the achievement of the organisation's goals. We add to this organisational perspective a societal perspective, where the employer's social responsibility is emphasised (see Chapters 12 and 13). There are also legal requirements, for example, laws concerning discrimination and the work environment, which employers must be in compliance with.

Reciprocity and adaptation are not applicable to certain groups only. In the first part of the book, more overarching questions which concern organisations in general were dealt with, in the sense that specific groups of employees were not identified. In the chapter on co-workership development (Chapter 1), focus is placed on *all* employees where general factors relevant to the development of co-workership were mentioned. Engström (Chapter 2), who writes about interaction patterns in organisations and the structure of meetings, also refers to the importance of participation in both the execution of work and in developmental work in the organisation, for everyone within the organisation. The discrepancies which Bjursell and Raudberget (Chapter 3) identify in the work done in knowledge transfer and product development in a technology firm are also of a general nature. Lindberg (Chapter 5) adopts a holistic perspective with respect to the promotion of creativity in organisations which includes every employee. In the majority of the chapters, mention is made of the heterogeneity present in organisations, which entails that the employees' individual conditions and interests should also be taken into account.

How then can the relevant adaptations be made, so that employee competence can be used in a beneficial way? In several chapters in the second part of this book, concrete recommendations for adaptations and changes are provided, based on the research reported on in each chapter. The point that is made is that different groups of people need different forms of adaptations and other arrangements. For example, people who have high-functioning autism need structure and clarity, and should be tasked to do one thing at a time (Chapter 12), whilst people who are specially gifted need a high degree of freedom (Chapter 14). For immigrant employees, social fellowship at the workplace is important, so they can quickly enter the society of their new country and learn the new language (Chapter 11). Employees who are on long-term sick leave (depending on which illness they are suffering from) are not able to be physically present at work, and thus need to determine for themselves when and where they are to complete their work (Chapter 13). All these different circumstances and conditions demand different adaptations and other arrangements from one and the same organisation. At the same time, the general principles and structures which apply to everyone within the organisation, also need to be developed, including co-workership, career planning, knowledge sharing, and how meetings are structured.

Consequences for HR work

Just as human beings are complex, the work to be done by the HR department and managers is also complex, in the promotion of the human resources within the organisation. Below, we summarise the factors which we believe are crucial to working successfully with these questions.

Knowing which adaptations and other arrangements which are suitable and how one should act demands *knowledge of human aspects*. This point is emphasised repeatedly in each chapter of this book. A HR specialist is expected, by dint of his or her education and experience, to possess a basic knowledge of how people function and of the interaction between people and organisations. An HR specialist's unique competence allows for the examination of problems from different angles; an approach which is supported by the breadth of training provided in academic HR training programmes (Ulfsdotter Eriksson, 2013). But general knowledge of these issues is often not enough. As mentioned earlier, different factors are at play, depending on the area and category, and thus specific knowledge of (i) how the particular situation may play out and of (ii) the conditions which govern each group of people involved is needed. This necessitates the HR specialist's continuous learning and active search for knowledge in those areas the specialist is assigned to work, or when a need is identified with respect to beneficial adaptations for employees or for candidate employees during the recruitment process.

Knowledge about for example gender equality, HBTQ issues, different disabilities, or specially gifted people is required in order to implement suitable arrangements or relevant adaptations of the work situation, but it is not enough. Heterogeneity was a feature of many of the groups discussed in several chapters. Differences exist, both generally between employees (Chapters 1 and 3), and between individuals within specific groups (Chapters 8–14). These circumstances cause that the person who is tasked with working with these assignments also needs to take into careful consideration each individual's needs. The HR specialist thus needs to have the ability to show empathy for the employee and his or her life situation (Bohlin & Eklund, 2013; Doorewaard & Benschop, 2003).

Since the various needs of the different groups are markedly different, different needs and arrangements might be put into opposition with each other, something which may result in conflict. The HR specialist should possess a holistic overview of the whole organisation, its operations, and its employees and take note of whether an arrangement that is made to adapt the work situation of a particular individual or group of employees will give rise to negative consequences for a different individual or group of employees. According to Swedish legislation, adaptations that are made for an individual employee, for example, with the aim of providing rehabilitation for the employee, may not worsen the work environment for the other employees (Iseskog, 2013). This may cause problems for employees who are signed off work with long-term illnesses. But this does not entail that there is reason to avoid suggesting unconventional adaptations; rather, changes must be tested to see if they provide acceptable solutions for everyone. In this context, the HR department has a *pedagogic* role in spreading knowledge about the needs of different groups, and with working with the attitudes held by managers and employees. The success of an adaptation or other arrangement rests on how well anchored it is with the people who are affected by the change. It is also important to share knowledge about structures and norms that are taken for granted; especially such structures and norms which may pose obstacles for groups or individuals to use their whole capacity within the organisation.

Damm and Dahte (2016) write about how today's HR managers perceive their role and the balancing act that is central to HR managers' work, as they link the organisation's operations to the individual's needs and way of working. A primary task in this context is to demonstrate to the organisation's top management that specific HR arrangements actually benefit the organisation, thereby allowing management to sanction the work done by the HR department. This authorisation is necessary before any HR arrangements can be implemented. Thus, it is not the case that various arrangements are merely put in place to satisfy the workforce collective as a whole, but rather a balance between human perspectives and economic perspectives is sought out, where the goal of maintaining a functional and successful organisation is the ultimate guiding light.

The mere gathering of information and obtaining an understanding of the situation at hand is not sufficient; *action* is needed too. In the questions that are addressed in this section, we note that, in some cases, unconventional arrangements can be necessary if change is to come about. In work on gender equality and HBTQ issues (Chapters 7 and 8), for example, it may be the case that challenging ingrained attitudes about gender and sexuality gives rise to feelings of insecurity in employees and managers, which, in turn, may cause opposition and criticism. Even in the context of adaptations at the workplace, for example, for people who are disabled, norms, regulations, and habits at the workplace might need to be suspended or ignored, thereby causing some kind of reaction in the employees (Chapter 12). In such cases, a professional demeanour and attitude, consisting of courage and integrity, is needed, in the sense that one "knows what one's goals is and one is able to act in accordance with one's convictions and resist external pressure" (Nationalencyklopedin, 2016). *Creativity*, in the sense of being innovative and being able to 'think outside the box', is also necessary in the creation of suitable adaptations or changes in an organisation. Creativity, imagination, and the ability to come up with ingenious ideas, together with a solid knowledge base and practical wisdom should stand the HR specialist in good stead as she or he works towards creating an inclusive workplace. *Practical wisdom* refers to Aristotle's concept of 'fronesis'; ethical awareness and the ability to know what a good action is and to perform the same, according to the situation (Damm & Dahte, 2016; Flyvbjerg et al., 2012)

Knowledge of one's self and one's own beliefs is foundational to being able to work with the questions raised in this book. Ahl (Chapter 7) emphasises the importance of initially examining oneself and one's beliefs with respect to gender, so that one then engage in the same process of 'consciousness-raising' with managers and employees. This is applicable to all HR work where attitudes, values, and beliefs are central. Many examples of such situations are provided in this book. A critical approach is crucial in this regard, which is informed by self-reflection and thoughtful examination of new trends and perspectives and relate this to research findings in the area and an ethical approach.

The adoption of a relational and holistic perspective on HR work, as is revealed above, includes several different dimensions. This observation brings us to the next challenge which we wish to share at this juncture, where we focus on the person's whole life and how we relate to other people using an ethical perspective.

Challenge 3: adopt and preserve a positive view of people and an ethical approach to HR work

The way HR specialists view other people in the organisation is foundational to HR work. It is also an ethical issue. Akademikerförbundet SSR (a Swedish trade union for HR professionals) has compiled a number of important ethical aspects for HR specialists to consider, given the perspective that people take up a central position in organisations (Blennberger, 2015). This union highlights the importance of HR specialists holding a positive view of employees. They should be informed by the belief that people possess "resources that enable them to learn, be active, and creative" (Blennberger, 2015: 9) and that employees want to participate in, and influence, their work.

The union also argues that the HR specialist should value diversity in work groups, where people with different perspectives, experience, and knowledge can come together. HR specialists are bound to prevent discrimination at the workplace too. The 'human value principle' is a guiding principle; people are highly valued and everyone is valued equally. Every person should be treated with respect and every person's life and the effort that they make is worth caring for. At the same time, everyone is responsible for their own life situation (Blennberger, 2015). The HR department is responsible for supporting the development of each employee, ensuring his or her well-being and equal treatment, and align these goals with what is beneficial and advantageous for the organisation's operations.

This perspective on human beings as part of the organisation and on the HR department's role forms an excellent foundation for implementing changes in structures and norms in organisations which may seem to be discriminatory. This includes the motivation to take special action to remove obstacles which prevent individuals from exploiting their inherent resources, in cases where they could contribute to the organisation's success and their own well-being. HR departments should adopt this human perspective and educate others in the organisation of the importance of certain human aspects to the organisation (Blennberger, 2015; Ulfsdotter Eriksson, 2013). Supporting the employees' development and well-being also strengthens the organisation's human resources; something which should benefit the organisation's operations.

This ethical perspective goes beyond one's own organisation, however. It includes all of humanity. Situations may arise where an ethical action may stand in opposition to what is financially advantageous for the organisation, at least in the short term. Employers, represented by managers and the HR department, are in a position of power over the employees, not only during work hours, but the employee's whole life can be influenced by his or her work situation. This may include how the employee is treated and what opportunities for development are offered to the employee. This, in turn, may impact on the employee's self-confidence and sense of professionalism. An awareness of this power relationship is necessary if the organisation is to act in an ethically correct way (Blennberger, 2015). Organisations which HR specialists work for, and represent, are a part of society, and cannot be considered as isolated islands that have no relation to their environment. From this viewpoint, HR work encompasses more than merely ensuring what is best for the organisation. In several of the chapters in this book, the importance of the cooperation between employers and social institutions is highlighted, and the relative importance of the responsibility that workplaces have with respect to including different social groups and providing them with the opportunity to create a good life for themselves. This will allow them to be part of the organisation and to contribute their abilities to the success of the organisation, and to society at large. The HR department should take an active role with respect to the organisation's social responsibility and ethical behaviour (Parkes & Davis, 2013). The HR department can play a key role when it is involved in the employee's life-cycle within the organisation. The HR function has grown out of a sociopolitical movement which was based on the idea of adopting humanistic values as a counter-weight against Taylorism's focus on technology and rationality (Damm & Dahte, 2016; Tengblad, 2000). The ethical and humane aspects are constantly present at the workplace, even though work conditions and problems change with time. Thus, we must continually work on these questions and establish the foundational ethical and humane values that we desire, in the prevailing time.

The competencies that are needed at HR departments to meet future challenges

Taking into consideration the three challenges that we have discussed above, the reader should acknowledge that future HR work will be complex in nature. Great demands are placed on HR as it shapes its professional identity and the practical aspects of the profession, and includes the competencies that are needed to deal with such complexity. Notwithstanding the fact that HR stands for *human resources*, we choose to place emphasis on the *human* aspect of the role.

Illeris (2011, 2013) expands on several elements of the concept of 'competence' which are crucial to work that is directed towards people, and are not usually included in traditional definitions of *competence*. By using Illeris' concept of 'competence', we will conclude by giving our view of the specific competencies which we consider to be necessary for the HR specialist if he or she is to be able to deal with current situations and challenges. Illeris' concept of 'competence' includes *a critical perspective, the potential to show opposition, combinatorial ability, empathy, creativity, imagination, flexibility,* and *intuition*. All of these elements of competence clearly appear in the three challenges which we formulated above, and we highlight this fact in the following discussion. To these elements we should add the broad theoretical foundation as the basis of all HR work, where knowledge of several different disciplines makes changes in perspective possible in those situations which the HR specialist deals with professionally.

In our first challenge, we emphasise the importance of how HR students and practitioners need to adopt, develop, and continually strive for a critically aware approach to prevailing conditions. In connection with the judgements and decisions which the HR specialist has to make in their daily work, the necessity of a *critical perspective* is made apparent (Illeris, 2013). Such a perspective includes a certain amount of thoughtfulness; thus we do not act without reflection or react according to what others expect from us, and neither do we do what is seemingly desirable to do, at first glance. The element of *competence* includes our ability to doubt and to sometimes dismiss a situation or conditions that we may be confronted with. The next element, *the potential to show opposition*, demands courage and the strength to go against something which may seem to be self-evident. This entails performing a different evaluation of a situation than the expected evaluation; something which is relevant to all of the challenges formulated above.

The importance of showing courage and the power to take action is highlighted in our second challenge, where we emphasise the importance of adopting a relational and holistic perspective on HR work. Knowledge and understanding of the different perspectives that are involved is needed if one is to develop a holistic perspective of the organisation, its operations, and employees. This also includes the evaluation of different situations when deciding between different interests within, and outside the organisation. Thus we note how the competence element which Illeris (2013) calls *combinatorial ability* is shown to be important. This element refers to the ability to combine information from different areas and different perspectives so as to, if possible, discover new opportunities and alternatives that were previously not thought of, thereby allowing for the emergence of new solutions. The ability to perform evaluations and judgements about new challenging situations by connecting different areas together, and explaining such situations from a pedagogic, sociologic, psychological, legal, and economic perspective (Ulfsdotter Eriksson, 2013), is thus an important part of the nuanced array of HR competencies.

To achieve this, additional elements of competence are needed, including *empathy*, *creativity*, *flexibility*, *imagination*, and *intuition* (Illeris, 2013). A holistic approach to HR work includes being responsive to different interests and needs in every situation. This responsiveness presupposes *empathy*; the ability to read and imagine what other people are feeling, to be able to understand how others are experiencing a situation, and to be able to adopt other people's perspectives, so as to achieve a nuanced understanding of each party who is involved in the current situation. *Creativity* is needed so as to be able to combine areas and perspectives in new ways and to allow for new opportunities to emerge. This ability is central to being able to deal with unforeseen and unknown situations and is crucial to being able to think along new lines. As shown in our second challenge, *courage* and *positive action* allows the practitioner to think 'outside the box', which, in turn, presupposes *imagination*. In this regard, suggested by Illeris (2013), we note the American sociologist, Wright Mill's concept of 'sociological imagination', which entails an ability to imagine that social conditions and existing circumstances can be different to what they immediately seem to be. *Imagination*, in this context, involves being able, in thought and action, to transcend prevailing conditions and, instead, think that things could be different. It is in this possibility of 'difference' that new pathways to change may be discovered.

Flexibility, as an element of competence, goes beyond the accepted understanding of flexibility as a preparedness for change, according to Illeris. Rather, *flexibility* allows one to let go of fixed routines, ways of working, and modes of understanding, and instead one has the freedom to form one's own thoughts and actions in relation to whatever changes and new situations one is confronted with. This interpretation of *flexibility* places emphasis on the ability of introspection (soul-searching) and the ability to develop an understanding of one's self and one's own views, something which we indicated in our second challenge. Introspection also breeds the ability to work with different 'awareness-raising' processes, with managers and employees alike.

In our third challenge, *Adopt and preserve a positive view of people and an ethical approach to HR work*, the competence element of intuition plays an important role. There is a risk that people might think that intuition is something irrational and unsystematic, similar to 'acting unconsciously'. Illeris' explanation of this element of competence is that, with experience, we can develop intuitive knowledge of an area. We can develop a comprehensive overview of our area, which, in turn, will allow us to act in the correct way without necessitating systematic thought. This can be related to the Aristotelian spirit of building good character and assuming good habits so as to be properly prepared to perform good actions in situations; such that the HR specialist will find themselves in during their professional practice (Flyvbjerg et al., 2012).

In summary, the HR work that is represented in each of this book's chapters is work which demands a continual balancing act which is conducted in a conscious and competent manner, where the HR specialist clearly possesses integrity. The balancing act does not entail going with the tide, or uncritically taking heed of the person who shouts the loudest. It is important to know where one stands, and which values inform one's professional practice. HR work has been performed in different ways in different times. The focus of the work has changed in step with developments in society and work-life, and included the zeitgeist with its inherent values and perspectives. How HR work will take shape in the future and what its focus will be is not obvious. In the literature on HR work, different ideas about the future are presented. One direction which emerges is the idea that HR work is moving towards a stage of market rationalism, with increased focus on customers and efficiency (Boglind et al., 2013). Another possible direction for HR work (in the opposite direction of market rationalism) is where HR work becomes more and more characterised by humanistic thought and social responsibility, where the employees' perspective is placed to the fore (Ulfsdotter Eriksson, 2013). The question is how we will relate to events as they occur. If the critical approach which was dealt with in the first challenge becomes established in the HR profession, then it will be possible to influence how the future will be.

References

Abrahamson, Eric (1996), Management fashion. *Academy of Management Review, 21*(1), pp. 254–285.
Antonovsky, Aaron (1987), *Unravelling the mystery of health: How people manage stress and stay well.* San Francisco: Jossey-Bass Inc, Publishers.
Bengtsson, Anki (2011), European policy of career guidance: The interrelationship between career self-management and production of human capital in the knowledge economy. *Policy Futures in Education, 9*(5), pp. 616–627.
Bergmo-Prvulovic, Ingela (2012), Subordinating careers to market forces? A critical analysis of European career guidance policy. *European Journal for Research on the Education and Learning of Adults, 3*(2), pp. 155–170.
Björkman, Ingmar & Stahl, Günter K. (2006), International human resource management research: An introduction to the field. In Günter K. Stahl & Ingmar Björkman (eds.), *Handbook of research in international human resource management.* Cheltenham: Edward Elgar.
Blennberger, Erik (2015), *Etik i HR-arbetet: Etisk kod för personalvetare.* [Ethics in HR work: A code of ethics for HR specialists] Stockholm: Akademikerförbundet SSR.
Boglind, Anders, Hällstén, Freddy & Thilander, Per (2013), *HR-transformation på svenska: Om organisering av HR-arbete.* [HR transformation in Swedish: The organisation of HR work] Lund: Studentlitteratur.
Bohlin, Henrik & Eklund, Jakob (ed.) (2013), *Empati: Teoretiska och praktiska perspektiv.* [Empathy: Theoretical and practical perspectives] Lund: Studentlitteratur.
Damm, Margareta & Dahte, Birgitta (2016), *HR – yrke, profession eller professionalism?* [HR – A job, profession, or professionalism?] Lund: Studentlitteratur.
Doorewaard, Hans & Benschop, Yvonne (2003), HRM and organizational change: An emotional endeavor. *Journal of Organizational Change Management, 16*(3), pp. 272–286.
Ekstedt, Eskil (2009), A new division of labour. The "projectification" of working and industrial life. (pp. 31–54). In Marie-Ange Moreau (ed.), in collaboration with Serafina Negrelli & Phillippe Pochet. *Building anticipation of restructuring in Europe.* "Work & Society", No. 65. Brussels, Belgium: P. I. E. Peter Lang. S. A.

Ekstedt, Eskil & Sundin, Elisabet (2006), Den nya arbetsdelningen – dimensioner och perspektiv. [The new division of labour – dimensions and perspectives] In Eskil Ekstedt (ed.), *Den nya arbetsdelningen: Arbets- och näringslivets organisatoriska omvandling i tid, rum och tal.* [The new division of labour: Work-life and business's organisational transformation in time, space, and language] Vol. 2006:11 (pp. 1–28). Stockholm: Arbetslivsinstitutet.

Fejes, Andreas (2010), Discourses on employability: Constituting the responsible citizen. *Studies in Continuing Education, 32*(2), pp. 89–102.

Flyvbjerg, Bent, Landman, Todd & Schram, Sanford (2012), *Real social science: Applied phronesis.* Cambridge: Cambridge University Press.

Haake, Ulrika & Löfgren Martinsson, Maria (2016), Personalvetarstudenters syn på HRD & anställningsbarhet. [The HR student view of HRD and employability] I Gun Sparrhof & Andreas Fejes (eds.), *Anställningsbarhet: Perspektiv från utbildning och arbetsliv* [Employability: Perspectives from education and work-life] (pp. 144–154). Lund: Studentlitteratur.

Hobbins, Jennifer (2016), Young long-term unemployed and the individualization of responsibility. *Nordic Journal of Working Life Studies, 6*(2), pp. 43–58.

Illeris, Knud (2011), *The fundamentals of workplace learning: Understanding how people learn in working life.* New York: Routledge.

Illeris, Knud (2013), *Kompetens: Vad, varför, hur.* [Competence: What, why, and how]. Lund: Studentlitteratur.

Iseskog, Tommy (2013), *Arbetsgivarens rehabiliteringsansvar.* [Employers' responsibility from rehabilitation] (6th edition). Stockholm: Norstedts juridik.

Jarvis, Peter (2009), Lifelong learning: A social ambiguity. In Peter Jarvis (ed.), *The Routledge international handbook of lifelong learning* (pp. 9–18). London & New York: Routledge Taylor & Francis Group.

McGuire, D. (2014), *Human resource development.* London: Sage.

Nationalencyklopedin (2016), *Integritet.* [Integrity] Retrieved from www.ne.se/ordböcker [2016-12-05].

Nilsson, Peter, Wallo, Anders, Rönnqvist, Dan & Davidsson, Bo (2011), *Human resource development: Att utveckla medarbetare och organisationer.* [Human resource development: Developing co-workers and organisations] Lund: Studentlitteratur.

Parkes, Carole & Davis, Ann (2013), Ethics and social responsibility: Do HR professionals have the "courage to challenge" or are they set to be permanent "bystanders"? *The International Journal of Human Resource Management, 24*(12), pp. 2411–2432.

Rubensson, Kjell (2006), The Nordic model of lifelong learning. *Journal of Comparative Education, 36*(3), pp. 327–341.

Sparhoff, Gun (2016), Anställningsbarhet: Ett tecken i tiden. [Employability: A sign of the times]. In Gun Sparrhoff & Andreas Fejes (eds.), *Anställningsbarhet: Perspektiv från utbildning och arbetsliv.* [Employability: Perspectives from education and work life] (pp. 25–36). Lund: Studentlitteratur.

Tengblad, Stefan (2000), Personalarbetets framväxt i Sverige? [The growth of HR work in Sweden?] In Ola Bergström & Mette Sandoff (eds.), *Handla med människor: Perspektiv på human resource management.* [Dealing with people: Perspectives on human resource management] Lund: Academia Acta.

Thompson, James D. (1967), *Organizations in action: Social science bases of administrative theory.* New York: Mc Graw-Hill.

Ulfsdotter Eriksson, Ylva (2013), *Personalvetenskap – som förhållningssätt.* [Human management – as an attitude] Stockholm: Liber.

INDEX

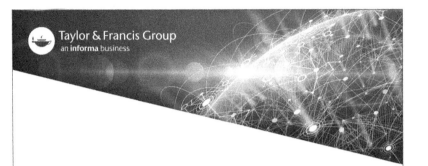